TIBET AND HER NEIGHBOURS
A History

Dalai Lama and Charles Bell seated.
Maharaj-Kumar Sidkeong Trul-ku of Sikkim standing behind.
Taken in Calcutta in 1910
Photographer: Johnston & Hoffman
1998.285.431 (BL.H.402-83)

TIBET AND HER NEIGHBOURS
A History

edited by Alex McKay

Edition Hansjörg Mayer, London

First published in 2003 by
Edition Hansjörg Mayer, London

Photography: Charles Bell Collection

Design: Olivia Koerfer and Hansjörg Mayer

Production: HaPaNa

Printed in Thailand by Amarin Printing & Publishing Ltd., Bangkok

Distribution:
Buchhandlung Walther König, Cologne
e-mail: order@buchhandlung-walther-koenig.de
Thames & Hudson Inc., New York
Thames & Hudson Ltd., London
River Books, Bangkok

ISBN 3-88375-718-7

CONTENTS

Bell's entry:
"Ya-so's for Maids of Honour with two assistants (left)".
Group outside decorated tents.
Women wear coral headdresses, turquoise inlaid amulet boxes (gau)
at the neck and waist, Lhasa style turquoise ear ornaments,
and strings of pearls, corals and other precious stones.
1998.285.156 (BL.H.133)

INTRODUCTION

Alex Mckay

Tibet today exists in three manifestations; the first is the Tibetan Autonomous Republic of China (hereafter, TAR). That is an administrative entity which includes the Lhasa-Shigatse heartland of the former Tibetan polity that was ruled by an incarnating succession of Dalai Lamas and which, during the period 1912-1950, functioned as a *de facto*, (although not *de jure*), independent state. (The TAR excludes, however, other areas that were under the control of the Dalai Lama during that period, with large parts of his domain having been transferred to neighbouring Chinese provinces such as Sichuan and Chinghai.)

The second manifestation is the Tibetan Government-in-exile, based in the north Indian town of Dharamsala, the residence of the current, 14th Dalai Lama of Tibet. Under the loose authority of that exiled government there is now a far-flung diaspora. This government and exile community, formed after the Chinese take-over of Tibet in the 1950s, represents a continuity with the previous Tibetan ruling structure and perhaps primary among its activities are those designed to preserve and maintain 'traditional' Tibetan culture and identity in a new setting.

The third manifestation of Tibet consists of a cultural zone stretching from Mongolia south through the Himalayas, and from an eastward zone situated in the Chinese-designated provinces of Sichuan, Yunnan and Quinghai, westwards into the Indian realms of Ladakh and even parts of the upper reaches of Himachal Pradesh and Uttarunchal. Throughout this zone, Tibet has historically exercised a strong influence, most notably in regard to the religious understandings deriving from the Tibetan Buddhist, but also Bon-po, systems and teachings.

We might also recognise a fourth manifestation of Tibet – a "Mythos Tibet" in which the actual Tibet is imagined as Shangri-La, a place beyond precise geographical definition, one located in the realm of fantasies of place. That Mythos Tibet is not, however, our concern here. The imagining of Tibet serves only to obstruct the understanding of historical realities, and it is with those realities that we are concerned. But to confront those issues is face the problem of the inherently political nature of studies of regions whose status is in dispute. The Sino-Tibetan problem – in which the Chinese government lays claim not only to actual current physical control over the formerly de facto independent state but also to historical authority there, while the Tibetan Government-in-exile claims traditional and popular sanction and disputes the Chinese historical interpretation – is ongoing. Thus control over historical 'facts' in this arena goes beyond academic dispute into the realms of politics and human rights.

The academic study of Tibet seeks, in as much as it is possible, to ascertain actualities, to deconstruct mythologies, and to go behind and beyond polemical and political interpretations of history. That politicians, with their ideological and day-to-day concerns may not accept the resultant findings is not the issue. While academics themselves have – and hopefully recognise - their own biases, preconceptions, agendas and world-views, their ideal is accurate representation of historical process. It is that representation of the history of Tibet, albeit approached from a variety of perspectives, that is presented here.

The papers included in this volume were originally presented at the History of Tibet conference organised by John Billington with the assistance of an academic committee comprising Professors Samten Karmay, Per Kværne, and Ernst Steinkellner and Dr Charles Ramble. The conference was held in St Andrews, Scotland, in September 2001. To John Billington and his assistants in the organisation of the conference, and to the members of the academic committee, we owe a vote of thanks. More than thirty scholars from Britain, Europe, Russia, Japan, India, Tibet, Nepal, Mongolia, New Zealand and the United States gathered for this meeting, and, in addition to the papers themselves, an attempt has been made to summarise the discussions that followed several of these papers, where those discussions add significantly to the understanding of the subject.

While the picturesque Scottish coastal town of St Andrews may be most famous as the "home of golf", the choice of it as the location for this conference was due to one man, Hugh Edward Richardson, retired diplomat and scholar. Richardson was a Scot who had developed an interest in Tibet even before he entered colonial service after his education at Glen Almond and Oxford. After an initial posting as an ICS officer in a Bengal district (of what is now Bangladesh), Richardson was selected as British Trade Agent in Gyantse in 1936, a position which was then, in effect, that of British Indian government representative in Tibet. It was an opportune time to begin service there as his immediate superior, Basil (later Sir Basil) Gould, the Political Officer in Sikkim, who was responsible for the Government of India's relations with Sikkim, Bhutan and Tibet, planned to establish a permanent British mission in the Tibetan capital, Lhasa.

Since the first British positions had been established in Tibet after the Younghusband mission in 1903-04, the British representatives had, for wider diplomatic reasons, been based at Gyantse, 120 miles south of the capital. This was clearly an unsuitable location for what was, despite its name, a diplomatic mission. But with the Political Officers able, since a ground-breaking journey by Charles Bell in 1920-21, to visit Lhasa on occasion, Gyantse had maintained its primary position as a forward 'listening post' in central Asia and centre of British influence. But in response to the Chinese establishment of a permanent mission in Lhasa after the death of the 13th Dalai Lama in 1933, a British-Indian mission in Lhasa became essential if the British were to continue to maintain an influence in Tibet.

Richardson thus served only briefly in Gyantse before joining Gould on a visit to the Tibetan capital, arriving there in July 1936. While Gould departed in February the following year, Richardson stayed on as head of the officially temporary British Lhasa Mission. He was subsequently to spend around 8 years in Tibet, including 3 years heading the mission after it passed to the control of the newly independent Indian government in 1947.

After his final departure from Lhasa in September 1950, just prior to the Chinese communist invasion, Richardson retired to St Andrews, where he devoted the rest of his life to the study of Tibet in all its aspects, most notably, in regard to its history. During the ensuing decades when Tibet was hidden behind the Bamboo Curtain, Richardson was one of a handful of scholars world-wide who maintained the field of study, and as Tibetan studies became increasingly popular in the late 1970s and early '80s he came to occupy an exalted position as the leading authority on Tibet in the English-speaking world.

It was in recognition of Richardson's work that St Andrews was chosen as the conference location, and the initial aim was to honour his status by dedicating the conference to him. At the time that the conference was planned, Richardson was ageing physically, although his mental perceptions remained as sharp as ever, and it was assumed that he would be able to take his place at the centre of the conference. But this was not to be. Richardson died in December 2000 and thus the conference became one of *in memoriam*, rather than *in celebration*.

*   *   *

The earliest manifestation of a recognisably 'Tibetan' state was that entity that emerged under the reign of King Srongsten Gampo in the first half of the 7th century A.D. Formed from the fusion of several tribal principalities in the riverine valleys of what is now central Tibet, this state conquered the neighbouring regions of Azha to the north-east and Zhang-zhung to the west, and over the course of the next two centuries, the new confederation rapidly evolved into the dominant power in Central Asian under the succession of kings known to us as the Yarlung dynasty. Until its collapse after the assassination of King Lang Darma around the year 842, Tibetan forces dominated the political control of a vast region between the Chinese, Arab and Turkic empires, and its strength and dominance was symbolised by its sacking of the Chinese capital of Ch'angan in 763 A.D.

The first three articles in our collection examine aspects of this formative period in Tibetan history. Helga Uebach's paper describes the extent of the Tibetan empire and discusses how the Tibetans were able to administer the vast expanse of territory under their control. She demonstrates that the various lands brought under the Yarlung sway in the initial phase of expansion – Zhang-zhung, Azha, Sumru and so forth – were to form the centre of the area that is culturally Tibetan down to the present day, and that the newly conquered regions were administratively absorbed into the Tibetan empire, providing an increased taxation and military conscription basis for further expansion.

The article by Guntram Hazard examines the history of the Kyichu region during the early period of the Yarlung dynasty to demonstrate that the residence of the kings and their council of ministers was not yet a fixed site. In line with Central Asian nomadic traditions, the royal household remained mobile. Lhasa did not become a fixed capital until as late as the latter part of the 7th century A.D., for prior to that period, it appears that the kings took to moving their winter and summer residences among the camps of the various tribal rulers who owed them allegiance.

In the following article, Tsuguhito Takeuchi discusses the evidence for Tibetan military administration of the central Asian centre of Khotan provided by Tibetan woodslips found in the Stein collection of the British library. This internal evidence for the conditions of military occupation of outlying provinces provides a fascinating glimpse of the actual conditions under which the soldiers served in their remote forts that oversaw the local administration.

The gradual introduction of Buddhism into the Yarlung kingdom during this period added a new element into the existing socio-religious situation, one that only added to the stresses inherent in a system in which powerful aristocratic factions limited royal prerogative. It appears that while Buddhism gained favour under royal patronage, competing elements closely associated with the pre-existing religious system(s) opposed the new faith. In the later Tibetan historiography this conflict is manifest in the understanding of the last Yarlung king, Lang Darma, as a persecutor of Buddhism who was assassinated by a Buddhist monk in defense of the faith. But as Samten Karmay's article demonstrates, it seems probable that the king was himself a Buddhist, whose murder was due to his desire for what we might today call a greater separation of church and state; a system in which the Buddhist clergy were not involved in politics nor given special state patronage.

The collapse of the Yarlung dynasty and the dissolution of the Tibetan empire was followed by a period of more than a century in which centralized authority was absent from Tibet. The subsequent gradual reconstruction of the state owed much to the unifying force of the Buddhist religion, which was deliberately and systematically diffused throughout Tibet under the patronage a new generation of rulers, and it was that faith that became central to the ideological identity of the recreated state. The primary impetus behind the widespread popularisation of Buddhism across Tibet (known to the Tibetans as the 'Second Dissemination of Buddhism', following its earlier introduction at court level), derived from the western regions, the erstwhile principality of Zhang-zhang.

The article by Roberto Vitali discusses the activities of the disciples of the Ngari Korsum (western Tibet) scholar Rinchen Zangpo, who, along with the great Indian *pandit* Atisha, was the primary figure in the 'Second Diffusion of Buddhism' in Tibet. Among the teachings that these less-known figures promulgated were those relating to Buddhist teachings on medical and veterinary sciences – aspects of immediate and obvious importance to the society of the time. These exemplify the many new ideas and practices associated with the new 'World Religion', that were systematically spread from India to central Tibet, *via* Zhang-zhung.

The Tibetan Buddhist state that emerged from this period gradually developed those characteristics that are commonly associated with 'traditional Tibetan society'. In this regard the reign of the 'Great Fifth' Dalai Lama (1642-1682) is particularly significant. Various sects had arisen which followed on different teaching traditions taken from late Indian Buddhism. While sharing certain defining characteristics (e.g. the *vinaya*, or code of monastic rules) these sects did compete for power and influence and several attained a dominant position during the 13-17th century. It was in the era of the 'Great Fifth' that the Gelugpa sect, with the aid of Mongol forces, became supreme, and it was also in this period that many other aspects of later Tibetan culture came to prominence – for example, the Potala palace became the supreme architectural manifestation of Tibetan culture. Of particular importance to Sino-Tibetan relations was the ensuing period in which Peking became increasingly involved in the complex affairs of the Tibetan and Mongol regions.

An overview of the socio-political developments in the critical 17th and 18th centuries is provided by Anne Chayet, whose survey brings us up to the eve of the period in which the Tibetan state became increasingly affected by Western modernity and the forces of imperial expansion – by both European and Asian powers. Tibet had become a Buddhist state, one in which virtually all aspects of society and politics were associated with Buddhist models, albeit with the specific characteristics that distinguish the Tibetan form of the faith. Thus its relations with its neighbouring Asian states were based on religious and cultural norms and understandings, and are difficult to express in modern Western political terms. But the increasing impact of Western modernity was to force Tibet to confront new and alien forces that were to act upon very different political concepts, secular, legalistic, and scientific and techno-logical. Tibet's frontiers were henceforth subject to definition on Western terms.

One example of the complexities of the traditional trans-border relations is provided in the article by Françoise Pommaret, who examines the relations between southern Tibet and Bhutan from the 18th to the early 20th century. The relationship between religious and secular understandings of territory and landscape is particularly apparent in regard to such frontier zones. The perignations of individual religious figures and the role of monasteries as centres of power radiating socio-political and economic influence were significant factors in the formation of territorial under-standings, while regional and trans-regional trade provided a crucial impetus to the development of elite authority. As Pommaret concludes, these trans-regional relations were a complex web of family, incarnation, and patron-lama relationships.

Tibetan religious influence was also highly significant in the Sino-Tibetan relationship, which was understood in terms of an inter-dependent association between *patron* (the Manchu Emperor) and *priest* (the Dalai Lama). One manifestation of the Tibetan role in this relationship was the establishment of a Tibetan Buddhist centre, patronised by the Emperor, in the Manchu capital of Peking (Beijing). This religious complex is discussed by Vladimir Uspensky, who demonstrates how Tibetan Buddhism gained its cultural dominance in the heart of Asia under Manchu patronage, and how monastic complex, text, and Buddhist *sangha* (the community of monks), prospered from its Peking centre and played a vital role in the Sino-Tibetan political relationship.

One aspect of Tibetan culture that developed of necessity during this period was the formation of an official style of Tibetan correspondence and in the following article by Hanna Schneider this development is examined and prospects for future studies based on this research considered. As with so many aspects of Tibetan Buddhist culture, the influence of classical Indian traditions is explicit. As the 'home of Buddhism' – and a region largely outside of political competition with Tibet - India occupied a particularly exalted place in Tibetan understanding, and many aspects of late Indian Buddhist culture were transferred wholesale to Tibetan culture, both as elite textual-based models and popular teachings and practices advanced by religious renunciates.

Our knowledge of the economic history of Tibet remains sketchy, not least because religious aspects have preoccupied Western historians of the region. John Ardussi's article draws on Tibetan sources to discuss the social and political implications of the ceremonial wealth distributions that were a feature of great festivals and public ceremonies. He demonstrates that these distributions were both a discharging of Buddhist requirements for charity and socio-economic rituals that clarified social and political relationships while also acting as an economic stimuli – one that came to influence early Western understandings of Tibet as a 'land of gold'.

Ardussi's article draws attention to the extent to which the Tibetan state – in common with many, if not all Asian political formations, existed not so much in terms of a territorial or ethnic entity, but as one in which ritual and social relationships were the fundamental expression of sovereignty and identity. This disparity between Asian and European concepts of the state has, since the imposition of the European model during the period of 'modernisation' in the mid 18th – 20th century, been at the heart of many of the fundamental intra-national disputes that continue to problematise the Asian region.

The article by Tirtha Prasad Mishra examines the unequal 1856 treaty between Tibet and Nepal that gave the recently emerged Nepalese state a degree of domination over Tibet. It was in the interests of both Nepal and China that Tibet should be subject to their interests, and even after Nepal came under British imperial influence the Kathmandhu government retained certain privileges in their dealings with Tibet. Despite this inequality, however, the treaty was of benefit to the Tibetans in demonstrating their separate political status, even in an era where Beijing was nominally the dominant power at Lhasa.

Integral to the historical development of Tibetan Buddhism was Mongolia, whose political, economic and religious relationship with Tibet is examined in the following article by L. Chuluunbaatar. While Mongolian armed forces assisted the various sects of Tibetan Buddhism in their earlier phase, most notably the Gelugpa sect, whose dominance owed much to Mongol arms, Tibet in return assisted the development of Buddhism in Mongolia, playing host to Mongol Buddhist scholars and providing the leading Mongolian incarnation, who was selected from Tibetan-born candidates. These close ties continued down to the time of the communist suppression of Buddhism in Mongolia in the 1920s, which preceded similar events in Tibet several decades later.

The article by Ishihama Yumiko discusses one aspect of the complex inter-relationship between Tibetan, Mongol and Manchu Chinese armies in the 17th century – the war of 1688-97 – and demonstrates that the three parties involved shared an understanding of the term 'Buddhist government' which they saw as involving a sym-biotic relationship between religion and state. Each justified their actions in terms of its appropriateness to this religious governmental system and this provided them with common diplomatic ground.

Essentially deriving from Indic Buddhist concepts of a 'Universal Emperor', the system of 'Buddhist government' underpinned the fundamental central Asian understandings of statehood up until the time of the collapse of the Manchu dynasty in 1911, although by that time the system was under severe challenge from the European Nation-state model. It is within that different conceptual universe that pre-20th century Sino-Tibetan relations must be located, with much of the tragic history of the 20th century due to the clash between traditional Buddhist and modern Nation-state models of government.

These articles indicate the variety of relationships that the Tibetan state entered into with its surrounding polities, but the complex nature of Tibet's relations with its neighbours still requires further analysis. While such studies have naturally been dominated by considerations of Sino-Tibetan relations, the Tibetan state dealt with numerous polities, and its foreign relations with its various neighbours involved both general and specific understandings and associations. On Tibet's frontiers during the 19th century were both great empires such as China and British India, and principalities such as Sikkim, Mongolia and Kashmir, each of whom were dealt with in specific contexts both before and after they too fell under the sway of the great empires of the period.

A third great empire entered into Tibetan consideration towards the end of the 19th century; that of Tsarist Russia. While Buddhists from the Kalmikia and Buriat regions had long maintained relations with their ultimate spiritual leader, the Dalai Lama, it was only in this period that the Russian state came into contact with Tibet, following the expansion of Russia into central Asia during the mid-19th century. Tibet now came to be caught up in the Anglo-Russian rivalry in the region – a contest popularly known as the 'Great Game'. The article by Alexandre Andreyev focuses on the intriguing figure of Agvan Dorzhiev, a Russian Buriat who became a key advisor to the 13th Dalai Lama. At a time when the Tibetan state was greatly in fear of the perceived threat from the British Indian empire that had absorbed so many of Tibet's minor neighbouring powers, Dorzhiev's attempts to draw Tibet into the Russian sphere of influence were viewed positively by the Tibetan leader. Russia seemed to the Dalai Lama to offer a neutral patron, one who would protect Tibet from British influence and also enable them to break free from the authority of China.

Andreyev demonstrates that Russia's generals played an active part in the relations between Russia and Tibet, dispatching secret missions there and perhaps even supplying military aid to the Tibetan state. The British, however, saw developments in this region through the lens of their Indian colony. They not only feared a threat to the security of India from the Russians, but considered Tibet to be within their sphere of influence and thus off-limits to Russia. Tibet's dealings with the Russians thus provided one of the primary justifications for their dispatch of an armed mission to Lhasa under the political control of Francis Younghusband. This mission fought its way to Lhasa in 1904 and forced the Tibetans to enter into formal relations with the British Government of India, which sought to use Tibet as a 'buffer state' protecting their Indian empire from subversion from the north – whether by Russia, or China. However, while the British did support the Tibetans in breaking free of all semblance of Peking's authority after the Chinese revolution of 1911, their refusal to acknowledge the actual independent status of the Tibetan polity – primarily for fear of upsetting China and thus damaging trade and diplomatic ties – was to have grave consequences for Tibet's future. Mongolia aside, no state recognised Tibet as independent and the ambiguous status of Tibet meant that when the Chinese communist forces invaded in 1950, the outside world effectively did nothing to protect it.

By the early part of the 20th century, the Tibetans had been forced to encounter various aspects of Western modernity. One manifestation of the pressures of modernity on the 'traditional' Tibetan system of government was the dispute between the Dalai and Panchen Lamas. The Panchen Lama, who was based in Shigatse, Tibet's second-largest urban centre, was in some senses the second-highest incarnation in the land. But, as the article by Parshotam Mehra indicates, he fled into exile in 1923 after disputes over the tax liability of the Panchen's holdings. New taxes imposed to finance the development and modernisation of Tibet's army – a policy in which they were encouraged by British India – upset the traditional relationships, and all attempts to resolve the issue failed. The exiled Panchen became prey to various Central Asian factions and the Chinese in particular were able to use him as a divisive force against Tibet's fragile state of *de facto* independence. They continued to use this weapon after the death of the 9th Panchen Lama in exile in 1937, and were able to exercise a large measure of influence over his successor both before and after the communist take-over of China in 1949.

The role of the 10th Panchen, who served under the communist regime until his death in 1989, remains controversial, with the extent to which he collaborated with the regime open to interpretation. His supporters would argue that he had done his best to protect Tibetan interests under circumstances more difficult than his critics could imagine. Final judgement, however, awaits access to sources now firmly closed to Western scholarship.

In addition to the British, other Western powers also had their interests in Tibet. While Nazi Germany's interests in that land were peripheral at best, a German mission did visit Lhasa in 1938-39 and met with the Regent who was then ruling Tibet during the minority of the 14th Dalai Lama. Balanced analysis of this mission has been hitherto unknown, but in the article by Isrun Engelhardt, drawing on German archives, the scientific nature of the mission is emphasised, and her research indicates that Nazi interests in the occult images by which Tibet has gained renown in the West have been much exaggerated. The mission's leader, Ernst Schaefer, was a serious scientist and apparently a reluctant Nazi, who enjoyed some popularity with Lhasa Tibetans. This new perspective is in stark contrast to the previously dominant views of some British-Indian officials, not least Hugh Richardson, then Head of British Mission Lhasa and an avowed opponent of the Schaefer mission.

In the following article, Warren Smith discusses the issue of Tibetan identity, arguing that communist Chinese policy in regard to Tibet is focussed on the destruction of a separate Tibetan identity and the assimilation of the Tibetan peoples into a Chinese culture. Smith discusses the various policies followed by the central government in regard to Tibetan identity and concludes that self-determination rather than autonomy should be the goal of the Tibetan exile movement as 'the history of Sino-Tibetan relations has demonstrated that meaningful Tibetan autonomy under China is impossible.'

China cannot, however, be seen as a single one-dimensional force. Within a broad consensus over Tibetan policy that has been continuous through dynastic, republican and communist periods of rule, different approaches to the Sino-Tibetan problem have been promoted by different individuals and tendencies within Chinese society. The need to ascertain and recognise the different strategies within China's actions in regard to Tibet is emphasised in the articles by Robbie Barnett and Melvyn Goldstein.

Goldstein's article focusses on analysis of one particular such strategic conflict, the dispute between two factions of the Chinese administration during the 1950s, a dispute with continuing ramifications in regard to Beijing's Tibetan strategies. This is a period of Tibetan history that is only now being closely examined, and Goldstein's work opens new ground with its illustration of the contrasting tendencies within Chinese policy and action.

Barnett's article focuses on the policies employed by Chen Kuiyuan, Party Secretary of the Tibet Autonomous Region (of China) from 1992-2000 and examines how these evolved during this period. The use of economic incentives, the transfer of (Han Chinese) population into the TAR, restrictions on religious expression and the denial of any 'special characteristics' to Chinese government in Tibet were all strategies employed in an attempt to overcome the forces of Tibetan nationalism and demands for democratic structures and expressions. Tibetan history itself was specifically identified by Chen as a battle-ground, with closer management of Tibetan intellectual expression instituted.

The intimate connection between history and political agendas that Chen acknowledged is of course, well-known, at least in general terms – as is clear from phrases such as 'the battle-ground of history', 'History is written by the winners' and so forth. In its specific manifestations this concept may be both clearly stated and explicit, as for example in the attempts to eradicate history made in Pol Pot's Cambodia. Equally its significance may only become apparent in a particular retrospective context. This is certainly the case within Tibetan studies, where apparently apolitical aspects of the past are, in today's political context inherently political; in one sense all study of Tibet may be seen as an affirmation of Tibetan separate identity. Thus while the culturally Tibetan regions of China remain firmly under central control, the very existence of an intellectual and academic field of Tibetan studies – both in China and the outside world – serves as a continuing reminder of the unique nature of the subject culture and history.

As the final article demonstrates, however, even apparently well-intentioned nations have not necessarily acted to Tibet's advantage. By the middle of the 20th century, Tibet had also begun to attract the attention of the government of the United States of America and as the article by Tom Grunfeld demonstrates, initial ties arising from the America's needs in World War preceded a period in which the Tibet issue became, in the American perspective, a part of the Cold War. One aspect of this was CIA aid to Tibetan guerilla fighters engaging the Chinese during the 1950s and '60s. But Nixon's rapprochement with China ended this aid and American support for Tibet was never given at a level significant enough to affect the Sino-Tibetan issue. Despite the popularity of Tibet as a 'cause' in contemporary America, ultimately, as Grunfeld concludes 'the United States has done more to betray the exile Tibetan community than to help them.'

*   *   *

The first articles in this volume concerning the early period of Tibetan history depict the functioning and development of a sophisticated and centralised empire, one that dominated Central Asia both militarily and culturally. The focus then moves to the Tibetan state during the period in which it developed and maintained those characteristics that we now associate with 'traditional' Tibet; that entity ruled by the Dalai Lamas (and, in fact for the majority of the time, their Regents). That state maintained a variety of forms of relationship with its neighbours, none of which, as we have suggested, can be easily defined in terms of the European model of the 'Nation-State'. Tibet's frontiers were defined only where that definition had proved necessary, and they were generally zones of cultural transition, rather than lines on a map separating cultures and races. Yet a distinct Tibetan entity existed, separate not only from China, but from Mongolia and Turkic Central Asia, from Nepal, Sikkim and Bhutan, as well as from Ladakh and many other distinct regions of what is now India. Its separate status was recognised by all of these parties at various times, although inter-state communication was generally on the basis of necessity rather than the kind of routine diplomatic communications favoured in the Western model.

Tibet as cultural centre also spread its influence into each of these neighbours, aspects of its language and religious culture remain there to this to day, and indeed many features of traditional Tibet are perhaps best preserved in its neighbouring regions. Similarly Tibet was only closed to outside ideas, cultures and foreign visitors at times when it considered itself under threat from those visitors, such as during its attempts to exclude Westerners in the 19th century and in its expulsion of Chinese officials in 1912-13 and again in the late 1940s. Otherwise Tibet's bazaars and trade centres were visited by traders and travellers from throughout the East; Russians and Armenians, Kashmiris, Assamese, and many others came for trade and pilgrimage.

Aspects of the culture of its neighbours were adopted, just as Tibetan culture spread outwards to those neighbours. Buddhism from India, the foodstuffs of the aristocracy from China, silks and brocades from Russia, all found their way into Tibetan culture, religious and material. The Tibetan state was thus a dynamic one, integral to the historical development of Central Asia, and firmly tied into the economic worlds of its neighbours. It is the fact that throughout its recorded history Tibet has preserved a distinct culture and identity, while maintaining political relationships with neighboring states, that enables us to speak of a *Tibetan* history, civilisation and culture.

The Great Prayer (Mönlam Chenmo) was instituted for the benefit of all Tibet by Tsongkhapa in 1409 and became part of the New Year celebrations. Thousands of monks from the great Gelukpa monasteries of Ganden, Sera and Drepung came to Lhasa for this event to spend several days reciting prayers. Bell's photograph shows some of them seated in a courtyard of the Jokhang, the most sacred temple in Tibet. 1998.285.212 (BL.H.185)

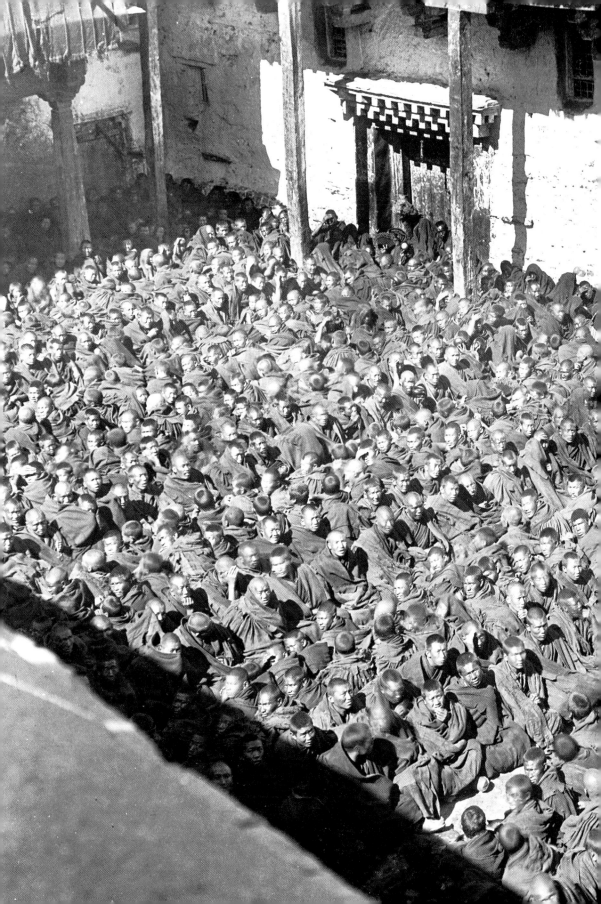

On the Tibetan expansion from seventh to mid-eighth centuries and the administration *(khö)* of the countries subdued

Helga Uebach

In the the early seventh century A.D. the Tibetans had started to subdue a number of surrounding countries. And thus they had laid the foundations for their future Central Asian empire in strategicaly important regions in the south west, north east and south east. By the mid eighth century most of the countries subdued are found integrated into the Tibetan empire. It is not surprising that the Tibetans brought a number of surrounding countries under their sway. Their equipment and military force was renowned. However, the question arises as to how they did control those vast territories, which many times outnumbered the size of the territory of Tibet proper.

The primary source which may furnish information to answer this question is the fragmentary excerpts of the Old Tibetan Annals in two versions. Annals I covers the period from the end of the reign of Songtsen gampo to 747 A.D. and Annals II supplies annalistic data from 743 to 763. Some information on the topic is also found in the Old Tibetan Chronicle.

With regard to the countries subdued like Zhangzhung, Azha, Sumru, Domä, Dschang and the less known Tongsö and Trom, there are attested two administrative terms, *phalö* and *khö*. The meaning of both terms has been disputed. There is more or less agreement among scholars, that phalö refers to a kind of census, probably the convocation of an assembly of heads of families. The term khö has been interpreted in various different ways. Its meaning was misinterpreted, too, by the rendering "gather an army" and the like. However, textual attestations collected from different sources prove that khö means "order" "right order", "order of the world", (*Weltordnung*) and with regard to the state its meaning is "administration", "institution", "settlement".

Both the terms phalö and khö not only are applied for countries subdued but are also applied for Tibet proper. It may therefore be useful to recall first the basic institutions of Tibet's state organisation.

A glimpse of the fundamental institutions of Tibet's state organisation

In the year 654 A.D. the Annals record: "The beginning of the account/writing of the great administrative (khö) arrangement was made by dividing the [population] into men obliged to military service and men obliged to civil service." The division of the population into these two groups seems to have been the first and fundamental decision in organising the state. Beside there was the territorial division of Tibet into "Horns", first into "Three Horns" ("Middle, Left and Right Horn", seen from North) and later on "Four Horns" ("Horn Supplement"), which constituted Tibet proper. Each of the Horn was divided into thousand-districts which again were subdivided into smaller units. The thousand-districts were the fundamental units for both military and civil administrative measures. Another important figure in the state organisation was the Conference gathered by the highest ranking councillor(s). It is first mentioned in 673 A.D. and used to be gathered annually in summer and in winter. The place where the Conference assembled changed. Though it remains unknown who exactly was entitled to participate in the Conference, it is obvious from the records in the Annals that mostly administrative, economical and fiscal measures concerning the Four Horns or a single Horn were made.

Observations on khö and phalö

Surveying the total of 17 textual attestations of khö in the two fragments of the Annals and one attestion of it in the Old Tibetan Chronicle it can be observed, that out of these, five attestations (seven when counting the overlapping years of the two Annals) refer to Tibet proper and eleven refer to countries subdued. Further on, the khö is carried out in the Conference gathered by the councillor(s). Since there are khö reported to have been made in the Conference in the summer term and in the winter term, obviously the presence of a great number of representatives of the population was not required. There are neither regular annual intervals for carrying out a khö nor is there regnal dependency. Only for Tibet proper there can be seen that specified khö were carried out:

> great khö or khö of the pastures (673 A.D.; 709 A.D. for the Left Horn),
> great khö of the soldiers, corresponding to khö of the Four Horns in Annals II
> (744 A.D.), khö of the pastures and fallow lands of the Four Horns (746 A.D.).

As to the phalö, it is throughout reported to have been "convoked" in the Conference of the winter term. Therefore it may safely be concluded that a great number of representatives of the population had been present, which in an agricultural society only was feasible in winter. For Tibet proper, the phalö is referred to twice. In summer of 743 A.D. the "wooden tablets of the phalö were laid down (in the sense of abolished)".

This perhaps refers to an unrecorded convocation of an earlier phalö, probably even to the above mentioned year 654 A.D. of the first khö. The second reference of the convocation of the "phalö of men obliged to military service and men obliged to civil service" is recorded for 743 A.D. It precedes the "great khö of the soldiers" carried out in 744 A.D.

Khö and phalö in countries subdued

Zhangzhung
The principality of Zhangzhung was situated to the West of Tibet, on the way of the route which led via Kashgar into the Chinese dominated Tarim basin. Therefore it was of great strategical importance for the expansion of the Tibetan empire. It was first subdued in the reign of Songtsen gampo around 634/640. A matrimonial alliance with a sister of Songtsen gampo and its ruler was concluded. According to later historiographies Songtsen gampo had also married a Zhangzhung lady. The alliance failed, Zhangzhung revolted and had been overthrown again. In 653 the Old Tibetan Annals report that a Tibetan governor of Zhangzhung was appointed.

For Zhangzhung it is reported that three khö had been carried out in 662, 675 and in 724 A.D. in Conferences assembled by the Tibetan councillor(s) presumably in hitherto unidentified places of Zhangzhung.

In 671 A.D. a Tibetan imperial princess went as a bride for a member of the ruling clan of Zhangzhung. Two years after the second khö, in 677 A.D. Zhangzhung again revolted and was overthrown again.

A phalö of Zhangzhung and Mard (Ladakh) was convoked in 719 A.D. in a conference in Tibet proper. Unlike in Tibet, where the phalö had been convoked in the year preceding the carrying out of the khö, obviously in order to gain actual data, in Zhangzhung the phalö preceded the khö by five years.

From later historiographies Zhangzhung is known to have been organised like a Horn (province), however, Zhangzhung never was called a Horn.

Azha
The Azha, a people of Mongolian origin, occupied a strategicaly important territory which stretched from the west of lake Kokonor as far as the border of the Tarim basin. Once this country was subdued, there was open access to attack the Chinese in order to take from them the control over the Silkroads and at the same time to cut them off their western dominions. The Azha were first subjugated by Songtsen gampo. Their final defeat took place in 663 A.D. In consequence many thousand families of the Azha took refuge in China. Defeating the Azha and preparing the administration does not seem to have been an easy task because the great councillor of Tibet is known to have stayed in the Azha country from 659 to 666 A.D., with only one year of interruption, when in 662 A.D. he was made the khö of Zhangzhung. In 689 A.D. a Tibetan imperial princess was sent as a bride to the then Azha ruler.

For Azha, as for Zhangzhung, there are reported three khö to have been made in Conferences in hitherto unidentified places of the Azha country, in 696, 714 and 742 A.D. According to the Annals in 727 A.D. the *tsenpo* Tri Detsugtsen had come to the

Azha country "in [order to exert] state power". On this occasion he had officially conferred the title *wön* to the Azha ruler, who was the son of the above mentioned Tibetan imperial princess. The phalö which was convoked in 734 A.D. preceded the khö of 742 A.D. by eight years.

Though very fragmentary, Annals of the Azha principality of this period have been transmitted. Their records show, that in the Azha country Conferences were assembled regularly.

Sumru

The Sumpa, a tribe of Tibetan stock, are enumerated in the Old Tibetan Chronicle among the allied subjects who had revolted when Songtsen gampo ascended to the throne. They were soon subjugated again by the tsenpo's councillor.

While tsenpo Tri Düsong and his army raided a number of Chinese prefectures, and allied with the Eastern Turcs, were successful in capturing Liang-chou or Ling-chou, the Tritse of the Annals, his councillors in 702 A.D. made the great khö of Sumru, during the winter Conference of Domä. This record is noteworthy in two accounts. First, the great khö of the Sumpa was made in an unidentified place in the conference of Domä. It implies that the Sumpa at that time administratively were part of Domä (see below). Second the Sumpa for the first time are found to be organised as a Horn [province]. It is unknown if this was a result of the great khö or if the Horn of the Sumpa was already organised at an earlier date, unrecorded in the Annals. With regard to the name "Horn Supplement" (= Forth Horn of Tibet), the Horn of the Sumpa is also called "Second Supplementary Horn of the Sumpa".

Domä

The region of Domä is first mentioned in the Old Tibetan Annals in 653 A.D. It is not a territory known to have been subjugated as a whole, but different tribes inhabiting the area are known to have surrendered. However, it is included here because it is not part of the Four Horns of Tibet, but obviously was administrated separately. This can be inferred from the fact that from 692 A.D. onward the place of the Conference of Domä in winter is regularly reported in the Annals. Moreover, starting from 755 A.D. there was a Conference in summer, too. All the place names of the conferences are provided, but apart from one exception, the places are hitherto unidentified. Therefore the exact location and the extension of Domä remains unknown. It may, however, be guessed that it bordered Sumru in the east and comprised parts of present day Kham and of Amdo south of the Yellow river.

The great khö of Domä was carried out in 715 A.D. Apart from the regular Conferences of Domä, there is almost no information in the Annals about the region. Since is was administrated separately it may be assumed that records of their administration were kept separately, too.

In documents dating from the period of Tibetan occupation of Central Asia there is the interesting reference to the office of "councillor of DomÍ".

Tongsö

The Annals record that in 730 A.D. the khö of Tongsö was carried out in a place of Domä. This is why Tongsö must formerly have been under the administration of Domä. The Annals II refer to Tongsö as the place whereto in 755 A.D. the servants of two disloyal councillors had been banished. Therefore it may be assumed that this hitherto unidentified area is situated on the far away frontier of Domä.

Trom

The great khö of Trom was carried out in a place of the Azha country near lake Kokonor in 741 A.D. It is a unique fact that it was done "in the presence of the tsenpo", this is Tri Detsugtsen who had set out to the north east of his realm for a military campaign and was victorious.

Trom poses a problem since it cannot be stated with certainty if it refers to a specific toponym like f. e. Matrom (Trom of Matschu, Yellow River) or if it refers to the special military provinces called *trom*. These trom, eight in total, are known to have been established at the borders of Tibet starting from Bruzha (Gilgit) in the south west along the southern part of the Tarim basin up to the north east to Kva-chu and Khartsen.

Dchang

The kingdom of Dschang (chin. Nan-chao) which comprised the tribes of the Black and White Myva is situated on the south east border of Tibet, in present day Yünnan. According to the Annals, it had been subjugated by tsenpo Tri Düsong in 703 A.D., but there is no attestation of a khö having been made in Dschang. Later there seems have been disaccord with Tibet. In the Old Tibetan Chronicle there is one attestation of khö dating from the second half of the eighth century. The Chronicle reports of resurrender and refers to the re-establishment of a "former *khö*". After this surrender, tsenpo Tri Songdetsen had officially conferred the title "younger brother" to the Dschang ruler Kaglabong (R. 748-779 A.D.) Having united their forces, the army of Dschang and of the Tibetans invaded the Chinese province of Ssu-ch'uan. By the end of the eighth century Dschang allied with China, the western part of Ssu-ch'uan, however, continued to be under Tibetan control.

In this survey concerning the countries subdued, unlike for the Four Horns of Tibet, the khö are not specified, apart from being termed great khö for Sumru, Domä and Trom. In Zhangzhung and Azha, where the making of the khö is preceded by the convocation of a phalö, certainly the division of "men obliged to military service" and "men obliged to civil service" was made. For the other countries subdued the same may be assumed, but it is unrecorded in the excerpts of the Annals. It goes without saying that men obliged to military service in general not only ranked high in Tibetan society but were needed in great number. Therefore reinforcement of the army by troops of subdued countries was essential for the Tibetans who often are seen fighting at a time on different far away fronts.

It has already been shown that the term khö is used to denote the administration and state organisation in general (from circa 654 A.D.) as well as to denote single specified administrative measures. In this context it is interesting to note that some later Tibetan historiographers basing themselves on records which reflect the later political situation of the second half of the eighth century supply detailed information on khö which may help to understand the use of the term khö. The information provided had in part already been detected from the Annals. They transmitted slightly varying catalogues of six khö and 36 (six to six) khö. Among the six institutions (khö) are enumerated the "boundaries of the Horns", the "thousand-districts of men obliged to military service, the groups of men obliged to civil service, the shares of territory of the country/the khö of the country, the three maternal uncles (i.e. the councillors related to the tsenpo by matrimonial alliance) and the councillor and/or the Conference and the three divisions of the heros.

Among the 36 institutions (khö) a catalogue of six institutions (khö) is contained which presents the names of five countries, one entry is missing. It enumerates Tibet along with Zhangzhung and Sumpa. Further the names of two other countries referring to a later period of expansion are provided.

Conclusion

In conclusion it can be stated that the Tibetans in the course of their expansion in countries subdued obviously applied the same administrative system as in their home country, the Three viz. Four Horns. The administration of countries subdued was carried out by councillor(s) of Tibet in a Conference in the countries each separately according to the same fundamental institutions as for Tibet. In countries where there was a local ruler, i. e. in Zhangzhung Azha and Dschang, he was left in office and in addition/or prior to the making of the khö, matrimonial alliances were concluded in order to strengthen the ties with Tibet and to set up the so-called *zhang-wön*, "uncle and nephew/father-in-law and son-in-law" relationship or a *tschen-tschung*, "elder brother - younger brother" relationship, as in Dschang. However, as soon as the khö is reported to have been made, these countries had become integral parts of the Tibetan empire. Moreover it can be stated that the countries subdued in the first wave of the Tibetan expansion for centuries continued to be part of Tibet and disregarding the actual political frontiers, these territories at present still count among the areas of Tibetan civilisation. In fact the extension of the Tibetan empire in the mid eighth century almost exactly corresponds to the area of present day cultural Tibet.

FURTHER READING:

J. Bacot, F.W. Thomas, Ch. Toussaint, *Documents de Touen-houang relatifs à l'histoire du Tibet*. Annales du Musée Guimet 51, Paris 1940, Paul Geuthner.
G. Uray, The narrative of legislation and organisation of the mKhas-pa'i dga'-ston, *Acta Orientalia Hungarica* XXVI, Budapest 1972, pp. 11-68.
Ch.I. Beckwith, *The Tibetan Empire in Central Asia*, Princeton 1987, Princeton University Press.
R.A. Stein, *Tibetan Civilisation*, London 1972, Faber and Faber Ltd.

LIST OF CORRECT SPELLINGS:

Amdo = A-mdo
Azha = 'A-zha
Bruzha = Bru zha
Domä = mDo smad
Dschang = 'Jang
Kham = Khams
Khartsen = mKhar tsan
khö = mkhos
Matrom = rMa grom/khrom
Matschu = rMa chu
phalö = pha los
Songtsen gampo = Srong btsan sgam po
Sumpa = Sum pa
Sumru = Sum ru
Tongsö = mTong sod
Tri Detsugtsen = Khri lDe gtsug btsan
Tri Düsong = Khri 'Dus srong
Tri Songdetsen = Khri Srong lde btsan
Tritse = Khri rtse
Trom = khrom
tsenpo = btsan po
wön = dbon
Zhangzhung = Zhang zhung

following page:
Bell's entry: "(s) Monk's sports at Gyantse, jumping."
1998.285.505 (BL.P.249)

The Kyichu Region in the Period of the Tibetan Empire: A Historico-geographical Note

Guntram Hazod

The history of the Kyichu region in the dynastic period begins with the conquest of the northern territories of Ngäpo (later Phenyü) under the Yarlung king Namri Songtsen, who in this connection established a residence on the Kyichu (in Gyama of Medro), where his son and successor Songtsen Gampo (d. 650 A.D.) was later born. The story (as told in later sources) continues with the departure of Songtsen Gampo, who at some point in the 630's built a personal castle in what was later to become Lhasa and then laid the foundation stone for the famous Lhasa temple.

In the secondary literature one often reads in this context of the foundation of the "capital Lhasa", a term however that for the dynastic period is somewhat misleading. Rather, the sources indicate a political landscape that was characterised by mobility, with the locations of residence of the royal household (*phodrang*) and council assembly (*dünma*) changing more than once every year. We have evidence of this from the annual entries in the *Dunhuang Annals*. As Uebach has already stated in one of her earlier works (1988), the majority of the dynastic places described in the *Annals* are to be located in the area of the so-called Central Horn of Uru and its immediately neighbouring areas (Uebach 1988). Uru thereby clearly assumed the leading political position among the provinces of Tibet proper (i.e. the area of the four Horn provinces, which were established in the period after Songtsen Gampo). Thus Uray noted that the assemblies that took administrative decisions for the whole of Tibet (such as the census records concerning all Horn provinces) were usually held in the Uru areas (1960: 49). A number of these important places were in the narrower Kyichu region, on which the following remarks will concentrate.

Kyi and Kyishö

In the earliest documents, the Kyichu area is subdivided into an upper and a lower Kyi (Kyitö, Kyime), definitions that are not, or are no longer in use in the oral tradition. (Also the name Kyichu is not very common; the river (the source area of which is considered to be the Nyenchen Thangla mountain range) is often referred to rather as Tsangpo (the name of the Brahmaputra), in the same way as some of the major tributaries are called "Tsangpos" (such as Medro Tsangpo, Drigung Tsangpo, Reting Tsangpo). In the literature, too, one finds Tsangpo (Tsangchab) as the name for Kyichu, an interesting fact which I will not pursue further here). Kyitö and - me are known to form two of the thousand-districts of Uru. The sources leave us uncertain as to what exactly upper and lower Kyi refer. It seems that the geographical extent of the Kyichu river (see Map) does not cover the historical boundaries of the Kyi region and the borders of the Kyi thousand district. According to the *Wangri* list, in which the allocation of the territorial shares of power to the emperor and various clans is noted (*KG* 186f.) the Kyitö - and – me thousand districts fall to the Wa clan, whose settlements are associated with the central Kyichu area (Richardson, p. 231). The *Annals* mention a range of dynastic places that are prefaced by Kyi as part of the name (*Table A*); according to the location of these places (as far as it is known) the Kyi region begins roughly at the later Lamo, or Ganden; the highest upriver Kyi place in the *Annals* that we know of is Kyi Lhä, just south of Ganden (see below). The locations north of here (on both sides of the river) are not, as far as we can see, listed as Kyi places, but are attributed to Medro, or Phenyü. Thus the royal residence place of Dzenthang situated north-east of Kyi Lhä (see below) is called Medro Dzentang and not Kyi Dzentang; opposite, on the other side of the river, the valley of Shog is given as Phenyü Shog etc. On the other hand, in the *Chronicles* Medro is also spoken of as the land of Kyi (DTH 116), perhaps only a geographical classification. It remains open as to whether the old Kyitö district included the Kyichu section of Medro (broken line on the map). The situation of the "Kyi places" in the *Annals* suggests that the Kyi region also included the valley areas south of the river (up to the ends of the valleys), as well as west and east of the lower Kyichu (a presumed exception is the Tölung valley, often abbreviated as Tö ("sTod") in the *Annals*).

Kyi ([s]Kyi) is later spelt as "sKyid", and from the early post-dynastic sources onwards one finds the form Kyishö (lower tracts of the Kyichu area); it is subdivided into the sections of upper and lower Kyishö, with the upper section apparently also being ascribed to northern Medro and the area of the Drigung Tsangpo; the lower Kyishö seems to include also the western part of Chushü which borders on Nyemo, and Tsang Rong respectively (cf. *DZ* 74; Lange, p. 50). The border between upper and lower Kyishö is at approximately the level of Ramagang (southwest of Lhasa). In the early 13th c. this Kyishö became the central territory of the Tshepa hegemony, whose rulers (with their seat in Tshe Gungthang near Lhasa) are also described as the "Lords of Kyitö and - me"

The borders of Uru

The border between Uru and the Left Horn (Yoru) in the south east, is given as Malalagyü (*DEU* 272, *KG* 186; the data refer to the 8th c.). This very probably refers to the Gökarla mountain range, named after Gökarla, one of the central passes on the way to southern Samye. The name Malalagyü of the texts is not known to the locals; the spelling possibly conceals the Malaya mountain of Indian religious geography, which was accepted here in the 8th c. and in the context of the Samye foundation.

One toponym that repeatedly appears in the sources as a geographical description for the areas south of "Malalagyü" is Ngamshö; to my knowledge it is mentioned for the first time in the *Washe* chronicle, where, in connection with the Samye foundation, Padmasambhava speaks of cultivating the sand[banks] of upper and lower (= western and eastern) Ngamshö and turning them into meadows (*DB* 13a). The toponym repeatedly crops up in the literature in connection with various places in southern central Tibet and it appears that it relates to the outlying areas north and south of the Tsangpo in the wider surroundings of Samye.

In this area of northern Yoru there are a number of dynastic places, such as those of On, the residences of Dragmar and Zungka, the places in Tra, Dol and Yar-drog (see Uebach 1988).

The eastern border of Uru is given as the not better known place of Shugpa in Ökha, the western as Shu in Nyemo; the northern boundary ran along the level of the not more precisely known area of Trag, which the *Annals* also list as a residence place (first for AD 658, the period of the rule of Ti Manglön). Among the dynastic places of northern Uru is also the residence of Merke (likewise primarily associated with *tsenpo* Ti Manglön), if the place is identical with the present-day Mer on the upper course of the Kyichu.

Like the other Horn provinces, Uru was divided into an upper and a lower half (Urutö, –me), as well as a number of district and administration units (*tongde, tshen*), which served for military organisation and the various forms of civil taxation (Takeuchi 1994). For Uru the sources variously give 10 to 13 thousand districts (*tongde*), and 10 to 17 further land units (*yüde, tshen* or *yüpöntshen*), the names of which partly relate to larger regions (such as Tölung, Lungshö, Damshö, Medro, Phenyü) and partly also refer to areas inside the *tongde*. Thus several *yüpöntshen* are to be ascribed to the chiliarchy of Kyi, such as those of Ze Chushü, Ngenlam (?), Balam (see below) and Sang (see map). The two (military) halves of upper and lower Uru, each under the command of a *rupön*, probably relate to northern and southern Uru. Thus the position of the *rupön* of Urume was entrusted to a member of the Wa clan, the same clan to which the district areas of Kyitö and Kyime were subordinate.

These Kyi districts certainly belong to the not more closely demarcated region of Urushö, which the *Annals* give as the geographical area of the assembly places of Rekam and Ciulung (see note on the map). From the *Wangri* list we learn that Urushöchen, "the great low tract of Uru", was the portion of territory that was directly subject to the monarch. It is not quite clear what is to be understood by this, but it seems that "great Urushö" can only refer to an area *in* Urushö. I presume that here the narrow area of Lhasa is intended, the position of which is defined in early post-dynastic sources as Uru Kyishökyi thil (centre of Kyishö in Uru) (*KK* 201). With the Ramoche temple Lhasa formed the centre of Uru.

Kyiro Chang
Perhaps the chronologically oldest Kyi toponym is Kyiro (Kyira), one of the pre-imperial principalities (*gyetren*), whose territorial god Kyilha Chamang appears in the list of the

nine territorial gods of united Tibet (Lalou, p. 202; Karmay, p.72). The centre is mentioned in Dunhung documents as "lC[h]ang(~ lJang) sngon" and other variants, "LJong sngon" in the *DEU* chronicle (p. 225). In the listing of the *gyetren* in the *Dunhuang Chronicles*, which clearly suggests a progression from west to east, Kyiro is placed between the dominions of the eastern Tsang (i.e. Nub and Myangro) and the northern Ngäpo (i.e. the later Phenyü) (DTH 80). A Dunhuang fragment that Richardson has worked on gives the seat of the Kyi ruling family as lower Kyi (1998: 28). Chang (= lCang, willow) is a very common place name in central Tibet and there is, for example, a "lCang-ngo" not far from Tagtse on the Kyichu (XD 93a); in relation to the lower Kyi, however, it is far more likely that ancient Kyiro Chang should be identified with the place of the present-day Chang ("lCang", also written as "lJang") on the right bank of the lower Kyichu; it is subdivided into Changtö and –me, which relates to the northern and southern section of the Kyichu valley, which at this point is extremely wide. One can also assume that the territory included the western mountain region of the present-day Chushü county, where there are also "Chang" places (Changra, Changri; XD 119a, 121a; Chushü is presumably approximately identical with the *yüpöntshen* of Ze Chushü). It is probably also this Chang that crops up again in the political landscape of the 11th c., after which Chang, together with the neighbouring territories of Trangpo and Lumpa and the northern Kyichu territories of Nyethang, Trib and Balam, became the residence of successors to the Yumten lineage. In the dynastic period the old Kyiro disappeared as an independent territorial unit; the toponym had obviously maintained itself in the old clan name Kyi, to which the one or the other of the Kyi places outside the Kyichu area may go back.

Royal residences and assembly places in Kyi
Not far north of Chang are the two western valleys of Nam and Bur, which have already been identified by Uebach as places of the winter assembly of the Kyi Nam and the Kyi Bur of the *Annals*. Kyi Bur lies more precisely above Ratö. Kyi is among the places in which the administrative decisions for all Horn provinces were taken, above all the carrying out of the *phalö census* (743 A.D.) (see Uebach in this volume). It is presumably identical with the residence of Namtong. Nam also appears in the list of the thirteen Bonpo assembly places (*dunä*) of Uru (*YU* 19f.) and is known as one of the stations of Padmasambhava on his way to King Trisong Detsen (*DB* 11a).

Also in Kyi is the assembly place of Lingring tshe, which seems to be identical with Kyi Lingtshe, also given in the *Annals* as Kyi Char Lingtshe (see also Thomas, pp. 48, 203, 254). This Char has not yet been identified; one also finds it in the name of the frequently mentioned winter residence Chargyi Changbu, which (as Uebach has already noted) obviously belongs to the Kyi area and should presumably be distinguished from the other Changbu places in the *Annals*, namely Tögyi Changbu and Nyenkar Changbu. Kyi Lingtshe may refer to present-day Kyipo Ling in Chushü (XD 119b).

Of the "Kyi places" of Kyi Chitshe and Kyi Dratshe there is so far no evidence. The well-known assembly place of Kyi Shomara, where according to post-dynastic sources the Tibetan laws were systematised (cf. e.g. Sørensen, p. 184), has been located by Uray (1972: 43) in Tölung (in the area of the Tölung river estuary), as a later source speaks of a Tölung Shomara. A Shomara is unknown here, however.

Likewise unknown in the local tradition is Ngenlam (the place of the residence of Ngenlam Tshesarpa (AD 701) and the area of the Ngenlam *yüpöntshen*), which according to some later sources is clearly to be located in the area of Tshe Gungthang on the Kyichu (Uebach 1988). Thus, for example, one source gives Tshabadru, the birthplace of Lama Zhang in Tshe, as Ngenlam Tshabadru (*LC* 181). Ngenlam also crops up in other contexts of the early Tshepa. The toponymic compound of Ngenlam-Lungpa-Räsum-Trib refers to the narrower Tshepa territory in Kyishö (*GK* 43a). The individual names are known (among other things from the list of the Bonpo *dunä* of Uru); with the exception of Trib their precise location involves some difficulty. Räsum is also mentioned as the centre of the early Tölung principality (Karmay 1996: 72), but also appears in the form of [Uru] Ngenlam Räsum (*YB* 20; *KT* 290; *BA* 173). Lungpa may relate to Kyishö Lungpa or to the not more precisely located *dunä* of Kyishö Lungnag (Uebach 1999: 265). A mount Ngenlam Tronpari is mentioned as one of the geomantic places in the founding story of the Lhasa Jokhang, with the words "in the east (of Lhasa)" (*KK* 214). It corresponds to the Balam Trumpari of other sources (*KG* 221; on Balam see below). Finally, Ngenlam is the place of the Ngenlam Jimogön temple, founded by Dring Yeshe yönten, one of the leading protagonists of the early *chidar* (later dissemination of the Buddhist Teaching) in Ü (11th c.). His group also called itself the Ngenlamtsho (Ngenlam community) after this temple, an alternative name of the so-called upper Dring community (Dring-tshotö), whose religious settlements lay in the region of Kyishö (*GY* 461). The position of the temple is still unclear, but presumably in Tölung, where the primary temple of the lower Dring community was situated (i.e. Drang Ramoche in lower Tölung). The Tshepa were later as it were to inherit these territories of Kyishö which had been converted to Buddhism by the Dring and it is conceivable that the association of the toponym Ngenlam with the area of Tshe goes back to this. But this is not the whole story of this apparently "wandering toponym". The original Ngenlam (also mentioned in connection with one of the nine Masang, an ancient group of clans, *DEU* 225) is probably to be sought in Phenyü, where the Ngenlam family was settled; this emerges indirectly from the Shö inscription, according to which, as is well known, the leadership of the bodyguard chiliarchy of Phenyü was given to this family (Richardson 1985: 21-23). Phenpochu, the main river of Phenyü, is also written as Phenpo Ngenchu (*NG* 295).

Lhasa, which appears in the *Annals* in the form of Rasai Shatshe (deer park of Rasa) is not recorded as an assembly place. As a residence place it is most closely associated with the figure of Songtsen Gampo, who chose it as the site of his *kukar* (personal castle). It was the traces left by this emperor that were later to make this place into a capital. The central position of Lhasa in dynastic times was presumably primarily of a symbolic nature and it was also a temple that functioned as the centre of Uru (see above). The first council assembly is noted as late as 673, so that we have no precise information of the early administrative function of Lhasa. Decisions were obviously made elsewhere. Thus in the period of the effective organisation of the kingdom (= the reign of Ti Manglön), it is mainly Merke and Nyenkar that are mentioned as the seat of the emperor, and the activities of the great councillor Gar Tongtsen Yüsung (the first administrative chief of Tibet proper) are recorded in connection with the places of Nyingdrung (in Damshung), Nyenkar (in Phenyü?), Mongphu (in Tölung) or Shomara.

According to local tradition, the seat of the minister Gar was in Trib (opposite Lhasa), where the locals call an ancient ruin "*lönpo* Gar tshang" (House of Minister Gar). It is said that Gar was banished here for three years by the jealous Songtsen Gampo after the minister supposedly had an affair with the Chinese princess Kongjo whom he had brought to Tibet. A "souvenir" of this journey was, among other things, the divinity Dzongtsen (Trib Dzongtsen), the territorial god of Trib who is at the same time regarded as one of the most powerful local gods of Kyishö. He is the partner of the protective goddess of the neighbouring Tshe Gungthang. As is so often the case, the events of the dynastic period appear to blend with a later story. The "Gar house" presumably goes back to the later Gar family, which provided the patrons and secular rulers of Tshe and had their seat in Trib (*GK* 29a).

Uebach has been able to identify the dynastic places of Kyi Lag (Lagi Buchung) and Balam (which in later sources are often mentioned together in the form of Lag Balam or also Balam Lag) relatively accurately with a valley to the east of Lhasa. Balam is more precisely the valley immediately to the east of Tagtse; it includes two valleys (Balam Shar and –Nub) that run into each other lower down. Lag is unknown today, perhaps it relates to one of the two "Balams". Balam is the setting of the well-known story of Vairocana and the smith and his wife, whom the Master met here on his way from Samye to Yerpa (*KT* 248f.). A dead cow plays a role in this, from which it is said the names Balam (cowpath) and Lag (dead (cow)) derive – certainly a later interpretation of the two place names. Balam Lag was among other things the home of Basenang, one of the most prominent representatives of Buddhism at the time of the Samye foundation; it was he who built a temple in lower Lag, in connection with which he succeeded in inducing his clan brothers (from the Wa clan) to distance themselves from Bon and to practice Buddhism (*DB* 15a). It is possible that behind Balam is the name of this clan, which is also written as "sBa", "'Ba'".

Worth mentioning at this point is a small temple in upper Balam Shar which the locals call Mani lhakhang. It contains completely undamaged paintings which indicate an old Kadmapa temple. To my knowledge this site has not yet been documented. Perhaps the foundation relates to the Balam Shatsha temple, built by Lume, called the Lag Balampa (BA 74; Szerb, p. 59).

The dynastic area of Kyi Lhä with the place Gangtshe, where in the 8th c. among other things the census of the families of the four horns was drawn up, relates in all probability to the Lhä (or Lhäbu) valley south of Ganden, known from the later Gelugpa account of Lhäbugön and Lhälunggön. The latter goes back to the settlement of the Dringtsho group from the 11th c. (*VS* 155; Uebach 1987: 147). It is this historical continuity, too, that leads us to exclude other Lhä places in the Kyichu region (cf. XD 90, 91, 104) as candidates in the location of ancient Lhä.

Dzenthang and Tratöthse
The oldest residence places of the Yarlung house in the Kyichu area are presumably Yarnön Dratötshe in Gyama and Medro Dzenthang, the location of the later Gelugpa monastery of Tsünmotshe situated east of Lamo. I have already discussed these in an

earlier paper (Hazod, forthcoming), and here I will only briefly summarise. Yarnön relates to the area of Gyama, for example expressed in the form Gyama Yarnön (the reversed form Nöngyi Gyama is also found in the sources). Nonlungpa is listed as one of the district units of Uru. Behind Nön ("sNon", "gNon") presumably lies the clan name Nön ("mNon"), one of the allies of Namri Songtsen. The assembly place of "mNon" (registered for the year 714) is certainly to be located in this area. Yarnön Dratötshe, where in 822 the Chinese-Tibetan peace treaty was signed by the Tibetan side, relates to the place Gyama *phodrang* Jampa Migyurling of the later sources, which Namri Songtsen coming from Yarlung built here and where Songtsen Gampo was later born.

From here Songtsen Gampo and his group later set off towards Lhasa, pausing on the (Kyichu?) river, where the king bathed and where for the first time the six-syllabic mantra appeared on a rock (Sørensen, p. 163). This episode from the classical Songtsen Gampo *vita* obviously corresponds with the entry of a later source according to which the court have encamped in lower Chenchen for some time, and where Thonmi Sambhota supposedly made the first offering of the letters (*yiphü*) to the king (*VS 166*), a tradition that is still maintained in Tsünmotshe today. The name Tsünmotshe relates to the "grove of the royal ladies" (and wives of Songtsen Gampo; more precisely the locals call it the place of the Chinese princess, who supposedly stopped here on her way to Lhasa). Dzentang of the *Annals* is the present-day Chenchenthang valley; Tsünmothse lies at the entrance to the valley below a towering rock; it corresponds to Dzen Khogna dolhakhang (stone *vihàra* of Khogna in Dzen[thang] (*VS ibd.*), which numerous post-dynastic sources indeed give as the place where Thonmi created the alphabet. One of the sources adds that this was then later completed in Lhasa (i.e. Lhasa *kukhar* Maru = Phabongkha) (Vitali, 23, 97).

Here it is not a matter of detailed questions of the historicity of the stories associated with these places such as whether Thonmi actually created writing here; the sources make clear that this section of the central Kyichu, in the vicinity of Gyama, form a significant pre-Lhasa period place of residence of the Yarlung house, in which period essential events concerning the formation of the empire are also to be dated, a fact that has already been alluded to by Richardson in relation to Gyama. He also established that the clans allied to the Yarlung king Namri Songtsen did indeed have their estates in this area around ancient Medro; the oral traditions of Gyama make it possible to conclude that Namri Songtsen came to Gyama from Yarlung via On, that is to say, the area of his allies, together with whom he was to drive the rival, the prince of Ngäpo out of his fortress (on this events see DTH 105f.; Beckwith, p. 205; Richardson, p. 128f.).

Zupug

The valley of Zibug in eastern Medro is also included in the network of connecting routes between the region on the Kyichu and the southern Tsangpo. The entrance of the valley lies east of Parab (most likely identical with the Bonpo *dunä* of Medro Barab) and runs south west in the direction of upper On and Gyama. In the wide central section of the valley, on the western side, above the village and monastery of Khargye, there is a remarkable complex of ruins which indicates an ancient residential building flanked by a tower. The place of the ruins is called Lingtökyang by the locals (*kyang* in the sense of "wild ass"); there are no further details about this place. It is just said that the ruins "have always been there". There is mention of another ruin further up on the eastern side of the valley which is said to refer to a place of the Chinese princess Kongjo. A number of things indicate that Zibug corresponds to the Zupug of the *Annals* (first mentioned for AD 688); it is evidently the Medroi Zurphug which a later source lists as one of the (eastern) halts of Kongjo on her way to Lhasa (*MK* 215b). The great ruins of Lingtökyang may relate to the Zupugi Kyangbutshe ("Wild Ass Grove"), known as one of the summer residences of Trisong Detsen (last registered in the *Annals* for the year 761). According to the *Washe*, in a pig year (presumably pig year 771), shortly before the Samye foundation, the Buddhists/Bon debate took place here (*DB* 13b). On the basis of the sources on Samye, Sørensen (pp. 572-577) has already made it clear that this place (which appears in various spellings in the later literature) can only be in Medro. It is the place of Medrozichen, the powerful *naga* (*lu*) king whose subjugation by Padmasambhava is described in several sources and who namely in Zurphü (= Zupug) offered the king his services (*SB* 29). There are several "Zichen places" in Medro, such as the Zichenthang plain on the Zichen river, summer residence of the nomads south west of Ruthog, who worship a Zichenlha as their territorial god. The name relates to the *zi* stone, which a forefather supposedly discovered on lake Zichen in the south-eastern mountains. Locals still speak of other Medrozichen places in the mountains, thus in Zibug too, where the Medrozichen place near the Gotshangla, the pass leading to On, is supposed to be. The spelling Zubug may be related to the *neri* Zudrug, the holy mountain on the western side of the Zichenthang.

In the texts, the snake-decorated Medrozichen is identified with Madropa, the *naga* king of Lake Anavatapta (the latter a name for the holy Manasarowa). He is among others a protective deity of the highly significant temples of Katshe (7th c.) and Lamo (11th c.) on the Kyichu; he later appears in the Tsongkapa vita and the founding story of Ganden and ultimately becomes one of the most powerful *lu* of the Dalai Lama period, making his arrival in Lhasa's Lukhang temple. The origin of this *naga* manifestation in Tibet goes back, I would provisionally say, to this local Zichen deity in Medro, which owes its popularity and supra-regional significance to the fact that it was here, at the beginning of the effective *ngadar* (early dissemination of the Holy Law), that the king had his residence.

The "mobile centre"
Zupug formed one of the six residence places and seven assembly places mentioned in the *Annals* for the period of rule of Trisong Detsen (*Table B*). The *Annals* break off in 763, so the number is very probably larger (for the period after 763, later sources give Zungka, Zupug and Dragmar as his residences). This number of alternative locations can also be carried over into the ruling period of other kings. The questions is, what is the reason for this constant change of location, which is so characteristic of the early Tibetan state organisation; what are the criteria for the choice of this or that place ?

From the *Annals* we learn that some areas were visited both in winter and in summer, whether as a place for the *phodrang* or for the *dünma*. With few exceptions, the *phodrang* and *dünma* always encamped in different places in each season, even if in relative proximity to each other (Uebach 1988; relative here means within the same province or Ru-half). Some places are visited several times at irregular intervals, others are only mentioned once or twice and then do not appear in the *Annals* again. In the report of a messenger to the Chinese emperor from the year 672, it is said that the Tibetan king moves around every spring and summer according to the availability of grass and water; in autumn and winter he lives in a fortified site, but here too prefers a tent as his actual residence (Stein, p. 127). This gives us a conception of the location of a royal household, but provides a false picture of a court and aristocracy leading a nomadic existence for economic reasons.

The places discussed in the Kyichu area are all in the side valleys; in the case of Zupug, Kyi Bur or Kyi Lhas, somewhere in the central or upper valley area. Other locations in the *Annals* are also rather remote. More precisely, the questions should perhaps be, what caused the royal family to set up camp in a hinterland such as Kyi Lhä or Kyi Bur? Unfortunately, we know too little about the clan-specific affiliation of these areas (a few data are to be found in the *Wangri* listing and in the statements on the *tongde* and military organisation). My supposition is that in the well over 30 residence places and almost 40 assembly places of Tibet proper it is largely a matter of the estates or homes of clans and aristocratic families who as ministers or other allies of the emperor belonged to the narrower circle of the *chabsi* (central government) and also in a sense to the circle of "king-makers". These groups alternated in offering the *tsenpo* their place as winter and summer residence and alternated in providing the place for the holding of the assembly. This produces the characteristic political landscape of an at least ostensibly decentralised state organisation whose internal cohesion, as it were, was guaranteed by the mobility of the centre.

Table A: "Kyi-places" in the *Dunhuang Annals*
(Su-R,Wi-R = places of the summer / winter residence
Su-A, Wi-A = summer / winter assembly places)

Kyi Nam (sKyi rNams (= [sKyi] sNam-stong ? - Wi-R 663)) > Wi-A 711
Kyi Bur > Wi-A 761, 762
Kyi Lagi Buchung (sKyi Glag gi Bu[~Pu]-chung) > Wi-A: 674, 685, 694; Su-A 685, 756, 762,763
Kyi Lagi Ruche (Kyi Glag gi Ryu-bye) > Wi-A 678 (Ba-lam > 677, 678)
Kyi Lhä Gangtshe (sKyi lHas Gang-ts[h]al) > Wi-R 704; Wi-A 724, 732, 733
Kyi [Char] Lingtshe (sKyi [Byar] Lings-ts[h]al) > Wi-A 704, 728, 746
Kyi Lingringtshe (sKyi Gling-rings-ts[h]al) (= sKyi Lings-ts[h]al, Byar Lings-ts[h]al ?) > Wi-A 692
Char[gyi Changbu] ([sKyi ?] Byar [gyi lCang-bu]) > Wi/Su-R (see *Table B*)
Kyi Chitshe (sKyi Phyi-ts[h]al) > Wi-A 756
Kyi Dratshe (sKyi Dra-tshal) > Wi-A 712
Kyi Shomara (sKyi Sho-ma-ra) > Wi-A 729, 731, 744

Further places situated in the closer Kyichu area: Onchangdo ('On-chang-do) > Wi-R 700, 702; Wi-A 702, 707, 708, 709. In Medro: Medro Keche (Mal-tro sKe-bye) > R 660; Medro Dzenthang (Mal-tro brDzen-t[h]ang) > [Su-]R 694, 713, 714, 761; Su-A 761; Medro Tam ([Mal-tro] lTam (= [Mal-tro] lTam gyi Ra-sngon ? > Su-R 671) > Su-A 714; Nön (mNon [= sNon / rGya-ma ?]) > Wi-A 714. In Zupug: Zupug [pho-drangding] (Zu-spug[i pho-brang-sdings]) > Su-R 758, 761; Su-A 688; Zupugi Zhongba (Zu-spugi Zhong-ba) > [Su-]A 694, Zupugi Kyangbutshe (Zu-spugi rKyang-bu-ts[h]al) > Su-A 713, 715.

Table B: Residences (Su-R, Wi-R) and assembly places (Su-A, Wi-A)
in Central Tibet as registered in the *Dunhuang Annals* for the reign of
Trisong Detsen (r. 756-797/802?) (the entries cease with the year 763)

Su-R	Wi-R
756: Zungkar (Zung-kar)	756: Zungkar
757: Babamgyi Yagrugong (Ba-bams gyi g.Yag-ru-gong)	757: Tögyi Changbu (sTod gyi lCang-bu)
758: Zupug	758: Chargyi Changbu (Byar gyi lCang-bu)
759: Tögyi Kho (sTod[-lung] gyi mKho)	759: Nyenkar (Nyen-kar)
760: Myangdron (Myang-sgrom)	760: ?
761: Zupugi phodrangding	761: Chargyi Changbu (= Zupug Kyangbutshe?)
762: Char[gyi Changbu]	762: Chargyi Changbu
763: Chargyi Changbu	763: ?

after 763:
Zungkar (~Zur-mkhar); Zupug Kyangbutshe (place of Buddhist/Bon debate in the pig year [771?]); Dragmar (Brag-[d]mar i.e. Brag-dmar 'Om-bu-tshal, Brag-dmar mTsho-mo-mgur; the places are mentioned in later sources as residences of the king during the period of the foundation of Samye in the 770s.

Su-A	Wi-A
756: Lagi Buchung	756: Kyi Chitshe
757: Tögyi Mong (sTod[-lung] gyi Mong[-kar ?])	757: ?
758: ?	758: ?
759: ?	759: Slo (= Lo ?)
760: ?	760: Ne-tso-lung
761: Medro Dzenthang	761: Kyi Bur
762: Lagi Puchung	762: Kyi Bur
763: Lagi Buchung	763: ?

Annals = Dunhuang Annals, in DTH, 13-75.

BA = Roerich, G. N. *The Blue Annals*. Delhi: Motilal Banarsidass 1995.

Beckwith, Christopher I. A Study of the Early Medieval, Chinese, Latin and Tibetan Historical Sources on Pre-Imperial Tibet. Ann Arbor: UMI Dissertation Service 1977.

Bellezza, John V. *Divine Dyads*. Dharmsala LTWA 1997.

DB = Wangdu, Pasang and H. Diemberger. *dBa'-bzhed. The Royal Narrative Concerning the Bringing of the Buddha's Doctrine to Tibet*. Wien: Verlag der ÖAW 2000.

DEU = *Chos 'byung chen mo bstan pa'i rgyal mtshan lde'u jo sras kyis mdzad pa*, Bod-ljongs mi-dmangs dpe-skrun-khang, Lhasa 1987.

DTH = Bacot, J. Thomas, F. W. and Toussaint, Ch. *Documents de Touen houang relatifs à l'histoire du Tibet*. Paris: Libraire orientale Paul Geuthner 1940.

DZ = Wylie, Turrell, V. *The Geography of Tibet. According to the 'Dzam gling rgyas bshad. Text and English Translation*. Roma: IsMEO 1962.

GK = Ngag-dbang bstan-'dzin 'phrin-las rnam-rgyal, *Gung thang dpal gyi gtsug lag khang byung rabs dang bcas pa'i dkar chag 'gro mgon zhal lung bdud rtsi'i chu rgyun* (written in 1782), copy of a ms of 76 folio kept in the library of the TASS, Lhasa.

GY = dPal-'byor bzang-po, *rGya bod yig tshang chen mo*, Si-khron mi-rigs dpe-skrun-khang, Chengdu 1985.

Hazod, forthcoming = Hazod, Guntram. The Royal Residence *pho brang* Byams-pa mi-'gyur-gling and the story of Srong-btsan sgam-po's birth in Rgya-ma, *in* H. Blezer (ed.), *Tibetan Studies*, forth-coming.

Karmay 1996 = Karmay, Samten. The Tibetan Cult of Mountain Deities and its Political Significance, *in* A. M. Blondeau and E. Steinkellner, eds., *Reflections of the Mountain. Essays on the History and Social Meaning of the Mountain Cult in Tibet and the Himalaya*, Wien: Verlag der ÖAW 1996, 59-76.

Kaschewsky = Kaschewsky, Rudolf. *Das Leben des Lamaistischen Heiligen Tsong-kha-pa Blo-bzaï-grags-pa (1357-1419)*. Wiesbaden: Harrassowitz 1971.

KG = dPa'-bo gTsug-lag 'phreng-ba, *Chos 'byung mkhas pa'i dga' ston*, Mi-rigs dpe-skrun-khang, Beijing 1986.

KK = *bKa' chems ka khol ma*, Kan-su'i mi-rigs dpe-skrun-khang, Lanzhou 1989.

Lalou = Lalou, Marcelle. Catalogues des principautés du Tibet ancien, *JA* 253, 1965, 189-215.

Lange = Lange, Kristina. *Die Werke des Regenten Saōs rgyas rgya mc'o*. Berlin: Akademie-verlag 1976.

LC = Ri-bo-che dPon-tshang, *lHo rong chos 'byung*, Bod-ljongs bod-yig dpe-rnying dpe-skrun-khang, Lhasa 1994.

MK = *Chos rgyal srong btsan sgam po'i maōi bka' 'bum*. Xining: mTsho-sngon mi-rigs dpe-skrun-khang, 1991

NG = Eimer, Helmut. *rNam thar rgyas pa*, 1.Teil. Wiesbaden: Otto Harrassowitz 1979.

Richardson 1985 = Richardson, Hugh. *A Corpus of Early Tibetan Inscriptions*. London 1985.

Richardson = Richardson, Hugh. *High Peaks, Pure Earth. Collected Writings on Tibetan History and Culture*. London: Serindia Publications 1998.

SB = *sBa bzhed*, Mi-rigs dpe-skrun-khang, Beijing 1982.

Sørensen = Sørensen, Per K. *Tibetan Buddhist Historiography. The Mirror Illuminating the Royal Genealogies. An Annotated Translation of the XIVth Century Tibetan Chronicle rGyal-rabs gsal-ba'i me-long*. Asiatische Forschungen 128. Wiesbaden: Harrassowitz 1994.

Stein = Stein, Rolf. *Die Kultur Tibets*. Berlin: Edition Weber 1993 (German ed. of *La civili-sation tibétain*).

Szerb = Szerb, János. *Bu ston's History of Buddhism in Tibet*. Wien: Verlag der ÖAW 1990.

Takeuchi 1994 = Takeuchi, Tsuguhito. Tshan: Subordinate Administrative Units of the Thou-sand-districts in the Tibetan Empire. In: P. Kvaerne, *Tibetan Studies*, vol. 2, Oslo: The Institute for Comparative Research in Human Culture 1994, 649-659.

Thomas = Thomas, Frederick William. *Tibetan Literary Texts and Documents Concerning Chinese Turkestan. Part II*. London: The Royal Asiatic Society 1935.

Uebach 1987 = Uebach, Helga. *Nel-pa paōóitas Chronik Me-tog Phreï-ba*, München: Bayri-sche Akademie der Wissenschaften 1987.

Uebach 1988 = Uebach, Helga. Königliche Residenzen und Orte der Reichsversammlung im 7. und 8. Jahrhundert. *In* H. Uebach and Jampa Panglung, eds., *Tibetan Studies*, München 1988, 503-514.

Uebach 1999 = Uebach, Helga. On the Thirty-seven Holy Places of the Bon-pos in the Tibetan Empire. H. Eimer *et al.* eds, *Studia Tibetica et Mongolica*. (*Festschrift Manfred Taube*).

Indica et Tibetica 34. Swisttal-Odendorf 1999, 261-277.

Uray 1960= Uray, Géza. The Four Horns of Tibet, *Acta Orientalia Hungaricae* 10, 1960, 31–57.

Uray 1972 = Uray, Géza.The Narrative of Legislation and Organisation of the mKhas pa'i dga' ston, *Acta Orientalia Hungaricae* 26, 1972, 11–68.

Vitali = Vitali, Roberto. *The Kingdoms of Gu-ge Pu-hrang. According to mNga'-ris rgyal-rabs by Gu-ge mkhan-chen Ngag-dbang grags-pa*. Dharamsala 1996.

VS = sDe-srid Sangs-rgyas rgya-mtsho, *Dga' ldan chos 'byung bai óârya ser po*, Krung-go bod kyi shes-rig dpe-skrun-khang, Beijing 1989.

Wasche = DB

YB = g.Yung drung bon gyi rgyud 'bum, in *Sources for a History of Bonism. Part 2*, ed. by Mitsushima, D. T. 1997.

XD = *Xizang zizhiqu Dimingzhi* [The Toponymical Record of TAR]. 2 Vols. Beijing 1993.

Suggested further Readings:

Beckwith, Christopher I. *The Tibetan Empire in Central Asia*. Princeton: Princeton University Press 1987.

Uray, G. The offices of the *bruō-pa*s and great *mðan*s and the territorial division of Central Tibet in the early 8th century. In *Acta Orientalia Hungaricae* 15, 1962, 335–360.

Uray, G. L'annalıstique et la pratique bureaucratique au Tibet ancien. In *Journal Asiatique* 153, 1975, 157-170.

Dalai Lama's bodyguard troops
In background carved building
1998.285.451 (BL.P.80)

Military Administration and Military Duties in Tibetan-ruled Central Asia (8th-9th century)

Tsuguhito Takeuchi (Kobe)

The Tibetan Empire ruled the Southern Route of Silk Road and most of the Gansu Corridor, including Khotan, Lob-nor, and Dunhuang, for over fifty years from the late 8th to the mid-9th centuries. The newly acquired territories were divided into several administrative units called *khrom*, where Tibetan military district governments were established. Tibetan armies, including Sumpas and Zhangzhungs, were sent and stationed there, and local peoples, such as Chinese, Khotanese, 'A-zhas, and Mthong-khyabs, were recruited *in situ* and incorporated into the Tibetan military system.

While the outline of the Tibetan administrative system became gradually understood, its details, e.g., how Tibetan armies were sent, how local peoples were recruited, what were their duties, and so on, remained unknown.

Among the Old Tibetan texts unearthed from Central Asia, the wooden slips from Miran and Mazar Tagh are the most informative primary sources for our concern, because many of them were actually used by military officials and soldiers. The largest collection of Tibetan wooden slips (hereafter woodslips) is the Stein Collection in the British Library, where about 2,200 items are housed. I started databasing and classifying them since last year. In this paper I wish to draw your attention to some of the woodslips regarding Tibetan military administration in Khotan with a hope to provide some substantial information.

1. Old Tibetan woodslips – two fold analyses: shape and content
One of the important characteristics of woodslips is their form or shape. The shape of a woodslip conforms with its function and usage.

2. Letter with seal case

plate-1 For example, these are two examples of a letter cover with a seal case, which is always at the left end. And the form of address is written from left to right.

plate-2a The content is written on the second and sometimes the third slip, which were combined together with strings.

plate-2b is a letter in another form; it was attached by string to present goods like an invoice.

3. Reuse and tools

Reuse is another important feature of woodslips. The surface of used woodslips was often shaved away to be reused as woodslips.

plate-3a But they were also reused for wooden tools, such as knives, spoons, spatulas, and so on.

plate-3b Sometimes one edge was rounded and charred, probably to make it soft. According to my colleague, they resemble those found in toilet ruins in Japan – so could be contemporary 'toilet paper'. Stein states in his journey report that the Tibetan ruins both in Miran and Mazar Tagh are distinguished by a bad smell, to which these scrapers may have contributed. So much for woodslips in general, but here I wish to focus on particular groups of woodslips.

4. *ri-zug* woodslips

plate-4a These are a particular type of tally sticks. One side is painted red. Several short and long notches are cut. Sometimes *nas* "barley" is written on them. A wedge is cut away at the right bottom corner. A string-hole is on the left. Nearly 80 of these items were found from Mazar Tagh. Thus, they form a group, which I call "*ri-zug* slips."

plate-4b On the left side are written place names, often ending with *rtse* "mountain peak." They are places for *ri-zug* or hill-stationing for watchmen. Thomas translates *ri-zug* as "mountain sickness." *zug* is the perfect stem of the intransitive verb *'dzug-pa*; it came to mean "prickle, sick" in Western dialects, which Jäschke learned at Kyerong. But, Tibetans would not get mountain sickness in the Taklamakan desert. Thus *zug* should be returned to its original meaning "settle, station." Around Mazar Tagh, there are many hills or *tâgh*s to which watchmen were sent to station for a certain period. I have identified 39 such *ri-zug* spots.plate-4bb.

plate-4c These watchmen were sent in a unit called *tshugs*, which is another derivation from the verb *'dzug-pa*. One *tshugs* consists of 4 men, *tshugs-pon* "commander," *'og-pon* "sub-commander," *byan-po* "cook", and *byan-g.yog* "assistant cook." The inclusion of two cooks may look strange, but is understandable because this is not a combat unit (by the way in 6th c. Japan, every soldier was accompanied by one cook during military campaigns).

plate-4d Now, back to the woodslips. How were they made and used? According to my colleague Prof. Tateno, a specialist of Japanese woodslips, in the process of making these slips, a triangular cut-away must have been made before cutting the right bottom wedge. And in fact we found those slips.

plate-4e This is the very first stage, where a *ri-zug* spot is written, but no notches or wedge cut away. The upper one is the next stage, where notches are cut. This shows how notches function: long notches are cut across all the way down to the

Plate 1

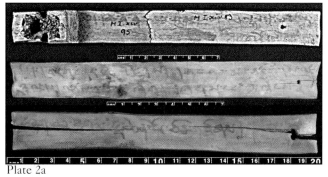

Plate 2a

Plate 2b

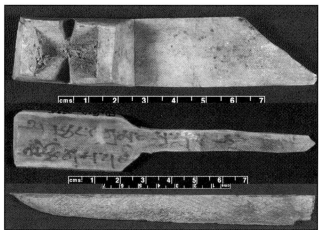

Plate 3a

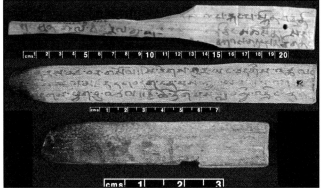

Plate 3b

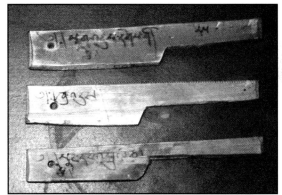

Plate 4a

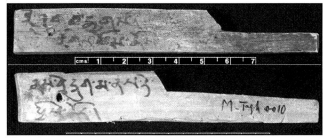

Plate 5a

Plate 5c

Plate 6a

A letter from the watchmen at Gling-rings to those stationing at Ho-tong gyu-mo
and other ri-zug spots westward to relay their request for provisions to Mazar Tagh.

Mazar Tagh   Ho-tong gyu-mo   Gling-rings

Plate 6d

At the bank of the river-confluence (of the Yurung-kash and Kara-kash),
the rear guard soldiers of Ngam-ru-pag [station].

Plate 8a

Report of the escape of a Khotanese watchman from Stag-bzhi

Plate 8b

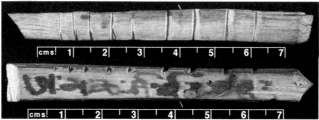

Plate 8d

bottom edge, while the same number of short notches are cut both at the top and bottom edges. That means: the long notches serve for later match-up or identification, while the short ones represent the number (i.e. amount) of grain.

Now, as to how were they used. When watchmen, a group of *tshugs-po*, set out for hill-stationing, they bring their provisions, but they need to receive more provisions later, for which they bring the cut-out wedge as a tally. So the tally was made and cut apart before the watchmen's departure. After a certain period, messengers called *so-slung* (N 1936) transport provisions to the hill-stationing spot together with the woodslip indicating their destination. When the messengers hand over the provisions to the watchmen, the latter had to show the tally (wedge part) for identification, which the messengers bring back together with the slip to the office in Mazar Tagh as a receipt. The slips were then kept in the office as records.

5. Periods of hill-stationing
In a few cases, these woodslips contain verso writings by the watchmen.

plate-5a, plate-5b A watchman named Zig-tsho received the provisions for hill-stationing. Sometimes they didn't receive the promised amount and wrote, "[We] have not received six *bre* of barley; [we] will receive [them] later."

plate-5c N 1541 seems to mention the provisions for hill-stationing for one month. But another text (N 1442) suggests that the amount of barley flour to be received was about one *khal* and 10 *bre* - which is not so much. I suspect that one month was rather exceptional, and that watchmen received provisions every two or three weeks.

How long, then, did watchmen have to be stationed on the hill? In one woodslip (N 1629) watchmen complain that they stayed as long as one year and two winter months, which is probably exceptionally long. They were probably stationed for within a year, during which they were supposed to receive provisions regularly.

6. Locations of *ri-zug* spots
plate-6a In spite of such a well organized military supply system, it is not surprising to find woodslips in which watchmen make urgent requests for extra provisions due to shortage. For example, this is a letter from the watchmen stationed at a hill named Gling-rings to the watchmen stationing at Ho-tong gyu-mo and other hills westwards to relay their request for provisions to the headquarters, Mazar Tagh. Incidentally, these slips give us hints as to the relative locations of hill spots. plate-6b mapAs we have seen, there were about 40 spots. Many of them were located to the east of Mazar Tagh, some to the north, and probably some to the west. To the south of Mazar Tagh, at the confluence of Kara Kash and Yurung Kash there was a station of rear-guard.plate-6c

7. How were Tibetan armies sent to Central Asia – *ru* and *stong-sde*
plate-7This is a list of watchmen of each *tshugs* and the *stong-sde* they belong to. For example, at Ho-tong gyu-mo is stationing a *tshugs* consisting of 2 Tibetans and 2 Khotanese. The two Tibetans, i.e., *tshugs-pon* and *'og-pon*, belong to different *stong-sde*, Myal-pa and Skyi-stod stong-sde, respectively.

In this way, Tibetan soldiers composing each *tshugs* belong to different *stong-sde*s, and even to different *ru*-s. They seem to have been selected intentionally from different *stong-sde*s (as in the case of Miran). But if a soldier on duty became sick, he had to be replaced by someone in the same *stong-sde* (N 2013). The replacement took place not in Central Tibet but in Mazar Tagh.

We may infer from these that the Tibetan armies were sent to Central Asia not *ru* but *stong-sde* as a unit, and that they were accompanied by their family and settled there. Soldiers were called for duty by turns, but while off duty they lived with their families. This supports Hugh Richardson's statement, "the military occupation of a great province lasting for nearly a century could not have operated without permanent bases and an efficient commissariat. The campaigning season was generally confined to autumn and winter and the Tibetans doubtless followed the Chinese practice of establishing military colonies where soldiers' families could live, and grain could be grown." (Richardson 1998: p. 172). The main military duties of soldiers during off campaigning periods were watchmen and scouts, while their non-military duties were farming and livestock herding (*dor* woodslips from Miran).

Thus, Mazar Tagh and Miran were military forts, but, like ancient Roman forts, they were also inhabited by civilians, including soldiers' families, merchants and so on. This is why administrative officials, such as *rtse-rje* "town prefect" and *mngan* "official of treasury" were placed there.

8. Tibetan administration of Khotan

plate-8a Now, what about local people, namely Khotanese, in Tibetan rule? As we have seen, people belonging to the administrative units called *tshard* and *srang* were recruited and incorporated into the units of Tibetan watchmen *tshugs* as auxiliaries. Not surprisingly, some woodslips report the escape and execution of Khotanese watchmen (N 1638, Contract Text 58).

The regime of the kingdom, on the other hand, seems to have been mostly retained.

plate-8b, 8c This is a similar type of tally stick, but is thicker with writing on three sides. Barley-meal and beer for the new year's [salary] for *spa* Sa-de fell short; [the amount] deficient was summed up and [written on this] tally stick which was divided into a "child", and the "child" was also given to *spa* Sa-de. *chang* and *bag-pye* are written on notches representing the amounts. This *bu* "child" must refer to the wedge or tally cut away from the right bottom corner, on which the same number of notches must be cut and the name *spa* Sa-de must be written. When he receives the barley and beer later, he has to present the tally. Thus, it served as a food ticket. *spa* is the title of a local Khotanese official.

plate-8d This is apparently a similar kind of *bu* or tally cut away from the main body of tally stick. Interestingly, it is a food ticket for *a-ma-cha*, the highest Khotanese official.

These woodslips together with other paper documents (e.g. P 1089 and Hedin contracts texts 10, 15, 38) clearly indicate that organisation beginning from the Khotanese king and *a-ma-cha*, down to the local officials such as *spâta* and *parsha*, remained intact under Tibetan rule (P 1089). But, as P 1089 also shows, the Khotanese king was headed by a Tibetan *blon* in charge of Khotan (*Li'i blon*); *a-ma-cha* and other high Khotanese officials were subordinate to a Tibetan *rtse-rje* (*rtse-rje chen-po*: N 1769) in Khotan. Tibetan *rtse-rje*s were both in Khotan and Mazar Tagh. But the highest Tibetan official was likely to be in Mazar Tagh, the headquarters of the

Tibetan administration in Khotan, from where he supervised Khotan to the south and frontiers to the east, north, and west.

Thus, it is most likely that small kingdoms, such as Khotan and Nanzhao, were allowed to retain their regimes under the Tibetan colonial domination.

9. Tibetan administration of Central Asia – Miran, Dunhuang, and Mkhar-tsan

In the other regions, military district governments or *khrom (chen-po)* were established in Tshal-byi, Kwa-cu, Dbyar-mo-thang, and Mkhar-tsan, where more direct Tibetan administrations were established. These *khrom*s were together put under the administration by the council of *Bde-blon* ministers.

Within each *khrom*, local administrative systems were mostly retained, and local officials held high civil administrative post, for example a Chinese *to-dog* in Dunhuang. But the posts of heads of administration of each town, i.e., *rtse-rje*s, were occupied by Tibetans.

On the military side, local inhabitants, such as Chinese, 'A-zhas and Mthong-khyabs were organized into *stong-sde*s. But the highest posts for each military unit (e.g., *stong-pon*) were mostly occupied by Tibetans, while local officials were appointed to be their assistants (e.g., *stong-zla*).

Head of a *khrom* "military district government" was *dmag-pon* "the highest-ranking military officer," but his title for the position was *ru-dpon*, which is equal to *ru-dpon* in Dbu-ru, G.yas-ru, *etc.* plate-9 (As I mentioned above, Tibetan armies were sent to Central Asia *stong-sde* as a unit but not *ru*.) The employment of the title *ru-dpon* for the head of a *khrom* in the frontier provinces may have implied an intention of the Tibetan government to eventually extend their *ru*-system to Central Asia, but it is a topic for another discussion.

I hope our preliminary examination of woodslips has shed some light on how Tibetan military administration in Central Asia, particularly in Khotan, was organized and functioned.

ABBREVIATIONS

Contract Text	Takeuchi, T. *Old Tibetan Contracts from Central Asia.* Tokyo, 1995
N.	IOL Tibet 'N' numbers, requisition numbers for Tibetan wood slips in the British Library.
Richardson 1998	Richardson, H. *High Peaks, Pure Earth*, London, 1998.
Tak.	Text number in Takeuchi, T. *Old Tibetan Manuscripts from East Turkestan in the Stein Collection of the British Library.* 3 vols, 1997-98, Tokyo–London

ri-zug "hill-stationing"

	pres	pf	
vi	'dzug	zug	be pricked in, stick to
vt	'dzugs	btsug	plant, prick, found, place
vi	'tshugs	tshugs	penetrate, establish oneself, settle

zug (pf stem of 'dzug) >   West dial. "pricks, feel a prick, sick"

                          >   settle, station

ri zug du mchis   (Tak 141)

ri zugi brgyags   (*TLTD* 2: 216, 234)

tshugs

	tshugs-pon	'og-pon
	byan-po	byan-g.yog

Plate 4b

Woodslip type 4 verso texts

N1180

    A. 'jag ma 'gur
    B. ri zug brgyags z[i]gs [tshos (/pos)] nos
    "Zigs-tsho (/po) received the provisions for hill-stationing."

N 1111

    A. $ /:/ stag skugs /
    B. nas bre drug ma nos te pyis nod
    "[We] have not received six *bre* of barley; [we] will receive [them]   later."
    six short notches and one long on verso.

N1541

    A. dgra yI cad /
    B. zla (/za) pa rI zugI brgyags / ryang rogs nos
    "Ryang-rog received the provisions of hill-stationing (for a   month?)."

N1442

    A. $ /:/ 'phrul gI mye long / kun snang rtse /
    B. glu gang gis phye khal gcIg dang bre bzhI nos / phyin bre [phye   dang] [
    "Glu-gang received one *khal* and 4 *bre* of flour; later [he will   receive . .] and a half *bre*."

Plate 5b

'bu gang   (Tib N 1678)

'bu sha[ng] [— khar]   (Tib N 1529)

'bum rdugs khri skugs 'jor   (Tib N 1109, 1606, 1833)

'bye ri snang dang [(Tib N 1450)

'jag ma 'gur   (Tib N 1180)

'phrul gI mye long kun snang rtse   (Tib N 1382?, 1442)

'phrul kyi rtse   (Tib N 1535)

bya mngas tshal   (Tib N 1625)

bye ma 'dor (/'dord) gi rtse   (Tib N 1344, 1546, 1630, 1826, 1832; Tak 247)

dag yo chad   (Tib N 1178)

dgra yi chad   (Tib N 1541, 1639, 1651, 1831, 1874)

dgra [byung] sh[o]r [tag] chad   (Tib N 1192, 1436, 1839)

dru gu 'joɾ   (Tib N 1153, 1370, 1438, 1577, 1782)

gling rings smug po tshal   (Tib N 1107, 1114, 1118, 1574, 1577, 1640)

ho-tong gyu-mo   (Tib N 1554, 1577, 1606?, Tak 247)

khrI skugs [cu] tshe   (Tib N 1425)

khu 'dus   (Tib N 1104)

khu (/khra?) 'dzin   (Tib N 1373)

khun [-u-]   (Tib N 1444)

legs pa yId bzhin sbyor   (Tib N 1504)

mjag ma mgur   (Tib N 1110, 1544, 1627)

mnga' ris byin gyi rtse   (Tib N 1117, 1376, 1838)

mye [sbyam?]   (Tib N 1378)

myes byIn cutshe   (Tib N 1507)

pe'u mar   (Tib N 1683, Tak 122)

rgyal ta gur   (Tak 164)

rke chad   (Tib N 1375)

rma? ca jig bag du   (Tib N 1783)

sk[i]d g[o] mkar   (Tib N 1677)

snang dang dprul ('prul) gyI rtse   (Tib N 1105, 1163, 1457, 1836)

snang dang mtong rtse   (Tib N 1449, Tak 47)

stag 'dus dgyes (/dges) gi rtse   (Tib N 1103, 1113, 1435)

stag bzhi bya ra sa   (Tib N 1164, 1536, 1606)

stag rtse khri skugs 'jor   (Tib N 1827, Tak 247)

stag skugs bye ri rtse   (Tib N 1106, 1111, 1112, 1601)

stag sras d[gyes gyi] rtse   (Tib N 1115, 1440)

ta ha'   (Tib N 1415)

tsang lang tshe   (Tib N 1542)

tshe'u chag   (Tib N 1108, 1439, 1600)

Plate 6b

List of Watchmen and their Regiments

N 1554
Ho-tong gyu-mo   2 Tibetans and 2 Khotanese
        tshugs-pon   Myal-pa [stong-sd   <G.yo-ru
        'Og-pon   Skyi-stod [stong]-sde   <Dbu-ru

N 1574
Gling-ring smug-po-tshal   2 Tibetans and 2 Khotanese
        tshugs-pon   Bzang-'ord [stong]-sde   <?
        'Og-pon   Lang-myi'i sde   <G.yas-ru

Tak 247
Stag-rtse khri-skug-'jor   3 Tibetans
        Mya tshes-kong   Grom-pa'i sde   <Ru-lag
        Lo-nan myes-chung   Myang-ro'i sde   < Ru-lag
        Snya-shur stag-bzang   Rtsal-mo-pag gi sde   < ZZ stod

Bye-ma 'dord   2 Tibetans and 1 Khotanese
        Phur-myi rke-dung   Yang-rtsang gi sde   < ZZ smad?
        Sro[sti?]-kro   'O-tso-pag gi sde   < ZZ stod
        Li ce'u-'do   *tshard* Jam-nya

Ho-tong gyu-mo   2 Tibetans and 1 Khotanese
        . .   Phod-kar gyi [sde]   < G.yas-ru

Tak 47
Snang-dang-mthong-rtse   2 Tibetans and 2 Khotanese
        tshugs-pon   . . .   < Sum-pa

Plate 7

khram-bu

N 1924

A1. $ /:/ lo sar gi bag pye dang chang   * * spa [sa de /]
B1. chad de snga slad sdoms te chad pa   * * chang * * bag pye
B2. khram ma bur bgos te bu yang
C1. yang spa' sa de la stsald /

Plate 8c

khrom	–	Tshal-byi, Kwa-cu, Dbyar-mo-thang, Mkhar-tsan		
rtse-rje	–	*to-dog*		
stong-pon	–	*stong-zla*		
ru-dpon	=	head of 4 *stong-sde*s in each *ru* head of a *khrom*	=	*dmag-pon*
administrative post				military rank

Plate 9

Bell's entry:
"(ar) Sera Monastery in summer. Taken from hill behind it."
1998.285.294 (BL.H.268A)

King Lang Darma and his Rule

Samten Karmay

In the post eleventh century Tibetan sources, the king Lang Darma (r.838-842) is usually described as a 'persecutor of Buddhism' and consequently he perished in what looks like a ritual murder performed by a Buddhist monk. The consequence of this action of the Buddhist monk was, as is well known, devastating for the Tibetan empire, because it gradually led to civil war and the disintegration of the whole country. The gravity of this can be measured by the fact that the country never recovered the unity of its former state.

These sources also portray the king as having an evil character, something compounded by his even being depicted with the head of a lion and his ministers with the heads of various other animals (Source No. 3, p. 365). The name Lang Darma is a nickname of the king. The word *glang*, which means ox, simply replaces the title Tri, the 'throne', hence king. The nickname is not attested in any of the early sources in which he was called Tri Darma, 'King Darma'. He was also known as Au Dunten invariably preceded by the titles *tsenpo*, the 'emperor' and *lhase*, the 'Divine Son'.

It is true that the name Au Dunten is a strange name. There is no precedent for this name among his predecessors in the De dynasty of Yarlung. The historicity of this person, who was the subject of so much fiction and legend after the eleventh century, has never been questioned. He was born around 803 and was a younger brother of King Ralpachen (r. 815-836). He was married to a woman from the family Nanam and another from Tshepong. In 838, aged 36, he succeeded his brother on the throne. He was therefore the 41st king in the line of the De dynasty and was the last emperor to rule over not only the whole of Tibet but territories beyond her frontiers, such as Dunhuang and its adjacent regions in China. Each of his two queens is said to have given birth to a son after the king's death, and there was therefore no heir-apparent in terms of the line of succession at the time of his murder. The late sources report a long controversy between two claimants to the throne. One of them was Ösrung who was born to the queen Tsenmo Phen of the Tsepong family. The names of the mother and son are referred to in several Dunhuang documents (PT 131, 230, 999) in contexts suggesting that the queen had taken the position of a sort of regent while her son was a minor. Ösrung finally managed to ascend the throne, but his kingdom was then plagued with civil war. Since the early documents do not refer to any royal descendant called Yumten, the son of the other queen according to the late sources, Hugh Richardson (1998: 49) has doubted whether this prince ever existed. The chief ministers of King Lang Darma were Wa Gyaltore Taknya and Dro Trisumje Taknang.

Unlike his elder brother, King Ralpachen, Lang Darma is not remembered for glorious deeds preserved in stone inscriptions or wall paintings. This may be because his reign was relatively short. The circumstances in which he succeeded his brother were very dramatic and violent. The court seethed with political intrigues coupled with the conflicts between the Buddhist ecclesiastic body and the imperial government. The Buddhist clergy was ever more demanding for what it seems to have considered as its share in the running of the country. It certainly was not content with just having a royal benefactor and staying away from politics. The prominence of the clergy taking part in the royal council (*mdun sa*) is attested already during the reign of Tri Srongdetsen (r. 755-797, b. 742), but it was under King Ralpachen that Buddhist monks succeeded in occupying ministerial positions in the government. This development elicited the resentment of the lay officials and finally led to events of assassination, suicide and execution in the court.

In Western works on Tibetan history King Lang Darma is described as the 'apostate persecutor of Buddhism' (Snellgrove and Richardson 1968: 247). As we shall see, this statement is of course based on late Tibetan Buddhist sources. A Dunhuang document, which is therefore a contemporary source, contains a prayer composed and recited on behalf of the king Au Dunten (Ariane Macdonald, Imaeda 1978: PT 134). To dedicate a prayer in this way to the current ruler was a normal practice, particularly in the Dunhuang region. Three other documents from the same place contain prayers of much the same formula on behalf of King Ralpachen (Ariane Macdonald, Imaeda 1978: PT 130, 132), particularly the document PT 1123 (Ariane Macdonald, Imaeda 1979).

I would like to present here a summary of the prayer (PT 134) and analyze its contents in order to assess to what extent the people felt and desired the well-being of their current ruler as well as to consider its religious and political implications. The manuscript is in the form of a scroll containing two separate documents and in the recent edition, the two parts are marked as I and II. It is part I that contains the prayer in 50 lines (1-50) and written in *dbu can* script. The last line (l.50) finishes with four Chinese characters (*zan pu yuan wen*, 'homage', 'prayer').

The title of the prayer runs:
"Offering of prayer on behalf of the Emperor, the Divine Son, Au Dunten".

It begins with a salutation on behalf of the emperor to the three Buddhist Ratna. This is followed by the formula of making offerings and confession. The confession is made on behalf of the ruler who in protecting Buddhism and in dealing with the affairs of state of a great empire, carried out political executions of those who became enemies. The prayer continues by beseeching Buddhas to continue their preaching, while the dependents of the ruler beg that the emperor may ensure his subjects are free in their worship and make them suitable for attaining salvation, capable of rendering benefit and happiness to other living beings; that the emperor may live long and not be influenced by others; that the miniature *tsha tsha* images and stupas that he has had made may remain for ever to be the object of offerings by gods, men and sentient beings; that he may attain the position respected by many high dignitaries; that he may meet no obstacles for his life and attain power in living long; that he may have temples and stupas newly built and those which were old repaired to remain as the object of offering and to preserve the Saddharma till the sun and moon stop turning; that by the power of meritorious work achieved in the past, or being presently or to be later engaged in, and by the blessings of the saints and those of the Dharmata, the emperor may be purified of all the bad deeds committed in previous lives, and accumulate the two kinds of meritorious action, overpowering all the kings of the eight directions.

It concludes: "We pray that the emperor may see no evil presages, that he is immune from the harm of obnoxious spirits and from all the opposing enemies and live an everlasting life; we pray that he may be given power and glory by Brahma, Indra, the four Lokapala, and the protectors of the ten directions; we pray that he may be immune from all the obnoxious spirits and that he be protected". From this summary of the document it should be evident that the prayer was composed and recited for the people who wished that the current ruler be in good health and had longevity and congratulated him on what he had achieved in the past and hoped to accomplish as the object of his policies both in the secular and religious spheres.

Although the document is about a prayer and does not necessarily contain a historical record of the ruler's deeds, it offers a strong suggestion of the kind of activities in which he had been and was currently involved. It indicates that the ruler had stupas and temples built and that he had the old and ruined ones restored. If the king was anti-Buddhist, as the late sources would have us believe, it is unlikely such a fervent prayer would have been composed on behalf of an 'apostate king'. In my opinion, the prayer also reveals the faith of the king as it does that of his colonial subjects in a conquered land as was the case of Dunhuang and its adjacent regions. It also incidentally brings to our attention the kind of Buddhism that was prevalent during the period. No divinities that would evoke Vajrayana are mentioned. This is because the practice of this vehicle became dominant in Tibet itself only in later centuries. It is interesting to note that the prayer desires political supremacy for the Tibetan *tsenpo* over all other rulers and becomes grandiloquent when it states that the *tsenpo* be given political power and glory by Brahma and Indra.

Paul Demiéville, who has studied a number of Dunhuang documents in Chinese (1950: 239-274, 280) which are similar in content to ours, shows clearly that it was common practice in Dunhuang at the time of Tibet's rule for the Chinese Buddhist monks to be ordered to compose such prayers and to recite them on behalf of the Tibetan military officials during ceremonies on important occasions. Demiéville further states that the Tibetan military officials, being Buddhist, wished to have prayers said and confession made of misdeeds committed in wars against China not only for themselves but also on behalf of their king and the regional military governor under whom they served. Demiéville also points out that the Chinese monks felt gratified by the fact that their foreign rulers felt repentance for their misdeeds in action against China while being careful not to show too much of their gratification.

It is possible that the prayer was composed during the early part of the *tsenpo*'s reign and that his policies about Buddhist establishments in the country later changed.

It is also possible that the people in Dunhuang, which was such a far-flung territory, were not quickly informed of what happened in the imperial court in Lhasa. However, neither of the cases is likely, because the content of the document is supported by another Dunhuang document (PT 840) which unmistakably states that Buddhism flourished in Tibet from the time of Lhase Darma to the time of King Ösrung. This document therefore in a way corroborates the content of the prayer, i.e. the king was a Buddhist and during his reign Buddhism suffered no persecution. Moreover, from the reference to King Ösrung in the document, it is evident that Buddhism continued to flourish even during the reign of this king. In other words, this document gives us no grounds for supposing that Lhase Darma was first Buddhist and then abjured; on the contrary, it suggests that he encouraged the practice of Buddhism not only during his reign but also right up to that of King Ösrung. This Dunhuang document therefore dates from after King Ösrung's ascent to the throne.

The inevitable question then rises: did the 'persecution of Buddhism' begin in Lang Darma's reign as late Tibetan sources assert?

From most of the late Buddhist historical sources (e.g. No. 1), one gets the impression that it was King Lang Darma who began to persecute Buddhism. However, from a close look at these sources (No. 1, pp. 411-28; No. 2, pp. 358-64), a somewhat different picture emerges. King Ralpachen, the elder brother of Lang Darma, reigned from 815 to 838. During his reign Buddhism gained a most remarkable ascendancy. As mentioned earlier, for the first time in Tibetan history, a Buddhist monk became a minister of the highest rank in the imperial government. This monk was the famous Drenka Palgyi Yönten, whose name appears as the first signatory to the peace treaty of 821-22 between Tibet and China, and it was he who was one of the chief negotiators on the Tibetan side.

King Ralpachen is described as being a weak person and a fervent devotee of Buddhism. He is accused of having left the affairs of state in the hands of his monk ministers. Whatever the case may be, the lay members of the government seem to have become discontent about the way in which the influence of the Buddhist clergy was becoming too strong. We read such expressions as, "If a lay official salutes the king 16 times the king simply ignores it"; "if he sees a religious person even at a distance, he salutes him" (Source No. 2, p.426). The lay officials were mostly from the powerful aristocratic families and a certain contingent was evidently not too happy about the clergy taking advantage of the devotion of the king and stepping into the secular sphere. We find such discontented statements as "the king reigns in accordance with Buddhism" (*chab srid chos dang bstun*) and "political power is given to the monks" (*dbang dge 'dun la phul*) (Source No. 1, p.75, l.3). The discontent of the lay officials grew to the extent that there arose the question of eliminating the king himself and restoring the secular state. It was thought, according to the sources, that it would be no use just eliminating the king, because there were other important religious personages within the royal family and also there was the powerful monk minister, all of whom would continue to run the government. One of the brothers of the king, called Tsangma, who is said to have been a Buddhist monk, was thought likely to succeed to the throne in such an event in which case, it was feared, the situation would be further aggravated. A very careful plot was then hatched and was carried through step by step. Tsangma was finally banished, though on what grounds it is not mentioned. As for the fall of the powerful monk minister, rumors were spread to the effect that he was having an affair with the chief queen, Nangtshulma, which in the end led to his execution. On hearing of the death of her lover, the queen is said to have committed suicide. Everyone who might have defended the involvement of the clergy in the affairs of state in the absence of the king had now been eliminated. The king was then assassinated by two of his own ministers while he was drunk and asleep.

It is hard to know whether all this has any historical substance, but certain elements, like the discontent of the lay officials about the clergy's involvement in secular affairs, the assassination of the king and the execution of the monk minister are all likely to have taken place.

It was in such circumstances that Lang Darma became the king of Tibet. Either he claimed the throne himself or he was chosen to succeed after the assassination of his elder brother. There were other brothers, but it was he who was in the end set on the throne probably for the reason that he supported the anti-clerical campaign. It would seem that he simply continued the policy of preventing the intrusion of the clergy into the political sphere.

The late sources allege that the king ordered statues to be removed from temples and monks expelled from monasteries. The same source also claim that the king was critical of the way in which the Chinese wife of King Srongtsen Gampo had conducted her affairs in Tibet and that he was particularly hostile to the image of the Jowo, calling it the 'Chinese statue' (rgya lha, Source No. 1, pp. 78-79). However, no contemporary evidence has so far been found for such allegations, but it does perhaps reflect the situation in which the king found himself in the face of the powerful clergy.

If he was a practicing Buddhist as the contemporary documents suggest, it would seem that the question of his 'persecution of Buddhism' did not concern his action against the religion itself as such, but against its institutions which were a powerful independent body enjoying special privileges. Already during the reign of Tri Srongdetsen, Buddhist monasteries like Samye were granted a certain number of households with landed property and animal stocks. These households were exempted from taxation by the government and their men were cleared from military recruitment. In the reign of King Ralpachen these privileges were further increased.

During the reign of King Lang Darma, Tibet was still ruling over Dunhuang and its neighbouring regions. The military governor of Dunhuang was the commander Zhang Trisumje, whose name appears as the second signatory to the peace treaty of 821-22. Paul Demiéville is of the opinion that it was primarily he who drafted the text of the peace treaty. The Dunhuang region was captured by the Tibetans in 787 and Zhang Trisumje was the military governor of the region when Lang Darma ascended the throne. Dunhuang and other north-western Chinese territories were still held by the Tibetans for eight years after the murder of the king and these territories only fell out of Tibetan hands in 848.

In general, the late Buddhist sources have hardly anything to say about these Chinese territories occupied by the Tibetans and the Tibetan military administration of the regions under the reign of King Lang Darma. Convinced that the king 'persecuted Buddhism', the authors of the late Buddhist historical works seem to have had no interest in history except to depict the king and his reign in a most degrading manner, thereby doing no justice to the political history of the period that runs from 838 to 848. We are told that the king was influenced by 'evil spirits' (*gdon*) and he was wicked and his ministers were bandits, so little comprehension is there of the historical facts. These accounts were of course written by Buddhist clerics and it is therefore perhaps not very surprising if they are so partial and ignorant of the facts since they were writing two centuries after the events in the belief that the king 'persecuted Buddhism' without giving any reasons that are plausible and logical.

This late version of the king's persecution of Buddhism is found in a Buddhist historical work which had been very influential on later works (Source No.1, pp. 1-65). It contains mainly historical accounts of the founding of the first Buddhist monastery, Samye. It is an extremely important work in spite of the vicissitudes of its versions. Its original version may well date from the ninth century (Cf. Wangdu, Diemberger 2000). However, it is mainly the 'addition' (*zhabs btags*, Source No. 1, pp. 65-92), which is the second part of the work and added to the main body of the text at a much later date, that served as the primary source for the late version of the account of King Darma and his rule. The name of the king containing the word *glang* is not given in this text. On the other hand, it curiously states that King Senalek had a nickname: Lang Jingyon, the 'ox that has a crooked neck' (Source No. 1, p. 69). This king was the father of Lang Darma.

This work was obviously written in the second half of the eleventh century, but unfortunately it remains anonymous for all its claims. Apart from being imbued with a partisan view, it is uncomfortably ignorant of the whole history of the last phase of the empire despite the fact that the king was still reigning over it. It is hard to give any credit to its contents concerning the rule of Lang Darma. Yet it is this version of the story of the king that has come to prevail in all later Buddhist historical works. It is already cited in Source No. 2 (p.503).

Amongst other historical figures and events it mentions Lotsawa Rinchen Zangpo (958-1055), Atisha arriving in Tibet in 1040, and Lha Changchubwö, and also the *Kalacakra* tantra translated in 1027 as well as a mass of other evidence that definitely proves that the work is posterior to the tenth century.

The ritual murder of King Lang Darma

We have no pre-eleventh century records of the killing of King Lang Darma. According to the late sources, the king was examining an inscription in Lhasa at the time of his assassination. The sources do not specify which inscription it was. Was it the inscription that was erected only two decades earlier during the reign of his elder brother and is today still preserved in front of the Jokhang, or was it the Zholdoring erected around 764 which still stands in front of the Potala? There were only two inscriptions that existed at the time in Lhasa. It is said that the king was sitting on the base of the inscription which was in the form of a tortoise when he was shot (Source No. 4, p. 427). This indicates that the inscription in question might be that of the Sino-Tibetan peace treaty because it has a rock base in the form of a tortoise.

In all the Tibetan historical works so far known, this is the only context in which a Tibetan examining such a thing is mentioned and it was Lang Darma! Did he want to know the records of the achievements of his predecessors inscribed on stone? We shall never know.

No Buddhist historians had ever bothered to read these inscriptions. Even Pawo Tsuklak Trengwa (1504-1566) did not do so, because he asks the readers of his historical work to insert the texts of the inscription of the Sino-Tibetan peace treaty in Lhasa into his work if the reader has occasion to copy them out (No. 3, Vol.1, p. 416). It took nearly eleven centuries for a Tibetan historian to take an interest in reading the inscriptions in Lhasa. This was Gedun Chöphel who examined them in the 1940s.

The late sources assert that King Lang Darma was so engrossed in reading the inscription that he hardly noticed his killer, who approached him in the guise of a court official. It is said that the killer had carried an arrow and a bow hidden in the wide sleeves of his cloak and pretended that he was saluting by bowing his upper body when in fact he was bending the bow in order to shoot. According to one source the arrow struck the victim in the forehead and, according to another, in the chest.

The way in which his murder took place has been glorified in favour of the murderer. There is no ambiguity about the identity of the killer of the king. All the late sources agree on this point. He is called Lhalung Palgyi Dorje. Nothing is known about this man.

The story of his slaying of the king is told in some detail, suggesting that he had a genius for crafty action and this has been construed as an heroic deed. It has provided an important theme, as mentioned earlier, for Buddhist tantric rituals. Indeed, the murder is described as a ritual accomplishment.

Late sources state that Lhalung Palgyi Dorje was in the hermitage of Yerpa practising meditation at the time when the king began to persecute Buddhism. Yerpa is an ancient Buddhist site situated to the east of Lhasa. One is often made to believe that Lhalung Palgyi Dorje was a tantrist by way of justifying his action, because in Buddhist tantric practices the practitioner is permitted to eliminate one's enemy if the latter is opposed to the doctrine to which one adheres. There are many stories in Tibetan Buddhist biographies that tantrists killed their opponents by magic and various other means. However, the presentation of him as a tantrist is contradicted by the story itself when it relates that Lhalung Palgyi Dorje ran away after the murder and found himself in Amdo where it is said that he was asked to participate in an ordination ceremony for some novices. The ordination ceremony needed at least five fully ordained monks to officiate and it was short of one. When Lhalung Palgyi Dorje was asked to come and participate, he refused to do so on the ground that had committed a murder and therefore was no longer a monk qualified to take part in such a ceremony.

The story that he was a monk and residing in Yerpa is supported by an inscription found in Yerpa. It is erected on a round rock base with the motif of leaves engraved around it, but unfortunately the upper part of the inscription is broken off and the fallen piece is missing. The lower part which stands on the base just described bears the words *dge slong dpal gyi rdo rje*, the 'monk Palgyi Dorje'. These are the only inscribed words on the stele. There is no doubt that the monk Palgyi Dorje is one and the same as Lhalung Palgyi Dorje. Lhalung is the name of a place in Lhodrag. Situ Chökyi Gyamtsho reports that near the monastery of Lhalung, a place was still remembered as being the birthplace of the monk when he visited the monastery at the beginning of the twentieth century (Source No. 5, p.253).

Moreover, in a Dunhuang document (Karmay 1988: 78, 80, IOL 689/2) the name Lhalung Palgyi Dorje is counted as the ninth Buddhist master (*dge ba'i bshes gnyen*) at Samye in a series that starts with Wa Yeshe Wangpo, the first abbot of Samye. This clearly suggests that he was either the ninth abbot of Samye or a high ecclesiastic connected with the monastery - therefore not only simply a Buddhist monk, but occupying a very high ecclesiastic position in the country.

In my opinion, based on this piece of the Dunhuang document, the murderer of the king was the ninth abbot of Samye. It would not be very surprising if the abbot of the monastery had taken such action against the king since the latter was hostile to the clergy.

The elimination of the king therefore definitely put an end to the conflict between religion and state, but then it threw the whole country into turmoil. The Buddhist clergy, however, continued its struggle though no longer under any single authority. It finally won supremacy in Tibet, so to speak, but Buddhism in Tibet never managed to reestablish an institution that would have a general authority over the subsequent development of the various Buddhist schools. Till very recent times when Tibetan Buddhists gathered together, there was not even a common prayer readily known to all.

Was Lang Darma Bönpo?

None of the Tibetan sources I have been able to consult has ever stated that the king was a follower of the Bon religion, and yet this idea has crept into some western works on Tibetan religions. Helmut Hoffmann (1961: 81) seems to be the first to suggest the king was a Bon practitioner, but he gives no sources for this statement. This seems purely a conjecture and is certainly very misleading. As we have seen, the conflict was about political power between the clergy and the secular authority and not the struggle between two religious establishments.

The Bon religion as a belief certainly existed in the ninth century, but it did not have an institutional form that put it in a position to compete with Buddhism. The latter was the state religion with monastic institutions and the benefit of imperial favour, even though one cannot exclude the likelihood that some of the ministers involved in the conflict had leanings towards the Bon faith.

Conclusion

If the pre-eleventh century sources concerning the rule of Lang Darma and his fall are to be taken seriously – as they must be, since some are contemporary and others closer to the events than those sources that were written during or after the eleventh century - a radical revision of this historical period will have to be made. The *tsenpo* Lhase Darma appears to have been sympathetic to a faction consisting of mainly lay ministers of the imperial government. This movement, which was led by the minister Wa Gyatore, viewed the government as weakened by the influence of Buddhism in its policies and particularly objected to the involvement of Buddhist monks in the government. However, there is a strong suggestion that the king himself personally remained Buddhist and during his reign Buddhism certainly continued to flourish.

The early sources give no suggestion that he persecuted Buddhist monks, but as he was against the involvement of Buddhist clergy in politics it is likely that he was not in favour of maintaining the special privileges of the Buddhist monastic establishments as had been the case especially during the reign of King Ralpachen.

Moreover, the late version of the accounts of Lang Darma and his rule are entirely ignorant about political events in the territories such as Dunhuang that were still under Tibet's rule during the reign of the king.

An inscription of the 9th century found at Yerpa bearing the name:
dge slong dpal gyi rdo rje, 'the monk Palkyi Dorje'.
(Photo: collection of Samten G. Karmay)

Wall painting in the Great Stupa of Gyantse, 15th century: figures from the
left, top 1. Tsangma, 2. Ralpachen, 3. Senalek, centre 4. Lahje Lhundrup, 5.
Tri Darma O Dumtsen, bottom 6. Tri Chenamo (not identified), 7. Ösrung.
(Photo: collection of Samten G. Karmay)

REFERENCES IN WESTERN LANGUAGES

Paul Demiéville, *Le Concile de Lhasa, une controverse sur le Quiétisme entre*
    Bouddhistes de l'Inde et de la Chine au VIIIe siècle de l'ère chrétienne, Paris: Imprimerie nationale de
    France 1952 [Bibliothèque de l'Institut des Hautes Etudes Chinoises, volume VII].
Helmut Hoffmann, *The Religions of Tibet*, London: George Allen & Unwin Ltd.,
    1961.
Samten G. Karmay, *The Great Perfection, A philosophical and meditational Teaching*
    of Tibetan Buddhism, Leiden: E. J. Brill, 1988a.
    Secret Visions of the Fifth Dalai Lama, London: Serindia Publications, 1988b.
    Btsan po lha sras dar ma dang de'i rjes su byung ba'i rgyal rabs mdor bsdus, Dharamsala: Library of
    Tibetan Works and Archives, 1986. This again appeared in *China Tibetology* (*Krung go'i bod kyi shes*
    rig), Peking 1989, 1, 81-103.
Ariane Macdonald (Spanien), Yoshiro Imaeda, *Choix de documents tibétains*, Paris:
    Bibliothèque nationale, Tome Ier, 1978; Tome II, 1979.
Pasang Wangdu, Hildegard Diemberger, *dBa' bzhed, The Royal Narrative*
    Concerning the Bringing of the Buddha's Doctrine to Tibet, Verlag der Osterreichischen Akademie der
    Wissenschaften, Vienna 2000.
Richardson, Hugh, *High Peaks, Pure Earth, Collected Writings on Tibetan History*
    and Culture, edited by Michael Aris, London: Serindia Publications 1998, 48-55.
Snellgrove, David, Richardson, Hugh, *A Cultural History of Tibet*, London:
    Weidenfeld and Nicolson, 1978.

SOURCES IN TIBETAN

1. *sBa bzhed*
(Rolf A. Stein, *Une chronique ancienne de bSam-yas: sBa-bzhed*, Paris: Adrien-Mainsonneuve, 1961)
2. Nyang-ral Nyi-ma 'od-zer (1136-1204)
Chos 'byung me tog snying po sbrang rts'i bcud, Lhasa: Bod ljongs mi dmangs dpe skrun khang, 1988 [*Gangs can rig mdzod* 5].
mKhas-pa lDe'u
3. *mKhas pa lde'us mdzad pa'i rgya bod kyi chos 'byung rgyas pa*, Lhasa: Bod rang skyong spyi tshogs tshan rig khang, 1987 [*Gangs can rig mdzod* 3].
4. dPa'-bo gTsug-lag phreng-ba (1504-1566)
Chos 'byung mkhas pa'i dga' ston, Vols. I-II, Mi rigs dpe skrun khang 1985.
5. Ka-thog Si-tu Chos-kyi rgya-mtsho (1880-1924)
Ka thog si tu'i dbus gtsang gnas yig (*Gangs can dbus gtsang gnas bskor lam yig nor bu zla shel gyi se mo do*), Lhasa: Bod ljongs bod yig dpe rnying dpe skrun khang 1999 [*Gangs can rig mdzod* 33].

INDEX

Bell's entry:
School at Lhasa, boy showing writing to teacher.
Backward write on broad wooden slates,
more advanced on narrow strips of paper.
Photographer: Rosemeyer
BL.P.299

On some disciples of Rinchen Zangpo and Lochung Legpai Sherab, and their successors, who brought teachings popular in Ngari Korsum to Central Tibet

Roberto Vitali

The work of the great translator (Lochen) Rinchen Zangpo (958-1055) and, to a lesser extent, his associate the minor translator (Lochung) Legpai Sherab (?-?), both active during the Second Diffusion of Buddhism in Upper West Tibet, has been the main focus of literary attention on the subject of the religious masters of Ngari Korsum. The accomplishments of their disciples have been largely neglected by the sources available at present, to the point that little is known about them.

In this short paper, I wish briefly to recall from oblivion the activities of a few of these almost forgotten but important disciples, who were instrumental in establishing in Central Tibet the teachings flourishing in the kingdom of Ngari Korsum especially because of the influence exercised by Rinchen Zangpo, Lochung Legpai Sherab and the lineage of enlightened rulers who left the throne to devote themselves to religion. These disciples were the main link between the religious renaissance in Ngari Korsum and the slightly less effulgent revival in Ü-Tsang which occurred separately and almost concomitantly. This insemination took place at a time of the history of Ngari Korsum when the kingdom was still at its apogee before a rapid decline occurred in the last decade of the 11th century and was complete by 1111.

The disciples of Rinchen Zangpo and Lochung Legpai Sherab are succinctly and diligently classified in the sources. In a passage of the middle-length biography of Rinchen Zangpo (*Rin chen bzang po'i rnam thar 'bring po* Dharamsala edition p.22 lines 12-13) a division of tasks between the two translators is mentioned, for it says that Lochen extended his competence as far as Purang while Lochung took charge of the translation work as far as Sakya. Reading this statement in terms of their disciples, it ensues that the biography hints at the fact that those from Ngari Korsum studied with

Rinchen Zangpo, while those who came from outside the kingdom studied with Lochung Legpai Sherab.

This is only apparently a clearcut and entirely admissible subdivision of the burdensome task of providing continuity to the newly introduced tradition of Ngari Korsum, because this passage is manifestly one of several interpolations that the text of the biography has undergone throughout the centuries. Although the middle-length biography of the great translator written by his direct disciple Guge Kyithangpa Yeshepal is the oldest and generally a most authoritative work on him, this work has been marred considerably in some parts by later textual interpolations.

It is obvious even to the most distracted reader, however, that such a share of responsibilities could not have occurred at that time, which is the early 11th century, because Sakya was founded only later, in water ox 1073.

I cannot explain with confidence the reasons which may have led to the interpolation of this passage distinguishing the disciples of Lochen and Lochung by their area of provenance, which is manifestly wrong. The available evidence concerning their disciples, which consists of several classifications proposed by later scholasticism, further disproves the idea that the students of Lochen and Lochung were divided along such lines. In fact, the later authors assessed the matter in a remarkably different way, though not ignoring the area of provenance of these students, for their writings betray a perceived need to articulate in greater detail a classification more summarily delineated in the earlier sources.

For instance, Jamyang Khyentse Wangpo, in his *mDo sNgags kyi lo rgyus dang rnam thar*, deals with the group of Rinchen Zangpo's disciples who were not originally from Ngari Korsum, showing that Lochen did concern himself with students from outside this kingdom. They belonged to the tradition which became known as *Yoga Meluk* (*Yo ga smad lugs*) because they were from Lower (*smad*, i.e. Central) Tibet and returned there to diffuse the teachings popular in Upper West Tibet.

Jamyang Khyentse Wangpo (ibid. p.259 lines 10-18) says: "The way [the tradition of Rinchen Zangpo] spread eastwards (*mar*) to Ü-Tsang [is as follows]. The earliest who went [to study] with lo chen was rGyang po Chos[kyi] blo[gros] of rGyang ro dPe dmar; then, Sum ston Ye 'bar of Shan; then, Ce zhar of Nyang stod; then, gZhon nu rgya mtsho, the father of dPang kha 'Dar chung; Brag steng ba of La stod and dMar ston Chos kyi rgyal mtshan of sGul phyi ru. Since mDog Kle ston, Bal Shakya rdo rje, and Thang ston Gong ge ba probably met lo chen [only] briefly, they mainly studied with lo chung. Since they diffused [*Yoga*] to the east (*smad*) in Ü-Tsang, this [tradition] is known as *Yoga Meluk*".

To check the validity of these assessments, the only solution is empirical. I will try to show how these differing interpretations are substantiated by evidence provided by the life of the disciples themselves, limiting myself to a couple of relevant examples.

The case of Dragtengpa Yontan Tsültrim is especially symptomatic. He was a little known religious exponent from Latö (hence not from Ngari), who had a major part in diffusing important teachings popular in Ngari Korsum beyond the boundaries of the kingdom. He is considered to have been a disciple of Lochung Legpai Sherab in some literary classifications, recalling the wrong statement found in the interpolation in Rinchen Zangpo's biography.

I have dealt with Dragtengpa at some length elsewhere [see Vitali, "Sa skya and the mNga' ris skor gsum legacy: the case of Rin chen bzang po's flying mask", *Lungta*

14, Spring 2001]. The evidence I was able to gather about him shows overwhelmingly that he was a disciple of Rinchen Zangpo from Latö, and thus this confirms that Jamyang Khyentse Wangpo's assessment is correct. In particular, Dragtengpa Yontan Tsültrim was responsible for transmitting the *Yoga* system of Ngari Korsum to the Sakyapa, as well as the cult of Mahakala Lord of the Tent, brought to Tibet by Rinchen Zangpo. He played a major role in the eventual transfer to Sakya monastery of Rinchen Zangpo's flying mask, a representation of this deity, which became its most revered image.

Kyangpu Treumar Chökyi Lodrö, the disciple who is undisputably reputed to have been the earliest student of Rinchen Zangpo, also upheld the tradition known as *Yoga Meluk*. He was from outside Ngari Korsum. Upon his return to Ü-Tsang, at an early stage of the Later Diffusion of Buddhism there, he founded the temple of Kyangpu at his native place Treumar in Nyangro/Gyangro, which became a stronghold of the *Yoga* tradition taught in Ngari Korsum. The period during which he studied with the great *lotsawa* in Ngari Korsum fell in between the master's first and second sojourns in Kashmir. Their meeting can be thus dated between 987 and 996. He had a further period of studies with Lochen, following the latter's return to Ngari in 1001 from his second sojourn in Kashmir.

The case of Kyangpu Treumar Chökyi Lodrö, who was from Nyangtö in Tsang, is illustrative of the efforts made by the local intelligentsia in bringing the religious system based on the *New Tantra*, ever since its introduction to Ngari Korsum, to other regions of Tibet.

Spreading the newly translated teachings from Ngari Korsum to other lands of Tibet gained momentum in the following decades of the 11th century (as it will be seen in the case of Zangkar lotsawa Phagpa Sherab). After Jowoje Atisha left Ngari Korsum for Ü-Tsang, there could have been a perception that the focus of religious activity had shifted to Central Tibet.

This change of focus may explain the reason for the later scholasticism's anachronistic inclusion of Sakya in the sphere of Lochung's influence, found in the text of Rinchen Zangpo's middle-length biography (was it of Sakyapa origin? Is it to be explained by the concern of this school for the ancient legacy of Ngari Korsum?). The re-assessment of a disciple like Dragtengpa as a student of Lochung rather than Lochen manifestly proceeded from the same view.

Here I will introduce only a few significant examples of the transference of teachings outside Ngari, which are evident from the lives of these disciples but hitherto neglected in the secondary literature. I will treat them with maximum restraint, given the limited space at my disposal, and postpone a more extensive treatment to another occasion. I will present them in chronological sequence, beginning with the disciples of Rinchen Zangpo who was an older contemporary of Lochung Legpai Sherab.

While Rinchen Zangpo is deservedly famous for his work as translator, being one of the most influential figures in the establishment of the *New Tantra* in Tibet, and for his activity as a relentless temple founder, his contribution to the adoption of Indian medical science in the Land of Snows is less well known. It is not immediately evident whether Lochen was a practising physician, and no indications or episodes in his several biographies allow one to presume whether he practised medicine like other great spiritual masters (for instance, the great *siddha* Ugyenpa Rinchenpel [1230-1309] who healed Khubilai Khan at his court, but also predicted his impending death).

To judge from his literary production, Lochen's contribution to the field of Tibetan medicine consisted in a few important translations. He put into Tibetan some medical works originating from India, which are included in the *Tangyur*, and favoured their diffusion in Tibet. These works are *Yan lag brgyad pa*, written by Lopön Pawo and its commentary *Zla zer*, composed by the Kashmiri *mahapandita* Dawa Ngönga. These texts are enough well known by the experts in Tibetan medicine and require no further assessment here. *mNga' ris rgyal rabs* (Vitali, *The Kingdoms of Gu.ge Pu.hrang* p.61 lines 6-8, and p.115) says that king Lhade invited the Kashmiri savant Dzanadhala to Guge Purang and Rinchen Zangpo worked with him on the translation of those two texts, which indicates that Lochen had developed an interest in medicine through his contact with the masters of Kashmir.

Rinchen Zangpo's contribution to the related field of veterinary science was the translation of a lengthy treatise on the treatment of horses, another subject of unquestionable relevance to the everyday life of the Tibetans. This text is entitled *rTa dpyad Sha li ho tra*, and it is also found in the *Tangyur*. All these works show another side of Rinchen Zangpo's personality, different from the one he is more famous for. He was not only a great master of learning and religious systems. He also contributed to the people's physical well-being and that of their animals. In fact, the existence of a group of his disciples known as the "four physicians of Purang", who were practising doctors, proves that Lochen was more than a mere theorist.

The reference to Purang in the collective appellative of these doctors is a sign that this region, rather than any other, was the centre of medical studies in the kingdom of Ngari Korsum.

The "four physicians of Purang" were Nyangde Sengedra, Shaka Tri Yeshe Jungne, Ongmen Ane, and Mangmomen Tshun.

Three of these four belonged to clans of Ngari Korsum, while the ancestry of the fourth is not clear. The Nyang clan is not documented as having settled in Upper West Tibet by the literary sources except those dealing with the history of the lineage of Purang doctors. The consistency of their presence in this land for no less than several decades (from Rinchen Zangpo to the advent of Bharo Chagdum to Guge Purang, on whom see below) proves that at least a branch was resident of Ngari.

Members of the Ong clan, to which the physician nun (Ongmen Ane) belonged, included Bönpo exponents from Ngari and Ong lotsawa, one of the early disciples of Phadampa Sangye (?-1117). He met the great *Zhije* master from India during the latter's visit to Ngari, the second of his five sojourns in Tibet.

The Mang clan gave ministers to the kingdom (from the Mangwer family of Mangwer Rinchen Sherab, one of Lochen's major disciples) and included Bonpo practitioners, a group of whom were active in Mustang during the period of the Later Diffusion of Buddhism in Tibet.

Mangmomen Tshun was the most outstanding master of the four, and he is said to have combined Rinchen Zangpo's theory and practice, which seems once again to confirm that Lochen was more than a translator of medical material. Mangmomen Tshun was responsible for the first phase of dissemination of the medical doctrines brought by Rinchen Zangpo to Upper West Tibet outside its boundaries, for he worked with most of the doctors then active in Ü-Tsang.

He also transmitted *Yan lag brgyad pa* and its commentary locally to members of one the most influential clans in the history of Ngari Korsum. The clan was the Che, and his disciple was Cheje Tipang. Members of the Che clan (also known as Chechen or "the great Che") intermarried with the royal family of Guge Purang. The kings Tsede and Sonamtse were born from mothers belonging to the Che clan.

For a few generations after Cheje Tipang, the transmission of Lochen's medical science was continued by former's family successors, which indicates that, after a first phase of insemination outside its boundaries, these teachings remained confined to Ngari.

Little is known about Nyang Sengedra, another of the "four physicians of Purang", but it seems that the transmission of medical science continued in his clan lineage for quite some time. In fact, a member of the Nyang clan studied with another great disseminator of medical science in Ngari Korsum. The latter was Kyebu Melha, a physician from Uddiyana, who is documented to have come first to Tholing, the capital of the Guge Purang kingdom, and then Purang, the centre of medical studies in these lands, during the reign of king Tsede.

His biography is originally found in the text entitled *sNyan brgyud be bum nag po*, seemingly not available outside Tibet. Kyebu Melha belonged to a noble family of physicians who professed an uninterrupted lineal transmission of medical tenets. His father Dzinamitra was an eminent doctor.

Kyebu Melha had fled Uddiyana because, as the physician of the local king, he had outraged the queen's modesty while he cured her of a disease. The king did not kill him, but amputated his hands, so that he could not practise anymore. He became known by the nickname Bharo Chagdum ("the nobleman with no hands") (not to be confused with the more or less contemporary Newar religious master of the same name, who was one of the main teachers of Ra lotsawa Dorjedrag [1016-?]).

Dzinamitra imparted all his knowledge to his son orally, and Bharo Chagdum is thus considered to have introduced an oral transmission of medical science to Tibet which was put into writing soon after.

His disciple in Ngari Korsum was Purang Nyangmen Ringmo, a member of the Nyang clan. Bharo Chagdum imparted to him the medical diagnosis of *Dhe skor*, its root and branches, and *Grang ba'i bcos thabs thur ma'i skor* ("the cycle of medical instruments as a curative method for cold-related diseases").

Bharo Chagdum then moved to Central Tibet and went first to Zhu Nyemo, taking Jowo Nyangmen Ringmo along with him. The latter was thus another exponent of the Ngari Korsum medical tradition, belonging to a family from Purang which had counted physicians in its lineage since the time of Rinchen Zangpo, who proceeded eastwards to disseminate medical doctrines first diffused in Upper West Tibet.

Bharo Chagdum had several groups of disciples in Central Tibet. The group of his "spiritual sons" (*thugs rgyud*) included Karchung Thazhi Shagge, who received *rMa rnams skor gsum*; Dragkyi Gyertön Chödrag, who received *Grang ba'i skor gsum*; Tölung Zeumenpa, who received *Brul tshe'i skor gsum*; and Yarlung Tongmen Tagchung, who received *Tsha grang rlung gsum*. Another group of disciples received teachings from him occasionally.

Bharo Chagdum's teachings kept being transmitted orally. Some of these teachings became known as *Dris lan skor tsho* (the "Cycles of Questions and Answers") and others as *Nag po skor gsum* (the "Three Black Cycles"), the latter being imparted only fragmentarily. Later, Trachi Bemen Wangyal, one of the disciples known as *thugs btags pa* ("those spiritually linked to him"), put them into writing.

It might seem that there was no transmission of Bharo Chagdum's teachings coming from Ngari, but this is not so because the two main disciples of Bharo Chagdum who are especially remembered in the tradition for their contributions to Tibetan medicine are Tongmen, the disciple from Yerpa who disseminated specific cures for different types of fever, and Nyangmen, the disciple from Purang who disseminated the use of a great number of medical instruments.

On the other hand, the transmission of Rinchen Zangpo's medical legacy continued uninterrupted through five generations of the Che clan after the "four physicians of Purang" until Cheje Zhangtön Zhigpo. He was a medical author and a master whose main disciple, Tsangtö Darma Gönpo, was from outside Ngari.

It was through this transmission that the teachings based on *Yan lag brgyad pa* reached Yuthog Yontan Gönpo the younger (1126-1202), who practised them particularly in the earlier part of his life. This Central Tibetan master was thus a *de facto* descendant of Rinchen Zangpo's medical lineage.

* * *

I wish to discuss briefly at least one disciple of Lochung Legpai Sherab, namely Zangkar lotsawa Phagpa Sherab. He mainly worked in Ü-Tsang but, being from Ngari, his activities there were rooted in his studies of the traditions prevailing in Upper West Tibet.

No major biography of Zangskar lotsawa Phagpa Sherab is available at present and one must piece together information on his life from different sources, but there is a hint in one work that an ancient *namthar* dedicated to him existed in the past. Finding it could prove to be important for the study of the Later Diffusion of Buddhism in Tibet.

In some ways, Zangskar lotsawa Phagpa Sherab followed in the footsteps of the masters of the Later Diffusion of Buddhism from Ngari Korsum, for he journeyed to the lands where the teachings originated to study them directly. Thus, he was well versed in the *New Tantras* (especially the *Yoga Tantra*), which he taught and practised by strictly observing the norms of *Vinaya*. This was in the best tradition of Ngari Korsum, as envisioned by the monk-rulers of this kingdom, according to whom *Tantra* had to be grounded in the norms of *Vinaya*. He disseminated these principles to disciples in central Tibet who were among the masters of *Vinaya* (such as Cha Duldzin, Balti Drachompa, and drubchen Nyiphupa).

He introduced to Tibet the transmissions of Namthösë and Chagna Dorje, defined as *Kha-che lugs* and *rGya-gar lugs*, after translating important texts on these subjects, as well as *Tshad-ma*, in Kashmir. He fulfilled the will of lhalama Yesheö by renovating the most important temples in Ü-Tsang built by the religious kings of the imperial period.

The account of Zangkar lotsawa's restoration of the Jokhang offers an insight into the obscure and controversial situation in Lhasa during the Later Diffusion of Buddhism, for it says that the major temple of Tibet was reduced, since the time of imperial Tibet, to a "beggars' nest" when he reopened it for religious practice.

He is also associated with the renovation of Samyë, also restored by his arch-rival Ra lotsawa Dorjedrag during the same period.

His mastery of the translations practised in Central Tibet set him on a collision course with Ra lotsawa. They clashed thrice and the last dispute proved to be fatal to Zangkar lotsawa. The first happened during the council of Tholing when Ra lotsawa foresaw the violent death of the Guge king Tsede, but the biography of Ra claims that Zangkar lotsawa's envy prevented him from removing this obstacle.

The second took place at Kyangbu, the stronghold of the Ngari Korsum culture in Tsang, when Zangkar lotsawa allegedly took away Thugje Chenpo, the *pandita* of Ra lotsawa, to help him complete the translation of *De-nyid dus-pa* left unaccomplished by Rinchen Zangpo. But the circumstances of the episode do not credit this version of the events.

The final dispute occurred following Zangkar lotsawa's purported disruption of Ra lotsawa's classes in Lhasa. According to his biography, Ra lotsawa assassinated him during a clash between their *yidam*s. In more down to earth terms, it seems that Zangkar lotsawa was poisoned at Chumig ringmo by Ra lotsawa who was jealous of his superior translation skills.

To sum up, Kyangbu Choskyi Lodrö, Dragtengpa, the several physicians of Purang, and in particular Zangkar lotsawa, as well as other disciples of the two translators not mentioned here, all contributed to bridging the cultural separation between Central Tibet and Ngari Korsum, a kingdom whose relative insularity was enhanced by its distinctive political status and its intelligentsia's direct interaction with the masters of the traditions newly established in India. The insemination of these teachings to lands beyond its boundaries was one of the historical factors which ensured the survival of the cultural legacy of Ngari Korsum after the kingdom's golden period came to an end.

In the following few lines I wish to mention briefly the sources used in this paper but not cited in the text in order to make Tibetan scholarship more accessible to a wider readership as requested in the guidelines for the Proceedings of the History of Tibet Conference.

One can see most *chos 'byung* and other historical literature to find out notions on the disciples of Rinchen Zangpo and Lochung Legpai Sherab which are quite sparcely preserved in this material. For the classifications of these disciples one can refer in particular to *Deb ther sngon po* and Mangtö Ludrub Gyatso's *bstan rtsis*. On Dragtengpa, the reader is requested to consult the bibliography of my "Sa skya and the mNga' ris skor gsum legacy: the case of Rin chen bzang po's flying mask" (*Lungta* 14, Spring 2001). On Kyangbu Chökyi Lodrö one can use *Myang chos 'byung* in particular. On the Rinchen Zangpo's "four physicians of Purang" and the other lineage holders of medical science in Ngari, apart from *sNyan brgyud be bum nag po*, the best source is *Gangs ljongs gso rig rig bstan pa'i nyin byed rim byon gyi rnam thar phyogs bsgrigs* by Byams pa 'phrin las, which should also be consulted for Bharo Chagdum. One needs also to look at the biographies of Yuthog Yontan Gönpo. On the clans of Ngari Korsum, one can check my *The Kingdoms of Gu.ge Pu.hrang*, *passim*. On Zangskar lotsawa, details about his life are scattered in a number of sources including several *chos 'byung*. Particularly useful is the material on Chana Dorje and Namtöse, but this is definitely not enough.

The bibliography I append to my forthcoming "Biography without *rnam thar*: piecing together the life of Zangs dkar lo tsa ba 'Phags pa shes rab" aims at being exhaustive.

Glossary

Balti Drachompa: sBal-ti dGra-bcom-pa
Bharo Chagdum: Bha-ro phyag-rdum (sic)
Cha Duldzin: Bya 'Dul 'dzin
Chagna Dorje: Phyag-na rdo-rje
Che/Chechen: Che/Che-chen
Cheje Tipang: Che-rje Ti-pang
Cheje Zhangtön Zhigpo: Che-rje Zhang-ston zhig-po
Chumig ringmo: Chu-mig ring-mo
Dawa Ngönga: Zla-ba mNgon-dga'
Dragkyi Gyertön Chödrag: sGrags-kyi Gyer-ston Chos-grags
Dragtengpa Yontan Tsültrim/Dragtengpa: Brag-steng-pa Yon-tan tshul-khrims/Brag-steng-pa
drubchen Nyiphupa: grub-chen Nyid-phu-pa
Guge Kyithangpa Yeshepal: Gu-ge Khyi-thang-pa Ye-shes-dpal
Guge: Gu-ge
Jamyang Khyentse Wangpo: 'Jam-dbyangs mkhyen-brtse dbang-po
Jokhang: Jo-khang
Jowoje Atisha: Jo-bo-rje A-ti-sha
Karchung Thazhi Shagge: sKar-chung mTha'-bzhi Shag-ge
Kyangpu Treumar Chökyi Lodrö: rKyang-bu sPre-u-dmar Chos-kyi blo-gros
Kyangpu: rKyang-bu
Kyebu Melha: sKyes-bu Me-lha (see Bharo Chagdum)
Latö: La-stod
Legpai Sherab: Legs-pa'i shes-rab
Lhade: lHa-lde
lhalama Yesheö: lha-bla-ma Ye-shes-'od
Lhasa: lHa-sa
Lochen: lo-chen
Lochung: lo-chung
Lopön Pawo: slob-dpon dPa'-bo
Mang: Mang
Mangmomen Tshun: Mang-mo-sman Tshun
Mangtö Ludrub Gyatso: Mang-thos Klu-sgrub rgya-mtsho
Mangwer Rinchen Sherab: Mang-wer Rin-chen shes-rab

Namthösë: rNam-thos-sras
Ngari Korsum/Ngari: mNga'-ris skor-gsum/mNga'-ris
Nyang: Myang
Nyangde Sengedra: Myang-'das Seng-ge-grags
Nyangmen Ringmo (Jowo): Myang-sman Ring-mo (Jo-bo)
Nyangro/Gyangro: Nyan-ro/rGyang-ro
Nyangtö: Nyang-stod
Ong lotsawa: Ong lo-tsa-ba
Ong: Ong
Ongmen Ane: Ong-sman A-ne
Phadampa Sangye: Pha-dam-pa Sangs-rgyas
Purang: Pu-hrang
Ra lotsawa Dorjedrag: Rwa lo-tsa-ba rDo-rje-grags
Rinchen Zangpo: Rin-chen bzang-po
Sakya/Sakyapa: Sa-skya/Sa-skya-pa
Samyë: bSam-yas
Shaka Tri Yeshe Jungne: Shakya Khri Ye-shes 'byung-gnas
Sonamtse: bSod-nams-rtse
Songtsan Gampo: Srong-btsan sgam-po
Tangyur: *bsTan-'gyur*
thadül: *mtha'-'dul*
Tholing: Tho-ling
Thugje Chenpo: Thugs-rje chen-po
Tölung Zeumenpa: sTod-lung Ze'u-sman-pa
Trachi Bemen Wangyal: Gra phyi'i Be-sman Byang-rgyal
Treumar: sPre'u-dmar
Tsangtö Darma Gönpo: gTsang-stod Dar-ma mgon-po
Tsede: rTse-lde
Ugyenpa Rinchenpel: U-rgyan-pa Rin-chen-dpal
Ü-Tsang: dBus-gTsang
Yarlung Tongmen Tagchung Tongmen: Yar-lung sTong-sman Thag-chung
Yuthog Yontan Gönpo: g.Yu-thog Yon-tan mgon-po
Zangkar lotsawa Phagpa Sherab: Zangs-dkar lo-tsa-ba 'Phags-pa shes-rab
Zhije: *Zhi-byed*
Zhu Nyemo: gZhu sNye-mo

DISCUSSION

One of the key issues confronting historians concerned with Tibet is that concerning sources. While that issue is obviously fundamental to all historical enquiry, it is particularly the case in dealing with Tibetan materials. The lack of historical data for the period prior to the 11/12th century is compounded by the religious and cultural nature of later sources. Accounts of voyages undertaken by individuals may, for example, represent visionary journeys, with a lack of distinction between these and reality as understood within the Western historical tradition. Similarly, problems with dating the indigenous texts compound the difficulty of understanding whether we are dealing with material reflecting contemporary mentalities or with later reconstructions of that mentality.

Thus, in confronting statements in the sources concerning the improbable life-spans of apparently historical characters, we are left with the question as to how to pull the data from all of these different lineages and their records together into some kind of coherent, chronologically extended narrative?

Discussants highlighted the importance of the need to ascertain the mental environment of the time, and acknowledged that it requires an understanding of Tibetan literary history and conventions to evaluate this material. It was further argued that the Tibetan historians were fully aware of the difference between vision and reality and having a certain critical viewpoint, under-stood certain statements as symbolic. In themselves attempting to reconstruct some kind of rationalised chronological sequence, they did not, however, want to overturn the understandings of the traditions within which they operated.

As to desirable future avenues of source exploration, it was noted that in regard to the 20th century, historians make considerable use of external sources; British, German, Russian, Chinese and so forth. Indeed, a considerable number of British reports from throughout Tibet, and Nepalese accounts retained in British records, remain to be analysed. But it was suggested that we need to examine the multitude of regional sources from within Tibet, and to consider both 'what the history for this period might look like from a different perspective' and whether we can put all of those regions into the same analytical framework. In that regard the importance of including Bhutan in considering Tibetan history was noted. That region was not a separate entity, but linked to Tibet through ties that included those of religion, family, lineage and teachings, and commercial economy.

There are too, other histories: what, one observer asked, of structural and cultural histories, of women's histories, and those of non-elite institutions? Clearly these were all areas in which considerable work was required.

Even the question of whether we should accept the 'catastrophic change model' of a sharp divide between pre- and post-1959 Tibet was raised. Here the use of oral sources is possible, and it was agreed that there was an urgent need to collect oral histories of pre-1959 Tibet while witnesses to that period were still alive. This task should be undertaken by interested historians of all backgrounds, foreign and indigenous.

Picnic party near Lhasa.
The game of dice sho is over and they are lunching inside the tent.
1998.285.171 (BL.H.148)

17th and 18th century Tibet: a general survey

Anne Chayet

The 17th and 18th centuries are usually considered as a comparatively well known period in the history of Tibet. That is certainly true as far as the general chronology and the main trends of home and foreign policy are concerned. In short, the 17th century is often described as the time of growth and triumph for the Gelukpas' power, and the 18th century as the time of its decisive conflict with the imperial power in China. During this period and through an attempt at centralism, Tibet entered modern times, though it has sometimes been denied.

One might say that the period began in 1578, when the Gelukpa Sönam Gyatso of Drepung monastery, was given the title of Dalai Lama by Altan Khan. The hostility between the Kargyüpas and the rising Gelukpas, the resulting struggles between the provinces of Ü and Tsang and the Mongol allies of both parties came to an end in 1642, when the Koshot prince Gushri Khan gave the Fifth Dalai Lama (1617-1682) temporal power over Tibet, but kept the sword in his truthworthy hands. Three years later, in 1645, the young pontiff started to build the symbolic monument of his power, the Potala. In 1644, the Manchus had ascended the imperial throne in Peking, and they invited the Dalai Lama and received him (1653) with high honours. The regent Sangye Gyatso carefully concealed the Dalai Lama's subsequent death (1682), to further Tibet's interests. But he was not able to secure powerful allies, free from ambition, to balance the growing Chinese influence. His relations with the Dzungar prince Galden were a part of his ruin, for the emperor Kangxi never forgave him. He was killed in 1705, and the Koshot prince Lhazang, from the Gushri Khan's line, came into power with the emperor's support.

By the end of 1717, the Dzungars stormed Lhasa and Central Tibet. The emperor Kangxi sent an army to Tibet (1720) and representatives to bolster his authority in Lhasa. After a provisional military government, a new government was organized with the Dalai Lama as nominal head (he was still a minor) and a council of ministers, under a discreet but firm imperial guidance. The Chinese garrison was withdrawn in 1723. In 1727, a civil war broke out, but a member of the council, Pholhanas, succeeded in pacifying the country (summer 1728). In September 1728, a small Chinese rescue force reached Lhasa. From now on, there were two *ambans*, imperial residents, in Lhasa, and a permanent Chinese garrison. Pholhanas became the head of the new government, while the Dalai Lama, implicated in the unrest, was exiled in Kham (1728-1735). Until his death in 1747, Pholhanas ruled Tibet in agreement with the Peking authorities. But with his son and successor, the situation soon came to a climax. An army was again sent from China (1750). The circumstances were different from what they had been in 1727-1728. The 1750 uprising were not a Tibetan internal affair, but seemed to be a rebellion against the imperial tutelage. The Dalai Lama then recovered a large part of what had been his temporal power in the Fifth Dalai Lama's time. But there were now the two *ambans* in Lhasa to control his activities, and the situation was to depend on the Dalai Lama's personality and on the *ambans*` abilities.

The 1791-1792 Gurkha invasions of Tibet, and the ensuing and costly campaigns to expel them, were much resented in Peking. In 1793, new regulations were issued, which limited and controlled the movements of pilgrims and traders, gave precise instructions concerning mintage and taxes, organized the Southern Frontier, and moreover gave the emperor and *ambans* a right to control the selection of high incarnate lamas, including the Dalai Lama and the Panchen Lama, to control their wealth and properties, to approve the designation of the *khanpos* of the great monasteries and list the clerical properties. It was the first unambiguous imperial intrusion into Tibetan religious life and traditions. Such are the main and extremely summarized events in 17th and 18th century Tibet. This leaves out, among other things, the persecution of the Jonangpa school (and of many religious opponents) after the Gelukpas' triumph, the administrative and land reform made by the Gelukpas mainly in Central Tibet, the wars with Ladakh and Bhutan, the rebellions of the Kukunor princes and of Jinchuan....

The main classical studies on the period, among which are the prominent works by Tucci (1949), Ahmad (1970) and Petech (1952-1972), focussed on Sino-Tibetan relations, which are undoubtedly a key to the history of modern and contemporary Tibet. Since the beginning of the 20th century, especially after the Simla Conference, the history of Tibet has often been investigated to substantiate the Tibetan claim to independence or to support the opposite Chinese thesis. When historians and diplomats tried to explain the ancient and often ambiguous relations between Tibet and China, they used sometimes the words 'suzerainty' and 'sovereignty', which do not have real meaning in Tibetan and Chinese traditions; they also used the word 'protectorate' which does not convey much more sense in this context. We have now to make a clean sweep of the rather unprofitable discussion about sovereignty, suzerainty or even protectorate, for the objective of a history of Tibet does not consist in finding among the Western political and historical concepts approximative equivalents to Tibetan and Chinese concepts.

The matter has to be, and has already been, investigated from a different point of view. The main point, though an obvious commonplace, is that Tibetan and Chinese cultures, being deeply different, consequently generated different concepts and different institutions. The concept of *chöyön*, for example, generally explained as "Lama-patron relationship", has often been discussed during the last few years as to its origins, its basic meaning and its evolution (Ruegg, 1991, 1995, 1997). This term appears frequently in the Tibetan historiographical and political literature of the period, mainly as a reference to the relations between the Dalai Lama and the emperor. It should certainly be interesting to know if the Tibetan religious and lay rulers of the period were aware that if the attitude of most of the Mongol princes was consistent with the *chöyön* principle, as described by the Tibetan documents, the imperial messages, as courteous as they usually were, did not mention it or gave it a much more restrictive interpretation. The imperial attitude concerning Tibet was not, during the Qing dynasty, what it had been during the Yuan dynasty.

The Yuan and Qing foreign dynasties did much for the Chinese empire, for both its development and its institutions. When the Manchus came to the Peking throne in 1644, they brought with them something of their nomadic past, their knowledge of the Inner Asiatic realities and their experience of the Mongols. After a period of comparative isolation, Tibet was again involved in Inner Asiatic affairs, through the religious and political relations established with the Mongols. By the mid-seventeenth century, Inner Asia came back to a greater extension, Peking and Lhasa being the two main poles of power, the third being more difficult to locate, for it consisted in fact in the more or less threatening power of the Mongol tribes hanging over the Qing dynasty and the Chinese empire, especially the Dzungar menace.

The Manchus at first did not consider the Tibetan question as the Ming emperors had considered it, but later on, their attitude became progressively more Sinicized. The Dalai Lama was highly respected, and he was considered an ally, at least as long as he was able to impose peace upon the restless Mongol neighbours of the Empire and to keep Tibet a peaceful and solid buffer state. But Tibet had no regular and well organized army (at least since Gushri Khan's death, 1656) and even then, the Dalai Lama could not have been its leader: such was the very peculiar kind of temporal power he had received. Tibet was therefore a weak point in the defensive circle of the Qing empire. After the Fifth Dalai Lama's death (1682), the regent Sangye Gyatso made a daring attempt to maintain his premonitory concept of a central, religious empire, but failed. On the other hand, the Manchus promoted the *tusi* system among the non-Han bordering populations of China; they appointed (or rather confirmed) and supported local native princes who spared them the expense of delegated administrators. This policy cost the Gelukpas most of their effective power in Eastern Tibet, while the Manchu maps kept this region out of Tibet proper. When, after the various periods of unrest in the 18th century, the Southern frontier of Tibet proved its weakness, the emperor edicted regulations with the hope of putting an end to the difficulties he had met with in Tibet. The fate of these regulations is a part of the history of the 19th century, but it can be said that the main reason for the Manchus' relative failure in Tibet might have been not so much their own loss of substance after Qianlong's reign, as their inability to find good administrators, Tibetans such as Pholhanas, and bannersmen.

From a political point of view, the period has been one of the turning points of Tibetan history. But it was also an important period for Tibetan civilization, in most of its aspects, even if some of them have still to be investigated and call for elucidation.

It is true that the economic and social history of Tibet has still to be written, as has been suggested by the anthropological and comparatively recent approach of some Tibetologists. Several brilliant sketches and studies have shed light, for example, on the main structures of administrative organisation, on the history of some families of the gentry, on the Tibetan system of mintage, or the organization of some pilgrimages. We know that during the 17th and 18th century, the populations of Central Tibet suffered two civil wars, a number of border clashes, the Dzungar and Gurkha invasions, they had to support the Chinese garrison and armies, and smallpox raged regularly. However, Central Tibet seems to have enjoyed an increasing social prosperity during the 18th century, even if shortages of grain, for example, have been recorded by the end of the century in the southern bordering districts which suffered from the Gurkha war. But we are still unable to give a statistical appreciation of these events and of their material consequences, and even a general, balanced and well documented description of them, though the analysis is in obvious progress. It is rather tedious and often disappointing work to hunt for that type of information in the written documents used by the historians (especially the biographical literature). And their authors, if they do sometimes mention economic matters, do it very seldom with the accuracy and precision that are wished for. There are, of course, fruitful exceptions. For example, regent Sangye Gyatso in his supplement to the Fifth Dalai Lama's autobiography gave many precise details concerning the evolution of the landed property and the new distribution of estates made by the Gelukpa government; in his history of the Fifth Dalai Lama's mausoleum in the Potala, he gave a very informative list of the workers engaged for the building. Inquiries made in the Tibetan Archives that have been gathered in Lhasa should provide much other information, especially in the field of agricultural productions, land revenue and taxes. Access to the Chinese Archives, that are so valuable in regard to Tibetan political matters, has become easier since some years; let us hope that the recently created Archives of the Tibet Autonomous Region will give easy access to the whole of their very rich collections.

We know that the map of landed property in Central Tibet, and the identity of the land owners and tenants, religious or lay, was notably modified as a result of the new Gelukpa government during the 17th century. This knowledge should lead to much new research or indepth investigations in various fields. Redistribution affected the oldest families and the well established principalities and many bordering districts, less heavily, though the new Gelukpa settlements were numerous in the whole Tibetan area, even, for example, in the Tatsienlou region, which was nevertheless incorporated into the Chinese province of Sichuan in 1720, one among many border rectifications Peking made during the first half of the 18th century. This field provides a good opportunity to make further inquiries concerning the history of the principalities of Eastern Tibet, and their economic and cultural development, and as a matter of fact there are an increasing number of studies concerning these regions. Another point of interest in connection with landed property is the question of the estates given to the Panchen Lama: examining their status could be a good way of studying the evolution of the opposition between Ü and Tsang after the 1642 events and we have to remember that their status became a matter of rupture with Lhasa in the beginning of the 20th century.

The period was also significant because of its artistic developments, especially in the architectural field. As it appears from the historical literature such as the Sangye Gyatso's *Vaidurya Serpo*, the Gelukpas made an impressive number of foundations and extensions, they also restored temples and monasteries. Many of them they had taken from other religious schools, they even fortified their settlements in Western Tibet. Their main achievement was undoubtedly the Potala, built between 1645 and 1648 by the Fifth Dalai Lama and completed in 1691-1694 by Sangye Gyatso. It showed a technical, but also economic and social prowess: workers and craftmen came from all the main districts of Tibet, as did the donors, either religious or lay. The collecting and transport of building materials was a bold enterprise that had never been seen before, even in the time of the building of such big monasteries as the Sakya Lhakhang Chenmo, and many technical innovations were made.

Moreover, after the heavy destructions suffered by Central Tibet in 1717-1720, or by Eastern Tibet during the Kukunor rebellion in 1723-1724, many temples and monasteries had then to be rebuilt. The Nyingmapa monasteries, the main victims of the Dzungars, were not favoured with government aid, as the other monasteries were, but the efforts made there, though sometimes necessarily restricted, presented the same technical standards that spread all over the country. Many of these technical innovations were dictated by the necessities of buildings much bigger than they were in the past and they mainly concerned carpentry work and the skylights. Their origin may be questioned, and an increased influence of Chinese carpentry cannot be denied.

These remarks can be considered as irrelevant in such a short survey of these two centuries of Tibetan history, but in their way they corroborate the fact that Tibet became involved in the evolution of the Chinese empire under Qing influence. China had an early but limited influence on the art and architecture of Tibet: it never became preponderant, except in some bordering districts of Amdo and Kham. The Qing emperors started a large campaign of foundation and restoration of Buddhist temples and monasteries in China that led to a somewhat standardized style. They also laid several notable "lamaistic" foundations in Peking, then in Mongolia. Since the 1578 meeting betwen the Dalai Lama and Altan Khan, many foundations had been built by the Mongol princes in Eastern Tibet and Mongolia, some of them benefited from imperial patronage, many of them from Tibetan skills. The local stylistic characteristics never disappeared, but from a kind of melting-pot (North-Eastern Tibet, Northern China, Mongolia), radiated a number of stylistic and technical innovations that can be traced in the whole "lamaistic" area. The use of the term "lamaistic" (and of course "lamaism"), strongly reproved of by the Tibetans themselves and by many scholarly Westerners, should in any case be limited to the period of the spread of Tibetan Buddhism in Inner Asia (17th-19th centuries), within and beyond the Qing empire, often with the support of the Qing emperors and sometimes under their supervision (particularly through the Lifanyuan, in charge of the Mongolian and Kukunor areas).

The period is also characterized by a great religious activity and a vast display of scholarship, from Bhutan to Mongolia, in spite of various wars and persecutions, especially against the Jonangpas and the Nyingmapas. There was a great need of books and teachers for the countries recently gained to the Law. The increasing number of colleges in the Gelukpa monasteries, either new foundations such as Labrang in Amdo, or older ones as Drepung near Lhasa, corroborates this fact. They received students from all parts of Tibet and Buddhist Inner Asia, but not without political attention: the Dzungar monks were carefully expelled from Central Tibet after the 1717-1720 events... Printing activity was increasing, in Central Tibet, as well as in Khams (Derge), Amdo (Kumbum, Labrang...), Peking, whose importance in the field is well established, and in Mongolia.

Significantly, the Tibetan Buddhist Canon had three editions during the period: in Peking (*Kanjur*, 1684-1692; *Tanjur*, 1724), in Narthang (Tsang, Central Tibet) (*Kanjur*, 1730-1732, the planks were engraved near Shelkar; *Tanjur*, 1741-1742), and in Derge (Khams) (*Kanjur*, 1731-1733; *Tanjur*, 1744). The 18ᵗʰ century was the Golden Age of Derge, whose very important and various production includes the 1737 edition of the *Sakya Kabum* (the collected works of the great Masters of Sakya), countless Collected Works, and the *Nyingme Gyübum* (collection of Nyingmapa *tantras*) edited by Jigme Lingpa (1730-1798). The history of the Derge principality, of its princes and of its monasteries, which has already interested several scholars, should deserve further studies.

When considering the titles of the works written by these Tibetan, Bhutanese or Mongolian Masters, one cannot fail to notice the number of works devoted directly to the basic study and the spread of the Law, that is to say works concerning the different categories of knowledge as described by the Buddhist tradition. These works deal with the "outer sciences", four of the five "major" sciences: grammar and linguistics, logic and dialectics, medicine, arts and crafts. It does not mean of course, that the mystic works, philosophical or canonical and non-canonical works and commentaries, works dealing with the "inner science" (*nang rig*), the last and highest of these five "major" sciences, were neglected during the period, and there is no question of making a list of the main works dealing with one or the other of the traditional sciences. But codification and diffusion were undoubtedly a real and constant concern during the period, as it was during all periods of development in Tibetan religious history. The Fifth Dalai Lama initiated and encouraged the development of an administrative language, that might be considered as an effort of standardization to help the Gelukpas' attempt at centralism as well as the general movement of diffusion. He also encouraged a renewal of interest in Sanskrit studies, which led, among others, to the translation of the Panini's commentary by Dar Lotsawa. This interest in the most ancient, and the most difficult system of the Sanskrit grammar was not entirely new in Tibet, but the other systems of Indian grammar had proved to be sufficient for the translation into Tibetan of countless Indian canonical texts that had been made since the 8ᵗʰ century. This renewal of interest led also to the compilation of lexicographical works such as the Tibetan-Sanskrit dictionary of Dokhar Tsering Wangyel (18ᵗʰ c.). Another important lexicographical enterprise was made in Peking with the 1741-1742 Tibetan-Mongol dictionary of Buddhist terminology. The greatest scholar of the period in the field of Sanskrit studies was probably Situ Panchen (1700-1774), corrector of the 1731-1733 Derge edition of the Kanjur, who then undertook the enormous work of revising the whole existing Tibetan translations of Indian literature concerning grammar, lexicography and philology. Such efforts at diffusing knowledge cannot be efficiently carried out without a sound textual basis, and there was in the 17-18ᵗʰ centuries a real and brilliant attempt at critical studies. This disposition can be traced also in the Kathog Tsewang Norbu's interest in epigraphy. It is less conspicuous if present at all in the other traditional sciences. Tibetan science did not enter modern times in all its fields in the course of 18ᵗʰ century. But what was done can be considered as a preliminary to the brilliant achievements of the Rimed movement in the 19ᵗʰ century.

BIBLIOGRAPHY

Ahmad, Zahiruddin, *Sino-Tibetan Relations in the Seventeenth Century*, Roma, Ismeo, 1970.
Petech, Luciano, *China and Tibet in the Early XVIIIth Century*. Leiden, E.J. Brill, 1972.
Ruegg, David S., "Mchod-yon, yon-mchod and mchod-gnas / yon gnas on the Historiography
        and Semantics of a Tibetan religio-social and religio-political Concept.", *Tibetan History and
        Language*, Wien, 1991, 441-453.
Smith, E. Gene, *Among Tibetan Texts*, Somerville, Wisdom, 2001.
Tucci, Giuseppe, *Tibetan Painted Scrolls*, Roma, 1949.

following page:
Bell's entry: "(co) Truptop Lama (e). Skull drum and
thigh-bone trumpet in hands, 2 skull cups, 1 holding beer
(c) and the other tea (d), bell and dorje in front of him;
ka-tam (b) (long pole) on his left." Hermit's band"
(Gom-tak) over right shoulder. These men wear long hair
like Sadhus. (e) Belongs to the Nyinma Sect. (c) for
offering to deities (lha) (d) which he drinks himself.
In this he may keep his food generally. (b) The minds
of deities dwell in the ka-tam."
1998.285.226 (BL.H.197)

Historical and religious relations between Lhodrak (southern Tibet) and Bumthang (Bhutan) from the 18th to the early 20th century: Preliminary data

Françoise Pommaret

Bumthang in central Bhutan is situated just south of the Lhodrak region in Tibet but separated from it by the Great Himalayan range. It is impossible to understand the history of Bumthang if research is not extended beyond the present-day political border. The history of the two regions should be put into perspective in the light of each other.[1]

Relations between Lhodrak and Bumthang have never been really explored, apart from a few notes (Aris: 1979). When researching this paper, I was reminded of the interest that Hugh Richardson, to whom this conference was dedicated, had in Lhodrak. Richardson was himself one of the 'discoverers' of the Kheype gatön, written by the great 16th century historian Pawo Tsuglag Trenwa and the woodblocks of this fundamental historical work had been kept in Lhalung monastery.

After a short geographical and historical background, I will present some data on relations between Lhodrak and Bumthang from historical and religious points of view in the 18th, 19th and early 20th centuries. This paper is a preliminary survey and this subject obviously calls for much more research.

I: Geographical and historical overview

Lhodrak is located in southern Tibet, and its border to the south is today common with part of the northern border of Bhutan. The ancient Lhodrak region is now divided into two counties: Tshome and Lhodrak, both belonging to the large prefecture of Lhokha (Ch. Shannan) in the Tibetan Autonomous Region (TAR).

Bumthang is an administrative province (*dzongkhag*) of the kingdom of Bhutan and is situated in the centre of the country. The present-day province encompasses roughly the traditional territory attributed to Bumthang that is composed of four main areas (Bum thang Dezhi): Chume, Chökhor, Tang and Ura.

Two high peaks considered to be the abode of deities dominate the landscape of these regions: Kula Khari (7,569 m; nowadays often wrongly transcribed Kula Gangri), which is situated inside Lhodrak, and Gangkar Pünsum (7,540 m), within Bhutan's borders.

Although separated by the Great Himalayan range, Bumthang and Lhodrak are linked by an ancient route that crosses over a pass, Monla Karchung (*ca*. 5,250m), which was the main - and much feared- thoroughfare.

Another pass, Lhodrak la (alt.?), slightly further east of Bumthang, leads into Lhodrak from the high valleys and 'hidden countries' of Pagsamlung and Khenpajong in northern Bumthang. Because of the difficult terrain, this path has never been much used as a route except by lamas looking for isolated meditation places.

This rapid survey would not be complete without speaking of Kurtö in the present-day Bhutanese Lhuntse province, to which Bumthang is closely tied economically, historically and linguistically. The valley of Kurtö is also situated south of Lhodrak and just south of the town of Lhakhang dzong where the famous Komthing temple and, also close by, the Lhodrakharchu monastery were founded. In this area, Kurtö and Lhodrak are not separated by a pass as the Lhodrak/Kuru river, a tributary of the Manas, cuts a gorge through the Himalayan range and flows directly from Lhodrak into Kurtö. To the east of the Kuru river valley, another pass, Böla (*ca*. 5,000 m), provides a link between Singye dzong in Bhutan and Lhakhang dzong in Lhodrak. Among the first travellers from Lhodrak into Kurtö recorded by written sources were three of the 'Vajra brothers' of Lhalung Pelkyi Dorje in the 9th century (TLNT: 45; Gyelrig: f. 42b, Aris, 1986: 58-59; D.G, 1994: 64).

This geographic information is essential to the understanding of how Bumthang and Lhodrak were connected religiously as early as the 8th century, if one is to follow the Pelliot Tibétain 44, the famous Dunhuang manuscript dealing with the teaching of the Vajrakila by Padmasambhava.[2] The two regions were also economically complementary, but pursuing this point would lead us too far astray from our present topic.

Bumthang seems to have been regarded with ambivalence by many Tibetans – a place of exile and a 'hidden country', a duality which is common to other borderlands of southern Tibet. The story of the exile of Khyikha Rathö in Bumthang is still alive in the oral as well as written traditions (Aris, 1979: 60-82).

Many great religious figures and treasure-discoverers who lived in Lhodrak visited either Bumthang or Kurtö, where they established temples and lineages which are still remembered today in Bhutan. Among the most famous were Ngotön Chöku Dorje (1036-1102), Lorepa Wangchuk Tsöndrü (1187-1250), Longchen Rabjam (1308-1363), Guru Chöwang (1212-1270), Ratna Lingpa (1403-1469) and Dorje Lingpa (1346-1405). It seems as if the 'Southern Valleys' were, for the religious figures of the 'Southern Rock', a privileged field for conversion and teachings, but also for matrimonial alliances.

Ngotön Chöku Dorje was a close disciple of the famous Marpa and he came from Sekhar Guthog, his home in Lhodrak, to the Tang valley of Bumthang where he established the temple of Langmoling (LCBS: f.91 a-b). Another Kagyupa lama,

Lorepa, founder of the 'Lower Drukpa', was active in Lhodrak where he restored the Lhodrak Kharcu monastery, and his memorial chorten (*dmar gdung*) was kept in Komthing temple. He visited Bumthang where he founded temples in Chödra and, just below, in Tharpaling, which became, one century later, one of the residences of Longchen Rabjam.

Guru Chöwang, who was from Neshi in Lhodrak, visited Bumthang and Kurtö where, according to Bhutanese texts (LCBS: 71b), he had a son who is at the origin of the lineages of Nyala and Lugkhyu in Kurtö. Ratna Lingpa, born at Groshul in Lhodrak, seems to have visited only Kurtö and a lineage in the village of Chusa in Kurtö still claims to descend from him.

From Ü in central Tibet, Longchen Rabjam went into exile in Bumthang where he stayed ten years, established several temples and fathered at least one son whose lineage is still known in Bhutan.

As for Dorje Lingpa, born in Dra (Ü, central Tibet), he spent most of his life in Lhodrak near Mt Kula Khari at a place called Layag Khyerchu, and in Kharchu. From Lhodrak, he made two or three long visits to Bhutan discovering texts. In Bumthang, he established temples and spiritual lineages and apparently fathered a son from whom at least one lineage claims to descend.[3]

It appears that the route through Monla Karchung pass, although testing, was not a major impediment to relations between the two regions, and lamas used to 'commute' with relative ease. For example, Pema Lingpa (1450-1521), the famous treasure-discoverer from Bumthang, visited Lhodrak twenty-five times and discovered texts in both regions. And this does not include the traders and ordinary pilgrims about whom nothing is known to date.

II: Bumthang and Lhodrak (18th to mid-20th century)

Although further research is needed, the historical elements already available at this stage raise interest in the study of Bumthang-Lhodrak relations from the 18th to the early 20th century.

One of the focal points of these relations was the monastery of Lhalung, to which Kathog Situ's guide to central Tibet (1999: 242-252) devoted an extended description. Interestingly, the historian Pawo Tsuglag, himself native to Lhodrak, did not dwell on this monastery in his Khepey gatön and the Desi Sangye Gyatso did not mention it either in his Vaidurya serpo. Thus far, its history remains patchy and subject to various interpretations, unless there is a historical text about Lhalung of which I am not aware.

The aim here is not to attempt a reconstruction of the history of Lhalung monastery, but this monastery could make a good case-study of the vicissitudes of a religious establishment. While Kathog Situ, in his pilgrimage guide, attributed one building to King Relpacen (1999: 244), Richardson (1998: 323) says that the original founding of the monastery is attributed to King Songtsen Gampo and that the 1st Karmapa, Düsum khyenpa (1110-1193), restored and enlarged it. Checking the Khepey gatön, I could not find clear evidence of this founding in the section devoted to the 1st Karmapa. Pawo Tsuglag simply mentions that the 1st Karmapa stayed in Lhalung when he was fifty years old (KPGT: 863).

It is necessary to raise here a point that is relevant to the subject. Richardson says that 'it remained in Karmapa control until it was taken over by the fifth Dalai Lama' (1998: 323), and that 'at first the Red Hat lamas were closely related to Lha lung in Lho brag' (1998: 339). In his own note for *Mk'yen brtse's guide to the holy places of central Tibet* (Ferrari, 1958: 139-140), Richardson remarks that the monastery 'is now apparently a mixture of 'Brug pa, bKa brgyud pa and rNying ma pa', and in his guide, Jamyang Khyentse Wangpo (1820-1892) himself states that Lhalung was 'at first a residence of the bKa' rgyud pa. Today it is under the protection of a series of incarnation of the verbal plane (*brgyud 'dzin gsung sprul*) of the descendants of Pad gling' (Ferrari, 1958: 58). Richardson also remarked that

> 'the seat [of the historian dPa'bo gtsug lag 'phreng ba] was formely at Lha-lung in Lho-brag, which had been founded by Dus-gsum mkhyen-pa in 1154, on what appears to have been the site of an older chapel, but this monastery was taken from the Karmapa by the Fifth Dalai Lama and the present Dpa'-bo lama lives at Gnas-gnang near mTshur-phu ' (1998: 339).

Indeed, at the time of the 5th Dalai lama several monasteries in Lhodrak - Nyingmapa as well as Kagyupa of different obediences - passed into the political control of the central government around 1648.[4] At first glance, here is a monastery that is said to have belonged to, depending on the period, different religious schools. This is not exceptional *per se* in the course of Tibetan history, but a monastery which, in the middle of the 20th century, was perceived as associated with several religious schools at the same time, is quite rare.

However, from this short historical sketch, it would be difficult for an outsider to assess the importance played by the region of Bumthang in the history of Lhalung. So far, it is not really clear how and when the monastery, from being a Karmapa monastery, became the main seat of the lineages of Pema Lingpa. Pawo Tsuglag, whose Karma Kagyupa lineage was affiliated to this monastery, does not appear to deal with the subject.

The seat of Pema Lingpa in Bumthang was Tamshing monastery, founded at the end of his life in 1501-1505 with the help of workers who were sent from Lhodrak by his patron (PLNT: 37b). However, his main seat was considered to be Lhalung and it was also the seat of his successive incarnations, the Peling Sungtrul[5] , as well as the Peling Thugse, the successive incarnations of his son, Dawa Gyeltsen.[6] The respective incarnations of these lineages of Pema Lingpa were very respected by the 5th Dalai Lama and paid several visits to Lhasa. (Ardussi: in press quoting the Dukula Gösang by the 5th DL). Both lineages were at that time close to the great Nyingma pa 'treasure discoverer' Terdak Lingpa (1646-1718) of the monastery of Mindröling, who was one of the 5th Dalai Lama's most revered masters. From the biography of the 2nd Gangte Tulku, a lineage descending from Pema Lingpa's grand-son, it appears that the 4th Thugse, Tenzin Gyurme Dorje, regained Lhalung from the 5th Dalai Lama in 1672 (TLNT: 48b, p.96 and Dukula quoted by Ardussi, in press), which suggests that Lhalung might have not been under the Peling school in the early 17th century.

Because of these lineages of reincarnations that had their roots in Bumthang, the connections between Lhalung and Bumthang became closer, especially from the

18th century. The relations constituted a maze of family connections, lineages of reincarnations and teachings passed back and forth. This is certainly not an unique occurence in the Tibetan world but as opposed to many instances, because of the details available in this case, they can be partly deconstructed with some accuracy.[7]

The list of reincarnations compiled in Tibet for the Manchus in 1814 and updated in 1820[8] gives the names and birth places of the Peling Thugse but, surprisingly, does not list the Peling Sungtrul, whose short collective biographies have been published in Bhutan.[9] Amongst the five Peling Thugse following the founder of the lineage (Dawa Gyeltsen, himself born in Bumthang), four were also born in 'Mon Bum thang'.

The 9th Peling Thugse was Thubten Pelbar (1906-1939). A hot-tempered man, according to the oral tradition, he was born in Bumthang in the chöje family[10] of Ogyenchöling, the son of Ugyen Dorje, the Jakar Dzongpon, head of the Bumthang district and first cousin of Bhutan's first king, Ugyen Wangchuck. The 9th Peling Thugse was, through his family, a descendant of both Dorje Lingpa and Pema Lingpa,[11] and his paternal grand-father, Trinle, from the Tamshing chöje family, had spent several years near Lhalung monastery.

The 10th Peling Thugse, Thegchog Tenpe Gyeltsen, born in 1951 in Dra in central Tibet, arrived in Bumthang, accompanied by several monks from Lhalung, in the early 1960s.

The Peling Sungtrul lineage was connected more directly with the family that would become Bhutan's royal family in 1907. The 8th Peling Sungtrul, Kunzang Dorje Tenpe Nyima (1843-1891), was born in Bumthang Wangdüchöling.[12] He came from the family of the Tamshing chöje and was the brother of the wife of Jigme Namgyal, the then Tongsa Penlop and father of Ugyen Wangchuck (1862-1926) who would become the first king of Bhutan.

Jigme Namgyal is said to have met his wife, Pema Chökyi, in Lhalung while she was staying with her brother, the 8th Peling Sungtrul, and married her according to the wishes of the Sungtrul. Jigme Namgyal had at that time reached the height of his power in Bhutan. In 1866, Jigme Namgyal restored the ancient Jampey lhakhang and added to it a temple dedicated to Kalacakra which was consecrated by his brother-in-law, the 8th Peling Sungtrul.

Jigme Namgyal's elder son, Trinle Tobgye, was sent to Lhalung as a monk but was recalled to Bhutan in 1877 by his father, who made him the Wangdüphodrang Dzongpon. As a young child, Ugyen Wangchuck himself learnt reading and writing with his maternal uncle, the 8th Peling Sungtrul, and when he became the Tongsa Penlop in 1882 after the death of his father, he always kept good relations with his uncle. In 1882, the Peling Sungtrul came to Bumthang to consecrate a stupa with a ritual for destroying future enemies and, in 1884, he built in one of the temples of Lhalung a memorial chorten for the Tongsa Penlop Pema Tenzin who was also his brother-in-law (Kathog Situ, 1999: 245).[13]

When the Peling Sungtrul died in Lhalung in 1891, Ugyen Wangchuck attended his funeral ceremony and invited one of the lamas who arranged the ceremony to visit Bumthang. Later, he had a silver chorten built for his uncle in Lhalung (Kathog Situ, 1999: 244).

The lama whom he invited was the famous 8th Bakha Tulku, Khamsum Rigzin Yongdröl. Like the Peling Sungtrul and the Peling Thugse lineages, the Bakha

Tulkus were, from the early 18th century, holders of the teachings of Terdak Lingpa, and therefore closely associated to the monastery of Mindröling. The Bakha monastery was at Sang ngachöling near Kanam, on the way from Powo to Pemakö.[14] At least from the end of the 18th century, they had an almost symbiotic relation with the Peling Sungtrul, Lhalung and therefore, Bumthang. The 6th Bakha Tulku, Rigzin Dorje, was born in Lhodrak (at Lhalung ?), the son of the 7th Peling Sungtrul, Kunzang Tenpe Gyeltsen (1763-1817). The 6th Bakha Tulku became one of the masters of the 8th Peling Sungtrul, who in turn became the master of the 8th Bakha Tulku, Khamsum Rigzin Yongdröl. At the death of the 8th Peling Sungtrul in 1891, the 8th Bakha Tulku became the 'throne holder' (khri 'dzin) of Lhalung monastery and the master of the 9th Sungtrul, Tenzin Chökyi Gyeltsen.

The 8th Bakha Tulku, Khamsum Rigzin Yongdröl, on the instructions of his master Jamyang Khyentse Wangpo, had Ugyen Wangchuck build the temple of Kuje in Bumthang, and, in particular, the three-storey-high statue of Padmasambhava Guru Zilnon to protect the country.[15] He also became the Master of Chants of Ugyen Wangchuck , who presented him with numerous gifts that helped the 8th Bakha Tulku to restore his own monastery in Powo.

The 9th Bakha Tulku's life was short but he had time to visit Lhalung and Bumthang. As for the present day 10th Bakha Tulku, his links with the lineage of Pema Lingpa and Bhutan are still strong. He visited Bhutan in 1996 and stayed in Tamshing monastery where he performed rituals.

One of his previous reincarnations, the 8th Bakha Tulku, was one of the 9th Peling Sungtrul's teachers, who lived in Lhalung. The 9th Peling Sungtrul, Tenzin Chökyi Gyeltsen (1894-1925), born at the Wangdüchöling palace, was the son of the sister of the first king of Bhutan, Ugyen Wangchuck and therefore the first cousin of the second king, Jigme Wangchuck.

The 10th Peling Sungtrul (1930-1955), Pema Ösel Gyurme Dorje, was born in Yardrok in Lhodrak and kept excellent relations with the royal family of Bhutan. A contemporary of the second king, he was invited at least twice to Bumthang, once in 1944 and then in 1952 when he performed the funeral rituals for the second king and the second king's aunt, Yeshe Chöden, the mother of the 9th Sungtrul, his previous incarnation. One of his teachers was the 9th Peling Thugse Thubten Pelbar, who was also related as we have seen, to the noble religious families of Bumthang.

The fact that two of the holders of Lhalung lineages were related to a powerful family of Bumthang that would become the royal family of Bhutan in 1907 is well demonstrated by the attitude of Ugyen Wangchuck when he travelled to Lhalung. There, in 1906, he received the British political officer to Sikkim, Bhutan and Tibet, J.C. White, with whom he had developed a friendship. White's description in 1906 gives an impression of a powerful man, perfectly at ease in Lhalung, having the camp pitched in the monastery's gardens, entertaining, sending messages and holding talks on Bhutan with the British. It also appears that, on the occasion of White's visit to Lhalung, the Tibetan official from the nearby Towa Dzong was not present in Lhalung, but simply sent a deputation on a courtesy call.[16]

In the course of the history of Bumthang and Lhodrak at that time, many more instances of interrelations could be brought forward. For example, even a Drukpa hierarch like the 5th Shabdrung , Jigme Chögyel (1862-1904), kept ties with Lhalung; he was in fact born in Dramitse (eastern Bhutan) in a family descending from Pema Lingpa, and his mother was the daughter of the Tamshing chöje in Bumthang.[17] The 5th Shabdrung was recognised when he was two years old by Nagchang Ugyen Yeshe Dorje, a lama who came from Lhalung, and his brother, Tenpe Nyinje, was recognised as the 7th Gangte Tulku.[18]

Conclusion

This short survey concentrates mainly on the relations between Bumthang and Lhalung monastery in Lhodrak, and more specifically, on the close-knit relationships between the most powerful families of Bhutan and the reincarnations of Pema Lingpa in the 19th and early 20th centuries. No doubt these connections gave the Bhutanese privileged access to Lhodrak and especially Lhalung. They had summer pastures and traded easily with this region: rice, madder, stick lac, paper, bamboo wares and medicinal herbs were exchanged for dried apricots, dried mutton, sheep-skins, wool, borax and salt. The Bhutanese also received teachings and blessings from Tibetan lamas who had found staunch and faithful patrons among the noble families of the region as early as the 13th century.

The interest on the part of powerful families from Bumthang in blessings and teachings was not restricted to lamas of the lineages of Pema Lingpa, although they were the most important for them. The case of Changchub Tsöndrü (1817-1857), an eccentric Tibetan lama who wandered all his life between central Tibet, Lhodrak and Bhutan, is examplary. A truly non-sectarian scholar and tantric practitioner, he exerted considerable influence first on the Tongsa Penlop Tshokye Dorje of Ogyenchöling, and then on the Tongsa Penlop Jigme Namgyal.[19]

It is also well known in Bhutan that Ashi Wangmo, the second king's sister, became a nun with the 15th Karmapa. And when Ngawang Yonten Gyatso (1920 - *ca.* 1963), the Sakyapa master from Ngor, visited Bhutan between 1936 and 1939, lavish gifts were showered on him by the royal family and he went back to Tibet very wealthy.[20]

These two regions, although belonging to two different countries, were, in the 19th and the first half of the 20th centuries, almost perfectly complementary in terms of religion and economy. This could not have been achieved without the family connections between the Pema Lingpa lineages and the most powerful families in Bumthang.

This short 'deconstruction work' shows that the age-old relations between Bumthang and Lhodrak were enhanced by three factors which combined into an intricate pattern and an influential web-family ties, patron-to-lama relationships and a reincarnation system inside precise religious lineages.

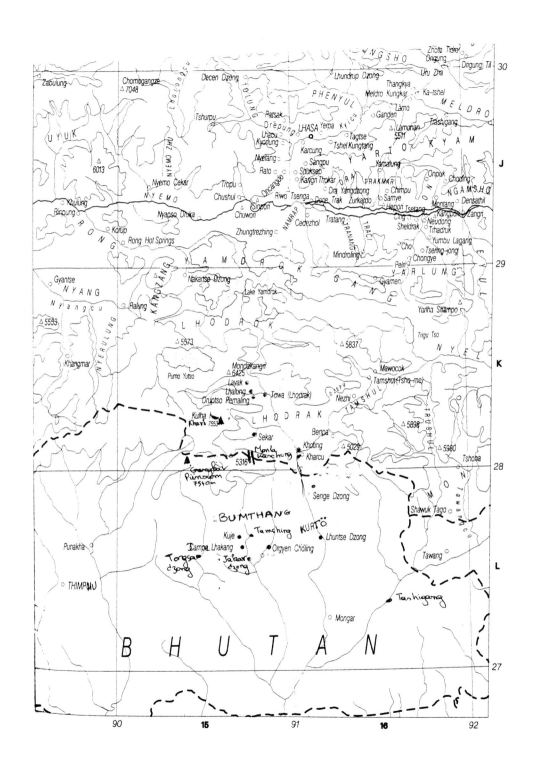

Genealogy Bumthang/ Lhalung

NOTE: Only historical figures important for this article are mentioned here.

- ____ blood line
- ,,,, several generations' gap
- = marriage
- red fonts: religious figures

- blue fonts: men
- black fonts: women

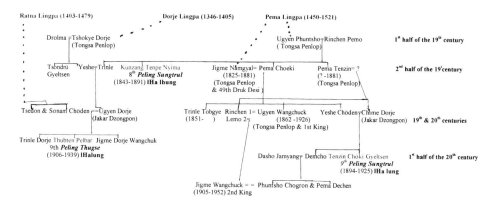

Ratna Lingpa (1403-1479)   Dorje Lingpa (1346-1405)   Pema Lingpa (1450-1521)

Drolma ₸Tshokye Dorje
(Tongsa Penlop)   Ugyen Phuntsho₸Rinchen Pemo
(Tongsa Penlop)   1st half of the 19th century

Tsöndrü ₸Yeshe₸Trinle   Kunzang Tenpe Nyima   Jigme Namgyal= Pema Choeki   Pema Tenzin= ?
Gyeltsen   8th *Peling Sungtrul*   (1825-1881)   (? -1881)   2nd half of the 19th century
        (1843-1891) **lHa lhung**   (Tongsa Penlop   (Tongsa Penlop)
                & 49th Druk Desi)

Tsedon & Sonam Chöden ==Ugyen Dorje   Trinle Tobgye Rinchen 1= Ugyen Wangchuck   Yeshe Chöden₸Chime Dorje
        (Jakar Dzongpon)   (1851-   )   Lemo 2₸ (1862 -1926)   (Jakar Dzongpon)   19th & 20th centuries
                        (Tongsa Penlop & 1st King)

Trinle Dorje Thubten Pelbar Jigme Dorje Wangchuk
        9th ***Peling Thugse***
        (1906-1939) **lHalung**   Dasho Jamyang₸ Demcho Tenzin Choki Gyeltsen   1st half of the 20th century
                9th ***Peling Sungtrul***
                (1894-1925) **lHa lung**

                Jigme Wangchuck = = Phuntsho Chogron & Pema Dechen
                (1905-1952) 2nd King

Reincarnation lineages ========
Master to disciple links +++++++++
Relatives ____

Pad gling gSung sprul   **rBa kha sprul sku**   **Pad gling Thug sras**

6th Pad gling gSung sprul   **6th rBa kha sprul sku**
Kunzang Tenpe Gyeltshen   Kunzang Rigzin Dorje
(1763- 1817)

7th Pad gling gSung sprul   **7th rBa kha sprul sku**
Pema Tenzin *alias*   Kunzang Dechen Choegyel
Choekyi Lodroe   (short life)
(1819-1842)

99

- Bla ma gsang sngags 1983. *'Brug tu 'od gsal lha'i gdung rabs 'byung tshul brjod pa sMyos rabs gsal ba'i me long*,'Thimphu.
- Chab spel Tshe brtan phun tshogs & al (eds.). 1991. *Bod kyi gal che'i lo rgyus yig cha bdams bsgrigs* (Gangs can rig mdzod series n°16), Lhasa: Bod ljongs bod yig dpe skrun khang.
- rGyal sras gZhan phan zla ba alias Bla ma Nges don rdo rje. 1982. *gTer chen rDo rje gling pa'i gdung brgyud O rgyan chos gling chos rje rim brgyud*, 18 ff. Unpublished mss.
- Ka thog Si tu Chos kyi rgya mtsho (1880-1924). 1999. *Si tu pa Chos kyi rgya mtsho'i gangs rjongs dBus gTsang gnas bskor lam yig nor bu zla shel gyi se mo do =Ka thog Si tu'i dBus gTsang gnas yig*, Lhasa: Bod jongs bod yig dpe rnying dpe skrun khang.
- Kun dga' dpal bzang po gzhan phan rol ba'i rdo rje. 1859. *rDo je 'dzin pa chen po 'phrin las mkha' khyab mchog gi rdo rje am Byang chub brtson 'grus kyi rtogs pa brjod pa ngo mtshar nor bu'i snying po* (= Byang chub brtson 'grus rnam thar), Tongsa dzong woodblocks, vol. ka, 172 folios. Thimphu: National Library.
- Pad ma gling pa & rGyal ba don grub *Bum thang gter ston Padma gling pa'i rnam thar 'od zer kun mdzes nor bu'i phreng ba zhes bya ba skal ldan spro ba skye ba'i tshul du bris pa* (= PLNT), Thimphu, 254 ff.
-1976. Kun bzang bstan pa'i nyi ma. *Pad gling 'khrungs rabs kyi rtogs brjod nyung gsal dad pa'i me* in *The Rediscovered Teachings of the great Padma gling pa*, vol. 14. Thimphu: Kunzang Topgay.
- dPa bo gtsug lag 'phreng ba. 1986. *Dam pa'i chos kyi 'khor lo bsgyur ba rnams kyi byung ba gsal bar byed pa mkhas pa'i dga' ston* (= KPGT), vol. smad cha, Beijing: Mi rigs dpe khrun khang.
- Ngag dbang (18th century)
Sa skyong rgyal po'i gdung rabs 'parung khungs dang 'bangs kyi mi rabs chad tshul nges par gsal ba'i me long. Known as the *Rgya lrigs*, manuscript, 54 folios. Dated 1728.
- Ngag dbang blo bzang rgya mtsho, 5th Dalai Lama (1617-1682). *Za hor gyi ban de ngag dbang blo bzang rgya mtsho'i 'di snang 'khrul ba'i rol rtsed rtogs brjod kyi tshul du bkod pa dukkula'i gos bzang* (cover title: *Ngag dbang blo bzang rgya mtsho'i rnam thar*).Vol. I. 1989 Vols. II-III, 1991 Lhasa: Bod ljongs mi dmangs dpe skrun khang.
- Padma Tshe dbang. 1994. *'Brug gi rgyal rabs 'Brug gsal ba'i sgron me "History of Bhutan by Lopen Padma Tshedwang"* (= D.G.). Thimphu: National Library.
- 10th rJe mKhan po bsTan 'dzin chos rgyal. 1973. *rGyal kun khyab bdag 'gro ba'i bla ma bstan 'dzin rin po che legs pa'i don grub zhabs kyi rnam par thar pa ngo mtshar nor bu'i mchod sdong (Gang steng sprul sku bsTan 'dzin legs pa'i don grub rnam thar)* (=TLNT). Reproduced from the rare manuscripts from mTshams brag monastery, Thimphu: Kunzang Tobgay. English title: *Biographies of two Bhutanese lamas of the Padma gling pa tradition.*
- 1988. *sPo bo'i lo rgyus*, Lhasa: Bod ljongs mi mangs dpe khrun khang.
- n. d. *Biography & writings of Zhabs drung Thugs sprul 'Jigs med chos rgyal*, Thimphu: National Library. 349 p.

Aris, Michael. 1979. *Bhutan: The early history of a Himalayan kingdom*. Warminster: Aris & Philips.
Aris, Michael. 1986. *Sources for the history of Bhutan*. Wien: Wiener Studien zur Tibetologie und Buddhismuskunde, n°14, Arbeitskreis für Tibetische und Buddhistische Studien.
Aris, Michael.1994. *The Raven Crown*. Serindia: London.
Ardussi, John. 1977. *Bhutan before the British*. Canberra Australian National University: unpublished PhD. In press. Wien: Arbeitkteis für Tibetische und Buddhistische Studien Universität Wien.
Bischoff, F.A. & Hartman, Charles. 1971. "Padmasambhava's invention of the Phur bu. Ms Pelliot Tibétain 44" in *Etudes Tibétaines*. Paris: A. Maisonneuve, 11-26.
Dudjom Rinpoche.1991. *The Nyingma school of Tibetan Buddhism*, G. Dorje & M. Kapstein (eds.). Boston: Wisdom Publications.
Ferrari, Alfonsa.1958. *Mk'yen brtse's guide to the holy places of Central Tibet*. Roma: ISMEO.
Imaeda, Yoshiro. 1984. "Memento chronologique (*bstan rtsis*) du calendrier bhoutanais", in *Tibetan and Buddhist studies commemorating the 200th anniversary of the birth of Alexander Csoma de Kôrös*. L. Ligeti (ed.), vol. 1, Budapest: Akademiai Kiado, 303-320.

Jackson, David. 2001. "The 'Bhutan Abbot' of Ngor", in *Lungta 14 Aspects of Tibetan History*, R. Vitali (ed.), Dharamsala, 88-107.

Kapstein., Matthew T. 2000. "The imaginal persistence of the Empire", in *The Tibetan assimilation of Buddhism. Conversion, contestation and memory*. New York: Oxford University Press.

Karmay, Samten. 2000. "Dorje Lingpa and his rediscovery of the 'Gold Needle' in Bhutan", *Journal of Bhutan Studies*. vol.2 , n°2 winter 2000, 1-34.

Pommaret, Françoise & Imaeda , Yoshiro.1987. "Le monastère de gTam zhing (Tamshing) au Bhoutan central", in *Arts Asiatiques*, tome XLII, 19-30.

Pommaret, Françoise. 1989, unpublished mss. "The age of Jigme Namgyal", *History of Bhutan*. Thimphu: Department of Education.

Richardson, Hugh.

1998. "Some monasteries, temples and fortresses in Tibet before 1950", in *High Peaks, Pure Earth: Collected Writings on Tibetan History and Culture*. London: Serindia, 302-329.

1998. "The Karma-pa sect: a historical note", in *High Peaks, Pure Earth: Collected Writings on Tibetan History and Culture*. London: Serindia, 337-378.

White, J. Claude. 1971 (reprint). *Sikhim and Bhutan 1887-1908*. Delhi: Vivek.

TRANSCRIPTION-TRANSLITERATION INDEX

Kunzang Dorje Tenpe Nyima	Kun bzang rdo rje bstan pa'i nyi ma
Kunzang Pema Rinchen Namgyel	Kun bzang Padma Rin chen rnam rgyal
Kunzang Tenpe Gyeltsen	Kun bzang bstan pa'i rgyal mtshan
Kurtö	sKur stod
Langmoling	Glang mo gling
Laya khyerchu	La yag khyer chu
Lhakhang dzong	lHa khang rdzong
Lhalung	lHa lung
Lhalung Pelkyi Dorje	lHa lung dPal gyi rdo rje
Lhodrak	lHo brag (Ch. Lhozhag/Luozha)
Lhodrak Karchu	lHo brag mkhar chu
Lhuntse	lHun rtse,
Longchen Rabjam	Klong chen rab 'byams
Lorepa Wangchuk Tsöndrü	Lo ras pa byang chub brtson grus
Lugkhyu.	Lug khyu
Marpa	Mar pa
Mindröling	sMin grol gling
Monla karchung	Mon la dkar/mkhar chung
Nenang	Gnas gnang
Neshi	gNas bzhi
Ngawang Yonten Gyatso	Ngag dbang yon tan rgya mtsho
Ngor	Ngor
Ngotön Chöku Dorje	rNgog ston chos sku rdo rje
Nyala	Nya la
Ogyenchöling	O rgyan chos gling
Pagsamlung	dPag bsam lung
Pawo Tsuglag Trenwa	dPa' bo gtsug lag 'phreng ba
Pema Chökyi	Padma chos skyid
Pema Lingpa	Padma gling pa
Pema Ösel Gyurme Dorje	Padma 'od gsal 'gyur med rdo rje
Pema Tenzin	Padma bstan 'dzin
Pema Trinle	Padma 'phrin las
Pemakö	Padma bkod
Powo	sPo bo
Ratna Lingpa	Ratna gling pa
Relpacen	Ral pa can
Rigzin Dorje	Rig 'dzin rdo rje
Sakyapa	Sa skya pa
Sang ngachöling	gSang sngags chos gling
Sangye Gyatso	Sangs rgyas rgya mtsho
Sekhar Guthog	Sras mkhar dgu thog
Shabdrung Jigme Chögyel	Zhabs drung 'Jigs med chos rgyal
Singye dzong	Seng ge rdzong
Songtsen Gampo	Srong btsan sgam po
Sungtrul	gSung sprul
Tamshing	gTam zhing
Tang	sTang
Tenpe Gyeltsen	bsTan pa'i rgyal mtshan
Tenpe Nyinje	bsTan pa'i snying rje
Tenzin Chökyi Gyeltsen.	bsTan 'dzin chos kyi rgyal mtshan
Tenzin Gyurme Dorje	bsTan 'dzin 'Gyur med rdo rje
Terdak Lingpa	gTer bdag gling pa
Tharpaling	Thar pa gling
Thubten Pelbar	Thub brtan dpal 'bar
Thugse	Thugs sras
Tongsa Penlop	Krong gsar spon slob
Towa Dzong	Do ba rdzong

Trinle	'Phrin las
Trinle Tobgye	'Phrin las stobs rgyas
Tshokye Dorje	mTsho skyes rdo rje
Tshome	mTsho smad (Ch. Comai/Cuomei)
Tshurphu	mTshur-phu
Ü	dBus
Ugyen Dorje	O rgyan rdo rje
Ugyen Wangchuck.	O rgyan dbang phyug
Ugyen Yeshe Dorje	O rgyan Ye shes rdo rje
Ura	U ra
Wangdüchöling	dBang 'dus chos gling
Wangdüphodrang	dBang 'dus pho brang
Yardrok	Yar 'brog
Yeshe Chöden	Ye shes chos ldan.

NOTES

[1] My thanks go to J. Ardussi and S. Karmay who provided me with texts and clues, as well as to Lopen Tsetenla from the Lhalung Dratshang at the Tamshing monastery in Bumthang, Kunzang Chöden, Ugyen Rinzin (*alias* Denma), and the people of Bumthang. Through their constant lively references to Lhodrak, they made me aware of the importance of this region for Bumthang. Unfortunately I was unable to consult the *lHo brag mKhar chu gdan rabs*.

[2] Bischoff & Hartman, 1971: 19 & 23; Kapstein, 2000: 158-159.

[3] Karmay, 2000: 1-34.

[4] I could not find any precise reference to this in the Desi Sangye Gyatso's *Vaidurya ser po* or the 5th Dalai Lama's autobiography. However this fact was stated in October 2000 by the old Umdze Tripola (d. 2001) who looked after the Lhodrak Kharchu monastery, first in Lhodrak and then in Bumthang.

[5] Pad gling gSung sprul lists
Imaeda (1984: 315 n.32).
1) Padma glingpa (1450-1521)
2) rGyal dbang bsTan 'dzin grags pa (1536-1597)
3) Kun mkhyen Tshul khrims rdo rje (1598-1669)
4) Ngag dbang Kun bzang rol pa'i rdo rje (1680-1723)
5) bsTan 'dzin grub mchog rdo rje (1724-1762)
6) Kun bzang bsTan pa'i rgyal mtshan (1763-1817)
7) Ngag dbang Chos kyi blo gros (1819-1842)
8) Kun bzang bstan pa'i nyi ma (1843-1891)
9) bsTan 'dzin chos kyi rgyal mtshan (1894-1913)
10) Ngag dbang chos kyi rgyal mtshan *or* Padma 'od gsal 'gyur med rdo rje *alias* Thub btstan chos kyi rdo rje (1930-1955)
11) Kun bzang Padma rin chen rnam rgyal nges don bstan pa'i nyi ma (1968-)
Ardussi (Wien: in press) gives a slightly different list
2) gsung sprul: bsTan 'dzin chos grags dpal bzang (1536-1597)
5) bsTan 'dzin grub mchog rdo rje (1725-1762)
7) Padma bstan 'dzin *alias* Kun bzang Ngag dbang Chos kyi blo gros (1819-1842)
8) Kun bzang bde chen rdo rje *alias* Nges don bstan pa'i nyi ma dpal bzang (1843-1891)
10) Padma 'od gsal 'gyur med rdo rje *alias* Thub bstan chos kyi rdo rje (1930-1955).

[6] Pad gling Thugs sras Lists
Pommaret & Imaeda, 1987: 29 n.3.
1) Thug sras Zla ba rgyal mtshan (1499-?)
2) Thug sras Nyi zla rgyal mtshan (?-?)
3) Thug sras Nyi zla klong yangs (?-?)
4) Thugs sras bsTan 'dzin 'gyur med rdo rje (1641- ?)
5) Thugs sras 'Gyur med mchog grub dpal 'bar (1701- ?)
6) Thug sras bsTan 'dzin chos kyi nyi ma (1756- ?)
7) Thug sras Kun bzang 'Gyur med rdo rje (1777- ?)
8) Thugs sras Zil gnon bzhad tshal (?-?)
9) Thugs sras Thub bstan dpal 'bar (1906-1939)

10) Thugs sras Theg mchog bstan pa'i rgyal mtshan (1951-) The 1939 date given in Pommaret &
Imaeda is a mistake for 1951.

•Ardussi (Wien: in press) gives a slightly different list

1) Thug sras Zla ba rgyal mtshan

2) unknown

3) Nyi ma rgyal mtshan (fl. early 17th century)

4) Thugs sras bsTan 'dzin 'gyur med rdo rje (1641- ca.1702)

5) Kun bzang bsTan 'dzin ye shes mchog dbyangs 'gyur med chos kyi rdo rje *alias* bsTan 'dzin 'gyur
med rdo rje *alias* 'Gyur med mchog grub dpal 'bar bzang po (ca. 1708- ca.1750)

6) bsTan 'dzin chos kyi nyi ma (ca. 1752-1775)

7) Two recognised rebirths in this generation:

a) Kun bzang rgyur med rdo rje lung rigs chos kyi go cha (ca.1780-ca 1825)

b) bsTan 'dzin ngag dbang 'phrin las

8) Kun bzang zil gnon bzhad pa rtsal (?-?), rebirth of 7a.

•As for Ka thog Situ (1999: 242-252), he does not give an exhaustive list but mentions some of the Pad
gling reincarnations while describing Lhalung monastery.

- Pad gling gSung sprul: 5th Ngag dbang Kun bzang rdo rje (probably an error for the 4th as the
  5th Pad gling gSung sprul Grub mchog rdo rje is also mentioned), 6th Pad gling gSung sprul bsTan pa'i
  rgyal mtshan, 7th Pad gling gSung sprul Ngag dbang chos kyi blo gros, and 9th Pad gling gSung sprul
  Kun bzang bstan pa'i nyi ma (an error for the 8th).

- Pad gling Thug sras 5th Pad gling Thug sras mChog grub dpal 'bar, 6th Pad gling Thug sras bsTan 'dzin
  chos kyi nyi ma, 6th Pad gling Thug sras 'Gyur med rdo rje (an error for the 7th as he also mentioned the
  7th Pad gling Thug sras as 'Gyur med rdo rje), 8th Pad gling Thug sras Zil ngon bzhad pa.
  Information on these lineages can be found in Dudjom Rinpoche (1991:735*).

[7] My information on this period come from the sources given in bibliography as well as from
oral testimonies.

[8] Bod kyi gal che'i lo rgyus, 1991: 327.

[9] The collective biographies of the Pad gling gsung sprul are found in The Rediscovered Teachings
of the great Padma gling pa, vol. 14.See bibliography.

[10]Chöje (chos rje) is a title given in Bhutan to a noble family descending from a prestigious religious
ancestor.

[11]His grandfather was Trinle, son of the Chöje of Tamshing while his grand-mother was Yeshe of
Ogyenchöling, the daughter of the powerful Tongsa Penlop Tshokye Dorje.

[12]Wangdüchöling would become the main palace of the future royal family. It was built in 1857-1860
by Jigme Namgyal (1825-1881), the Tongsa Penlop and father of the future first king. He was then the
strong man of Bhutan.

[13]Ka thog Situ (1999: 244) mentions this lama wrongly as the 9th Sungtrul. He was the 8th Sungtrul. Ka
thog Situ also calls Pema Tenzin the Temporal Ruler of Bhutan (Druk Desi). Pema Tenzin was Tongsa
Penlop but never Temporal Ruler.

[14]For the rBa kha lineage, see the sPo bo'i lo rgyus, 1987: 103-106.

[15]Pommaret, Oslo: in press.

[16]White, 1971: 206.

[17]Zhabs drung 'Jigs med chos rgyal rnam thar, 23 sq. and sMyos rabs, 356-358. The exact identity of this
lama still eludes me.

[18]This lineage descends from Pema Trinle (1564-1642?), the grandson of Pema Lingpa, and its seat is at
Gangte monastery in the Black Mountains, where western and central Bhutan meet.

[19]Byang chub brtson grus rnam thar, ff. 98a-107b; 122 a&b; 154b-170b. I am preparing a summary of the
life of this lama according to his biography.

[20]Jackson, 2001: 95-96.

Bell's entry:
"Four performers in the Kyormo Lung-nga theatrical troupe.
of these four are men, including the second from the right."
1998.285.177 (BL.H.154)

The 'Beijing Lamaist Centre' and Tibet in the XVII – early XX century

Vladimir Uspensky

The origins

Under the Manchu Qing dynasty (1644-1912), Beijing, which was originally and primarily a Chinese city as well as the administrative centre of the Empire, also became a major religious centre for the peoples professing Tibetan Buddhism, especially the Mongols. This historical and religious phenomenon came into being through a coincidence of many factors. The Manchu empire was a vast multi-ethnic state and Tibetan Buddhism formed an important component of Manchu spirituality. It was also the policy of the Manchus to accept the diversity of the peoples under their rule and to develop ways to communicate with each group in a manner that was meaningful to them.

Geographically, the 'Beijing Lamaist[*] Centre' was not encircled within the walls of the capital. It included the numerous lamaist temples and monasteries on the Wutaishan Mountains in the Shanxi Province, temples of Jehol – the favourite Imperial summer residence, temples of Mukden (Shenyang) – the original capital of the Manchus and the temples of Huhehota and Dolonnor (Chin. Dolun) in Inner Mongolia.

The 'Beijing Lamaist Centre' of the Manchu dynasty grew out of two principal historical roots.

The first "root" was the millennia-long pattern of relationship between China and its "barbarian" neighbours. These so called "barbarians" included the ethnic ancestors of several peoples: the Mongols, the Tibetans, and others, including the Manchus themselves. The prototypical Chinese strategies for Sino-"barbarian" contacts survived in their core until the early twentieth century. In particular, the capital of the Chinese Empire had to be seen as the centre of gravity by "barbarian" chieftains.

107

Other characteristics that were routinely observed in the Qing Dynasty included obligatory annual visits of Mongolian princes and incarnated lamas to the Imperial court to present tribute and convey greetings to the emperor for the New Year. Visitors would also be expected to perform offering prayers and religious services for his longevity.

The second "root" was the historical precedent of a special attitude held by the Imperial court towards Tibetan Buddhism. This special attitude had first been shown by the Mongol Yuan dynasty (1271-1367). A privileged position had been held by the lamas of the Sakya School throughout the whole period of Mongol rule in China. Moreover, fourteen lamas received the highest possible title of "Imperial Preceptor" (Chin. *dishi*), and a special "Bureau of Buddhist and Tibetan Affairs" was created. At that time the first Tibetan temples were built in Dadu, the Yuan capital situated on the site of modern Beijing.

The conquering Mongol dynasty was well disposed towards Tibetan Buddhism. By the thirteenth century the Tibetans had not only received Buddhism from India where it was dying out, they had adapted it to create a unique culture of their own which was permeated with Buddhism. It is not an exaggeration to say that for the peoples of Central Asia – with a numerically small population but occupying vast areas of land characterised by severe climate and physical features – Tibetan Buddhism became a non-antagonist alternative to Chinese culture. Chinese culture had been created by a much greater nation, whose influence stretched forth in all directions. For these peoples, adopting Chinese culture would have meant losing their identity and becoming Chinese themselves. On the other hand, adopting Tibetan Buddhism did not entail an assimilation by the Tibetans. It was not possible for the peoples of Central Asia to simply adopt Chinese Buddhism, which was profoundly and inseparably integrated into Chinese culture as a whole. The Manchus who tried, though not very successfully, to maintain their ethnic individuality and to avoid inevitable Sinicisation, used Tibetan Buddhism to this end. However, the numerous privileges given by the Mongols to Tibetan Buddhism in general and to some of its clerics in particular had finally led to disappointing results. As an historical model, it would not inspire the Manchus. The Mongol-supported Sakyapa rule in Tibet was overthrown by the Tibetans themselves even earlier than the Yuan dynasty was overthrown by the Chinese. The last Mongolian Emperor is said to have been more interested in Tantric practices than in state affairs, and this preoccupation was perceived to have contributed to his dynasty's demise.

The traditional, very pragmatic Chinese approach to all sorts of religious teachings, which regarded them primarily as being either useful or harmful in terms of the interests of the State, was also true in regard to the Manchu policy towards Tibetan Buddhism.

An overview

Buddhism can exist only if the Three Jewels (Skt. *tri-ratna*) are present. These are the Buddha, his Teaching (the Dharma, or Law), and the Order (Sangha, or community of the monks). Defined symbolically, the jewel of the Buddha can be statues or drawings of the Buddha venerated as objects of faith; the jewel of the Dharma is the word of the Buddha, written or printed; and the jewel of the Sangha is the community of the monks and nuns supported by a congregation of lay believers.

In Manchu Beijing, Tibetan Buddhists could not only take refuge in the Three Jewels but had a variety of opportunities by which to accumulate merit through the performance of pious deeds. The following is a brief overview of the "Beijing Lamaist Centre" from this Buddhist perspective.

1. The Buddha Jewel

Tibetan and Mongolian sources say that there were twenty eight lamaist temples and monasteries in Beijing; a modern researcher claims that there were as many as fifty three. These temples were built and very generously supported by the Imperial Court throughout the seventeenth and eighteenth centuries; later, however, the support diminished as the internal situation of the empire worsened.

The holiest image in Beijing was the statue of the so-called Sandalwood Buddha, which was placed in the lamaist Hongrensi Temple. According to legend, it was made during the lifetime of Shakyamuni Buddha and received his personal blessing. The most luxurious temple was the Yonghegong Temple built by the Qianlong Emperor on the site of his father's princely palace and his own birthplace. It was consecrated in 1744 and until today remains a functioning monastery and one of the most famous tourist sights of modern Beijing.

These temples were full of Tibetan-style Buddhist images produced in enormous quantities in the imperial workshops of Beijing. Most of the bronze statues were produced in Dolonnor and then brought by caravans to Central Tibet, Amdo and Mongolia. Unsurprisingly, as these were produced by Chinese artisans, the Tibetan-style images inevitably acquired visible Chinese features. Museum curators have noted that a considerable proportion of "Tibetan bronzes" are in fact Sino-Mongolian in origin.

2. The Dharma Jewel.

The Tibetan Buddhist Canon is traditionally divided into the Kangyur in 108 volumes, which is regarded as containing the real words of the Buddha, and Tengyur in 225 volumes which is a collection of commentaries on the Buddha's word by Indian sages. Its emergence, printing and wide dissemination became possible through the support of the Imperial Court of Beijing.

At first, a comparative catalogue of Chinese and Tibetan Buddhist texts was prepared under the Mongolian Emperor Khubilai Khan (reigned 1271-1294). Around 1310, with the financial support of the Mongol rulers, a manuscript copy of the Canon was produced in the Tibetan Narthang Monastery. In 1410, when the Mongolian dynasty had already been overthrown by the nationalist Chinese Ming dynasty, the Kanjur was printed for the first time, either in Beijing or in Nanjing.

Under the Manchus, a new set of wooden blocks were produced in Beijing in 1684-92. After publishing this edition, the Kanjur was printed in Beijing four more times: in 1700, 1717-20, 1737 and in ca. 1765.

As for the doubly voluminous Tenjur, a manuscript copy was prepared by the Fifth Dalai Lama Ngawang Lobsang Gyats'o and the Regent Sangyé Gyats'o. The manuscript was delivered to Beijing at the request of the Kangxi Emperor (reigned 1661-1722). In his turn, the Emperor was requested to provide a copy by a high Mongolian incarnated lama. Following this a lavishly designed edition was printed in 1721-24.

A great number of separate canonical works were also printed in Beijing. These ranged from a pocket-size Heart Sutra in Tibetan with both Manchu transcription and Chinese translation, to the Perfection of Wisdom Sutra in a Hundred Thousand Lines, a work comprising sixteen large volumes. The latter text was printed twice in Tibetan and twice in Mongolian. Many collected works by the Dalai Lamas, the Panchen Lamas, and authoritative Tibetan lamas were also printed, as well as many separate texts on various subjects of traditional Tibetan Buddhist study.

Beijing was also the place where thousands of Buddhist texts were translated from Tibetan into Mongolian. Almost all books in Mongolian printed in the Qing Empire were printed in Beijing, including the Kanjur in 1718-20 and the Tengyur in 1742-49.

Many Buddhist texts were translated into the Manchu language from Tibetan and Chinese and printed in Beijing in the form of Tibetan-style books (loose leaf pages wrapped in cloth). Even the Manchu Kanjur was compiled and printed in 1772-1790.

The Tibetan and Mongolian books were printed mainly in the Songzhusi Temple, while the Canon was printed at the Imperial printing shop. These books were mainly purchased by visiting Mongolian lamas for their home monasteries; however, the copies of the Buddhist Canon were not for sale and were only distributed as imperial gifts. Copies of the Canon were distributed throughout the empire and also reached Central Tibet.

Buddhist studies were also undertaken in Beijing in the eighteenth century under imperial patronage. These studies resulted in the publication of voluminous multi-lingual dictionaries of Buddhist terminology, glossaries of Indic names occurring in Buddhist texts, collections of Sanskrit *dharani*s (magic formulae), as well as reference works about the correct transcription of Sanskrit letters and words.

3. The Sangha Jewel

About one thousand lamas permanently resided in Beijing in the eighteenth and nineteenth centuries and these were, for the most part, Mongols. The Department of Tributary Territories (Chin. Lifanyuan) was in charge of them, whilst the Ministry of Rites was in charge of the Chinese Buddhist monks, *hoshang*s. The hierarchy and staff schedule of every monastery and temple were strictly fixed. The Chief Administrative Lama ruled the whole Beijing Lamaist Centre through four ruling lamas and fourteen abbots. From 1712 Beijing was made the permanent residence of one "living Buddha"; this was the Changkya Khutugtu, [Khutugtu (Mong.) – title of the highest clergy given to eminent incarnated lamas], whose successive incarnations enjoyed great honour and fame throughout Manchu rule. Changkya Khutugtus originated from the Amdo/ Kukunor area (modern Qinghai and Gansu Provinces of China). Several other incarnate lamas from this area (the so-called "Eight Great Khutugtus of Kukunor") served in Beijing and occupied the highest positions in the local lamaist hierarchy. Through many years of contacts unique relations were established between these lamas. For example, in one incarnation one lama was the teacher or assistant of the other while in the next "generation" it was vice versa.

All scheduled lamas received a salary from the government. For example, according to the regulations dated 1816, in the Yonghegong, the largest monastery of Beijing, there were four custodians who received two taels of silver per month, 246 lamas who received two taels and 254 lamas who received one tael. Since this monastery was also the only monastic college in Beijing, at the time of its foundation the Seventh Dalai Lama, Kelsang Gyats'o, (1708-57) sent 18 expert lamas from the Drepung and Ganden monasteries to teach the Dharma. By Imperial decree, the position of the abbot of the Yonghegong was always reserved for a person from Central Tibet. Moreover, in 1746 by order of the Qianlong Emperor, an annual great Buddhist festival was introduced and conducted in his presence. The prayer festival was modelled after the Lhasa Monlam. This included public debating by lamas, the taking of vows by novices, and well attended prayer ceremonies.

All lamas who permanently resided in Beijing, both high and ordinary, belonged to the "Yellow Hat" Gelugpa School. Though the Gelugpa predominance was firmly established in Central Tibet, Amdo and amongst the Mongols, it was important for Beijing lamas of the seventeenth and eighteenth centuries that the Imperial capital did not give rise to any impulse that could damage the hegemony in Tibet. The interest in the teaching of the Nyingmapa School that was demonstrated by Prince Yunli (1697-1738) – the head of the Department of Tributary Territories – caused great anxiety among some top Beijing lamas. When in 1732, having received permission from his brother-emperor, Yunli invited to Beijing the Black Hat Karmapa and the Red Hat Karmapa, both died mysteriously and almost simultaneously as they were approaching the capital.

The number and grandeur of lamaist temples in Beijing and the scope of their activities were in contrast to a relatively small community of lay believers who sponsored and supported them. However, amongst these sponsors were many representatives of the Manchu Imperial house, the foremost being the Emperors themselves. It goes without saying that such lay believers were by far more influential than any other possible donors, and they could practice the "perfection of giving" and other Buddhist virtues on a very lavish scale. The building of eleven replicas of the great Tibetan temples: the Potala, Trashi Lhunpo, Samyé, Tholing and others in the summer imperial residence of Jehol serves to illustrate the possibilities of imperial patronage. Almost all Beijing lamaist temples were generously financed through the Imperial Household, which also supplied them with candles, incense and other things required for conducting rituals. Moreover, major temples were allocated with lands, which gave them a systematic rental income. Beijing temples also received substantial donations from Mongol princes and high lamas who were obliged to regularly visit the capital. On the one hand, Imperial patronage ensured the well-being of Beijing lamaist temples; on the other, this prosperity quickly diminished as the Manchu dynasty began tottering and then collapsed.

Contacts with Central Tibet

The "Beijing Lamaist Centre" was not an island isolated from the part of Central Asia whose population confessed Tibetan Buddhism. It was obviously highly connected to Mongolia and the Amdo/ Kukunor area, not least because the lamas running the temples of Beijing had principally originated from there. However, active contacts with Central Tibet were maintained without interruption as Tibetan lamas visited Beijing and Beijing lamas visited Lhasa.

During the Qing dynasty, Beijing was visited three times by the highest Tibetan incarnate lamas, and each visit symbolised an important turn in the empire's history. The Fifth Dalai Lama visited China in 1652-53, soon after the Manchu dynasty established itself in Beijing and while it was still fighting to consolidate its power. The aim of this visit was to bless the newly established dynasty. The Emperor had invited the Dalai Lama at the request of the powerful Mongol chieftain Gushi Khan, whose military intervention in Tibet established overwhelming Gelugpa supremacy. The Dalai Lama arrived accompanied with a retinue of 3,000 persons and, besides Beijing, visited Mukden, where he conducted services at the graves of the founders of the dynasty. He also made a pilgrimage to the Wutaishan Mountains which are regarded as an abode of the Bodhisattva Manjushri. To host the Dalai Lama, the now destroyed "Yellow Temple" (Chin. Huangsi) was built in Beijing. During this visit diplomatic relations between Beijing and Lhasa were established, and the Emperor and the lama exchanged titles.

For a hundred years after this visit the central concern of the Manchus was to establish their total control in Central (or, Inner) Asia. This resulted in highly costly wars with the Jungar Mongols, who were their rivals in this area. In many cases the role of the Dalai Lama was regarded as pivotal by the Manchus. To this end top Beijing lamas were sent continuously to Tibet, mostly with Imperial edicts urging the Dalai Lama to undertake certain steps in regard to the Jungar Mongols. In some cases the actions of the Emperor towards Beijing lamas who sided with the Jungars was very severe: e.g., the Ilagugsan Khutugtu, the former Chief Administrative Lama of Beijing, was publicly executed in 1697 for his anti-Manchu activities. The Ministry of Tributary Territories recommended to the Kangxi emperor that the First Changkya Khutugtu be executed by strangling for his "inappropriate behaviour" when he was sent on a mission to attend the enthronement of the Sixth Dalai Lama in 1697-98.

The Beijing lamas T'ukwan Khutugtu and Kangyurwa Khutugtu participated in the enthronement of the Seventh Dalai Lama in 1720 which was conducted by the Manchu-Mongol armies. Subsequently the Changkya Khutugtu Rölpé Dorjé accompanied this Dalai Lama to Lhasa in 1734-35 from the latter's confinement in Gartar in Sichuan Province. The Changkya Khutugtu, Rölpé Dorjé, is also said to have influenced the Qianlong Emperor not to introduce direct rule in Tibet and not to establish a Chinese-style administration there after the revolt in 1750, but instead to make the Seventh Dalai Lama both the spiritual and secular ruler. When the latter passed away in 1757, Rolbi Dorje was sent to Tibet to supervise the discovery of the new Dalai Lama, the first one whose authenticity was approved by Beijing. The Third Changkya Khutugtu Yeshé Tenpé Drönmé (1787-1846), had the opportunity to undertake his Buddhist education in Tibet. Later, when he was the Chief Administrative Lama of Beijing, he visited Central Tibet in 1841-42 as an imperial messenger bringing a diploma and seal from the Emperor to the Eleventh Dalai Lama. These missions normally included governmental officials and lamaist clerics from Beijing in the travelling party, and besides other tasks, collected information about the internal situation in Central Tibet which was later reported to the Emperor.

The Third (Sixth) Panchen Lama, Lobsang Pelden Yeshé, visited Beijing in 1780 when the might and splendour of the Qing empire was at its height. That year the Qianlong Emperor celebrated his seventieth birthday and it was a suitable occasion to acknowledge the achievements of his reign. The geopolitical tasks which had been laid down by his ancestors were accomplished and all the borders of the empire were "pacified". A new Trashi Lhunpo Monastery was built in Jehol especially for this visit. The Emperor received several religious ordinations and bestowed generous gifts on his Tibetan guest. Numerous Mongolian nobles and lamas came to pay homage to the Panchen Lama, also bringing gifts and donations. The visit was darkened with the sudden death of the Panchen Lama. The Emperor ordered a marble stupa be built in his memory, while his earthly ashes were sent to Tibet with all the gifts received and even further donations for the funeral. The quantity of gifts was so great that this sudden increase in the wealth of Trashi Lhunpo Monastery enticed the Gurkhas to invade and sack it in 1791.

While visiting Beijing in 1908, the Thirteenth Dalai Lama T'ubten Gyats'o witnessed the death agony of the Qing dynasty. The almost simultaneous deaths of the Guangxu Emperor and his notorious aunt, the empress dowager Cixi, occurred during his stay in the capital. The Dalai Lama came to Beijing by train and stayed at the same Yellow Temple where the Fifth Dalai Lama stayed 256 years before. However, things had changed substantially since that time. In 1900 while the Boxer uprising was suppressed by European powers, Beijing suffered looting and destruction, on a scale much more severe than that of 1860 in the course of the "Third Opium War". The Sandalwood Buddha disappeared and thousands of wooden-blocks from which the Buddhist Canon was printed in Tibetan and Mongolian were utilised by European soldiers as excellent fuel.

The Sixth (Ninth) Panchen Lama Lobsang T'ubten Ch'ökyi Nyima, who left Tibet after a conflict with the Thirteenth Dalai Lama, stayed in Beijing in 1925-26. His residence was the Fuyusi Monastery, which had been built on the site of the palace where the future Kangxi emperor spent his early childhood.

Though the visits of these highest lamas were extraordinary events, regular "tributary missions" from the Dalai Lama and the Panchen Lama arrived at Beijing each year. In the early nineteenth century these missions were not allowed to exceed forty men. So as to carry the gifts and other luggage, the Dalai Lama's embassy was allotted 160 mules and the Panchen Lama's 120 once they had crossed the border of China proper. However, in case the members of these missions had too many personal things, the party was allowed to hire at the government's expense an extra 100 mules for the Dalai Lama's mission and 80 mules for the Panchen Lama's. The Qing government had to accept the fact that each such mission also carried commercial goods; although it tried to limit this amount to 20 packages. These Tibetan missions were not allowed to make contact with the local Chinese population and had to proceed straight to Beijing. After staying in the capital and attending customary rituals and receptions, these missions went back to Tibet loaded with a fixed set of gifts from the Emperor and purchased goods.

Conclusion.

The "Beijing Lamaist Centre", being a creation of the Manchu emperors of China, played an important and visible role in the religious developments which took place in Tibetan Buddhism in general, and played an even more prominent part in maintaining contacts between the Imperial Court and the Mongols and the Tibetans. To a large extent, it served the religious tastes of the comparatively small but pre-eminent social group of the empire. It was also a place where prayers were recited and rites performed for the benefit of the Emperors and of the empire. Its political aspect has always been well known. Since Buddhism served as a basic foundation of the culture and worldview of the Mongols and the Tibetans, it was important for their relationship with these groups that the Manchu emperors take on the appearance of being Buddhist rulers. Tibetan affairs were not handled by Manchu officials only, but top Beijing lamas also served as advisors and were often sent on missions to Tibet by the emperors. Those lamas, who belonged to the same cultural background as the Buddhist hierarchs of Tibet with whom they communicated in the same language, were able to contribute substantially to maintaining the balance between different parts of the empire. At the same time every Tibetan who came to the capital - for whatever purpose - did not feel isolated from his religion.

Within a few decades of the fall of the Qing dynasty the "Beijing Lamaist Centre" dwindled, adversely affected by the turbulent events which followed in China. Many temples were destroyed and many things relating to Tibetan Buddhism in Beijing were soon lost and forgotten. However, the "Beijing Lamaist Centre" left an enormous heritage, primarily thousands of volumes of Buddhist texts in Tibetan, Mongolian and Manchu, and thousands of Buddhist statues and paintings.

The Tibetans had inherited Buddhism from India. Buddhism provided inspiration throughout the subsequent centuries of relatively isolated historical development, and the Tibetans built an outstanding civilisation founded on it. Proselytising is in the nature of Buddhism, and thus Tibetan Buddhism could not have been confined within the Tibetan plateau. Moreover, any outstanding achievement of human mind and spirit needs many different kinds of support in order to become widely accepted. Such support ranges from popular belief to donations of gold and silver. "The expansive wind-swept, cold, dry, northern plain which comprises two-thirds of the area of Tibet," where "there are no trees" and "snow may fall in summer" (quotations from the Encyclopaedia Britannica), according to a Tibetan saying, was rich in one thing – the Dharma, i.e. Buddhist teaching. In a rare coincidence, this Tibetan richness is acknowledged everywhere, both in the East and the West. Through the strategic activities of Tibetan lamas belonging to different schools, Tibetan Buddhism spread and gained dominance throughout the heart of Asia, from the Himalayas to Eastern Siberia. It had firmly established itself in Beijing from the thirteenth century. Historians agree that traditional China was at its height under the Manchu Qing dynasty. At that time Tibetan Buddhism also flourished as never before and was capable of inspiring the creation of such an outstanding edifice as the "Beijing Lamaist Centre".

FURTHER READINGS

David M. Farquhar. "Emperor As Bodhisattva in the Governance of the Ch'ing
Empire." – *Harvard Journal of Asiatic Studies*, 1978, vol. 38, No. 1, pp. 5-34.
Terese Tse Bartholomew. "Thangkas of the Qianlong Period." – In: *Tibetan Art*
(*Towards a Definition of Style*). Ed. by J.C. Stinger and P. Denwood. London: Laurence King, 1997, pp. 104-17.
Evelyn S. Rawski. *The Last Emperors: A Social History of Qing Imperial Institutions*.
Berkeley, etc.: University of California Press, 1998.
Xiangyun Wang. "The Qing Court's Tibet Connection: Lcang skya Rol pa'i rdo rje
and the Qianlong Emperor." – *Harvard Journal of Asiatic Studies*, 2000, vol. 60, No. 1, pp. 125-63.
Susan Naquin. *Peking: Temples and City Life, 1400-1900*. Berkeley, etc.: University
of California Press, 2000.

* Though the word "Lamaism" is regarded by many as an unsuitable name which may lead to a false
idea that it denotes a religion differing from some sort of "true Buddhism," here it is used since it clearly
suggests the notion of "Tibetan Buddhism." When speaking about Tibetan Buddhism in Beijing, it is not
possible to speak just of "Buddhism", because this would necessarily include the more numerous Chinese
Buddhist establishments. Also, ethnic Tibetans constituted a minority of Tibetan Buddhists residing in
Beijing, the bulk of them being the Mongols.

following page
Lama and Postmaster seated in front of carved screen/wall. Lama holding rosary.
Bell's entry: "(j) Buriat Lama (right) and Tibetan Postmaster General."

The Formation of the Tibetan Official Style of Administrative Correspondence (17th-19th century)

Hanna Schneider

Illa vis autem eloquentiae tanta est, ut omnium rerum, virtutum, officiorum omnisque naturae, quae mores hominum, quae animos, quae vitam continet, originem, vim mutationesque teneat, eadem mores, leges, iura describat, rempublicam regat, omniaque, ad quamcumque rem pertineant, ornate copioseque dicat.
(Cicero, De Oratore Lib. III. cap. XX, 76)

The study of Tibetan letters and diplomas in their original context has, over the years, attained an increasingly important status within the scope of more detailed, in-depth research on authentic, primary sources of Tibetan cultural and administrative history. Whereas studies in both theory and practice of Tibetan diplomatics have, over the past twenty years, already led to encouraging results, it may be maintained that the development and practice of Tibetan epistolary theory, the basic science providing the means and methods of proper investigation into the external and internal structure of letters, their contents, and corresponding characteristics of syntax and style is a topic still deserving more particular consideration.

The present article's principal aim is to provide a first outline of the development of the official style employed in Tibetan administrative correspondence as exemplified within the letter-writer, or yigkur namzhag manuals of the 17th through 19th century C.E.

The historical background

The consolidation of the Tibetan state under the sovereignty of the Ganden Phobrang government during the second half of the 18th century necessitated, and was, in return, fostered through the reorganization and re-adaptation of a renewed, efficiently working administrative apparatus[1]. Formed after the year of 1651, the structure of this new government was remarkable and innovative in the sense that, for the first time in Tibetan political history, the maxim of 'chösrid sungdrel' – religious and temporal rule united – and its concept of a state to be held in its best possible balance through granting both the religious as well as the secular branches of its society a proportionate, ideally steady share in judicial and administrative procedure was actually implemented with the clear view to harmonize and settle these two sectors, the more so as the actual events of the middle of the 17th through the first half of the 18th century had clearly shown that neither side, monastic nor secular, was at that time in a position to rule by its own and sole authority, without at least including the other.

The theoretical buildup of the re-constituted government of 1651 and after entailed a re-centralization of stately cum religious power in the hands of the upper hierarchies of the Gelug tradition with the respective Dalai Lamas in the foremost position, in accordance with the overall status already held by the 'Great Fifth'.

On the secular side, the Kashag, or council of ministers, usually consisting of either four lay members, or of three laymen plus one ecclesiastic, emerged as *the* effective body within the performance of the actual, day-to-day affairs of state.

The council of ministers, provided with considerable decisive powers on its own, at the same time acted as an informative and influential link between the different levels of stately bureaucracy. Furthermore, it also functioned as some kind of 'inter-mediate' supreme cum appellate court.

Apart from these two strengthend institutions, the structure of this new government clearly reflected a symmetrical set-up of offices and sub-offices on either side, thus creating that kind of proportional balance that laid the foundation to its continuance till 1951, over the ensuing two hundred years to come.

As is generally accepted, the period during the mid-seventeenth through mid-eighteenth century was not exclusively a time of political unrest and change and consolidation – it was also a time of elaboration, and of vivid activitity in the various fields of human knowledge.

Within the Indo-Tibetan context, in a world where the natural sciences and the humanities were, by common consent, accepted to form a whole that was not to be separated from each other, this universal world-view was deeply embedded in the original notion of 'dharma', wherein religion, the sciences, ethics, law, the fundamentals of life, and existence per se formed an integral, non-inconsistent whole, whose parts might nevertheless be studied and described individually, through the best possible means of reasoning and rhetoric.

The standardisation of the Tibetan official letter style

Tracing the sources of the historical and stylistic development of Tibetan rhetoric of the period leads us back to the Vth Dalai Lama Ngawang Losang Gyatso, in whom we find that ideal of a synthesis of worldly and religious-scholarly activity take an active shape – in which he engaged, certainly in order to pursue his own scholarly interests, but at the same time with the clear view of shaping events, to give Tibet a strong inner standing, to centralize worldly and religious power in the hands of his own tradition, the Gelug – and also in the awareness that through such a symbiosis of religion, science and politics, each element could only fortify the other. The Great Fifth was also strongly conscious about the important part rhetoric would play in the achievement of that goal.

Equipped with the scholar's keen interest in language and lexicography, and with the awareness of the important role of rhetoric in mind, Ngawang Losang Gyatso vividly engaged himself in the systematic study of Tibetan and Sanskrit poetics and lexicography, which led him to develop his own, authoritative writing style that may be called 'applied Kavya', a highly complex, metaphorical, poetic language adapted to the demands of both scholarly and administrative style.

No wonder, therefore, that his extensive written correspondence, reflecting 17th century political and religious interrelations inside Tibet, between Tibet and its neighbours, and the heterogeneous levels on which these mutual interactions took place, have ever since been held in highest esteem, in recognition of the important role this man played in the shaping of Tibet's history, for the political implications even the formulaic parts convey, for his reputation as an outstanding scholar of his time, and for the complex, erudite Kavya style of his letter compositions.

A somewhat sad reality to the historian, but nevertheless important in terms of the development of Tibetan administrative letter-writer theory is the fact that the letters of Ngawang Losang Gyatso were not preserved in their original length; for the first time in Tibetan epistolary history, only the formulaic parts, viz. inscriptio, or heading, exordium, or introduction, and the conclusio, i.e., the ending part of the corresponding letters have become incorporated into this work[2].

Formulaic letter collections of this kind were, similarly to the editions of official letters and formula books of Near Eastern and occidental traditions, also compiled with a clear view to preserve them as sources for historical and literary research, and as model letters to be handed down to and copied by future generations of letter writers.

Consequently, a great number of the formulae, as well as stylistic elements employed by the Great Fifth have been copied within various yigkur namzhag manuals of the times to come, and thus even become preserved within the vast range of modern Tibetan letter- writers that have subsequently been published since the early sixties of the 20th century.

With the foundation stone of Tibetan epistolary theory and its reputation as a literary genre once established, a large number of Tibet's outstanding scholars of the 17th through 19th century felt inclined to compose yigkhur namzhag manuals: Jamyang Zhadpai Dorje Ngawang Tsöndrü (1648-1721), Sumpa Khanpo Yeshe Paljor (1704-1788), Jigme Lingpa Rangjung Dorje (1729/30-1798), Ngulchu Dharmabhadra (1772-1851?), Kongtrül Lodrö Thaye (1813-1899), and Mipham Gyatso (1846-1912). All these letter-writer texts form part of the Sungbum or Collected Works of the respective authors.

The Tibetan official letter style as reflected within the Tibetan letter writer, or yigkur namzhag manuals

Within Tibetan letter-writers, high priority is given to the exact, precisely prescribed framework of the exterior and interior parts of the letter, itself giving clear testimony of the order of precedence befitting the mutual respect existing between addressee and recipient, originator and beneficiary.

The external framework comprises the description of the material letters may be written on, which is usually paper[3], the format, the measures of the side margins as well as the spaces of respect to be maintained between the upper margin and the inscriptio[4], between inscriptio and exordium[5] and between the conclusio, or ending part of a letter and the lower margin of the piece of paper the respective letter is written on.

It furthermore comprises the type of script to be employed[6], the size of the script, the line spacing, the manner of how to set the so-called 'guwang', or formula of respect underneath the inscriptio at the beginning and underneath the conclusio at the end of the letter, as well as the technique of folding and sealing it, the procedure of affixing the sealing wax and the final process of imprinting the 'thagdam' signet, i.e., a small round seal, upon the sealing wax.

The criteria of the external framework are especially dealt with by Mipham Gyatso, and by Norgye Nangpa Wangdu Tshering, late 19th century author of a standardised letter-writer in official use up to the early fifties of the 20th century.

This letter-writer by Norgye Nangpa was published in blockprint form (67 fols.) in Kalimpong in the year of 1888, and published in a revised and enlarged form by K. Tharchin, *ipso loco*, in 1954[7], then also containing an edition of Norgye Nangpa's (?) manual of official seals[8], but, to our regret, without the replica of their proper imprints.

The external framework

I give here a short summary of the directions given by Norgye Nangpa within his model letters, to convey to the reader an impression of the style in which these guide-lines are composed:

Within letters addressed to the Dalai Lama - the exact title here is Gongsa Khyabgon Gyalwai Wangpo - as sovereign of the state, the guidelines for all those addressees holding the rank of a Kalon or a lower rank hereof are the same:

> 7 sor, or finger's breadths for the side margins;
> 1 tho, that is, the span between the thumb and the extended middle finger plus 8 sor for the space of respect between the upper margin and the inscriptio;
> 1 tho, 4 sor for the space of respect between the inscriptio and the so-called guwang formula to be set in three steps, and underneath the formula 'zhabs' of the inscriptio.
> The space to be maintained at the lower margin depends on the rank of the addressee.
> Even though, in most cases, due to the respect the addressee owes to this exalted recipient, the paper ought to be cut in a way that the lower ends of

the letters might just remain safe, it would be inauspicious to do so.
Therefore, 1 1/2 sor should be maintained there.

The size of the script ought to be a small as possible, the line spacing should not extend 1 sor-tse, i.e., the measurement of a nail's tip.

Abbreviations, additions to and corrections of the context are to be avoided.

The letter, once written, should be folded as precisely and as minutely as possible, first in small horizontal creases from the bottom to the top, then bent three times from the right side to the left side, in a way that the part formed by the innermost bend comes to measure three sor, or finger's breadths (cf. fig. 1). The letter, once folded and bent in the prescribed order is entwined with a paper band, in nine turns. (cf. fig.1) The thus affixed paper band is stabilized at the front and backsides, the thagdam signet being impressed upon the previously applied sealing wax.

As for letters addressed to the Panchen Rinpoche (Kyabgon Kunzig Panchen Rinpoche), no distinctions are to be made here, as the compiler maintains that Dalai Lama and Panchen Rinpoche, respectively 'Jina father-and-son' are of equal rank. Within letters addressed to the regent holding the highest position of stately power during the vacant period between the succession of consecutive Dalai Lamas, – the Kyabgon Sikyong Rinpoche, if he belongs to the ecclesiastical branch, or Desi, if he is a layman, for all spaces of respect, 1 sor has to be substracted from what has been said above.

Subsequently, the following addressee-recipient-relations are dealt with:

Appeals and letters, addressed to the Kashag or to one of the four Kalon – other titles employed here are Shape, or Sawang Nampa.

Letters to monastic convents.

Letters, written by normal secretaries of the own chancery, by Dzongpons (district governors, 4th rank), or administrators of government estates (Zhidod), 6th or 7th rank, addressed to a recipient holding the 4th rank.

Letters, written by an addressee holding the 4th rank, addressed to a Jasag Thaiji, resp. letters, written by a Se nampa or by a normal secretary to the Kashag addressing a recipient holding the 4th rank - i.e., the addressee addresses a recipient of slightly higher rank (cf. fig. 2).

Letters, exchanged between addressees and recipients of equal rank.

Letters, addressed to a person of slightly lower rank.

Letters, addressed to a person of lower rank.

Letters, addressed to a recipient of still lower rank.

The internal framework

The internal framework treats the internal, precisely defined parts of a letter, their set of fixed corresponding formulae as well as the exactly prescribed usage of personal titles befitting each individual addressee.

The schematic disposition of a Tibetan letter is as follows[9]:

The inscriptio, or heading of the letter, is followed by the 'guwang', or formula of respect, itself leading to the exordium. This is the introductory part of a letter, comprising the so-called captatio benevolentiae, that is, the formulaic part of a letter aiming at achieving the recipient's attention and 'benevolence'.

The narratio, forming the main part of a letter, the formulation of which is largely relies on the addressee's motive and purpose is due to individual formulation and therefore not dealt with within the letter-writers.

The petitio, the part where the addressee puts forward his request is followed by the conclusio, or ending part of the letter, and, finally, by the date of issue.

Letter-writers particularly emphasize on the importance of the correct formulation of the inscriptiones as immediate reflectors of the rank of the recipient as well as the individual degree of respect the addressee owes to the former, or the reverence the addressee is willing to express.

The main reason why that much emphasis is put upon the inscriptio is that it is *the* part of a letter where the whole range, and not just some of the formulae pertaining to the titles of the recipient are to be formulated in due order.

The criteria of the exact wording and order of these titles nevertheless also serve as an effective means for the evaluation of the authenticity of a specific letter.

Furthermore, letter-writers also give testimony of the political standing, as well as the rhetorical treatment of such semi-independent political entities within the Tibetan state as the kingdom of Derge in eastern Tibet, or the principality of Sakya, domain of the Sakya school of Tibetan Buddhism.

Thirdly, they reflect the variegated political relations to as well as the rhetorical treatment of outside powers such as the Ambans, representatives of the Ch'ing emperors' court at Lhasa and at other strategically significant places of the country, as well as the sovereigns of the surrounding countries of Ladakh, Nepal, Sikkim and Bhutan.

It seems worthwhile here to note that neither the Ch'ing, nor the Mughal emperors, nor the representatives of the British Raj are directly dealt with throughout Tibetan official letter-writer theory.

Conclusion

The classification and evaluation of Tibetan letters and diplomas according to the standards of western epistolary and diplomatic theory is a field that may be worked efficiently, on account of the compatibility of the two traditions, the striking similarities with regard to the historical line of development, and the close connection between epistolary and rhetorical theory here and there, i.e., the significant role rhetorical theory has also played throughout Tibetan letter-writer history in shaping both style and arrangement of the different parts of a Tibetan letter enabling us to examine them according to the rules of the five standard rhetorical divisions known to us in the West.

In my subjective point of view, this factor reveals a close, yet, of course, independent affinity to the classical western rhetoricians', e.g., Marcus Tullius Cicero's (106-43 B.C.E.) concepts of stately and rhetorical theory, concepts originally inherited from classical antiquity which, once imparted to the world of Roman thought shaped the Occident's traditions of state, laws, administration, rhetoric and their related areas in manifold ways.

It is this affinity of thought that allows us to analyse Tibetan concepts of state, law and administration according to the categories of classical western diplomatics without artificially tilting one system against the other.

As research in Tibetan epistolary theory of the 17th through 19th centuries is still in its infancy, the primary objective for the years to come is to make the sources of the Tibetan letter-writer genre accessible to historical and literary investigation.

Besides, careful examination of the formulaic parts of the Vth Dalai Lama Ngagwang Losang Gyatso's official correspondence will certainly open up new insights into 17th century political and religious interrelations inside Tibet, as well as between Tibet and its neighbours, and the heterogeneous diplomatic levels on which these mutual interactions took place.

It will then be equally important if, and how examples of written correspondence accessible within published western sources actually reflect these theoretical precepts within the practice of day-to-day chancellary usage.

Lastly, the question as to what extent the close relationship between the theory of Tibetan letter writing and the rhetoric of the time took a formative role in the shaping of the Tibetan juridical language of the 17th through 20th centuries still awaits being answered in detail.

BIBLIOGRAPHY

Ahmad, Z., 1970. *Sino-Tibetan Relations in the Seventeenth Century*, SOR XL, Roma.
Black's Law Dictionary 1990. St. Paul, Minn: West Publishing Co. (6th ed.).
Goldstein, M.C., 1989. *A History of Modern Tibet, 1913-1951*. Berkeley, Los Angeles, London.
Petech, L., 1972. China and Tibet in the Early XVIIIth Century. *T'oung Pao* Vol I, Leiden.
Petech, L., 1973. *Aristocracy and Government in Tibet 1728-1959*. SOR XLV, Roma.
Richardson, H.E., 1962. *Tibet and its History*, London.
Schneider, H., 2002. "Tibetan Legal Documents of South-Western Tibet: Structure and Style". In: Blezer, H. et al. (eds.).*Tibet, Past and Present. Tibetan Studies I. Proceedings of the 9th IATS Conference, Leiden 2000*. Leiden, pp. 415-27.
Smith, E.G., 2001. *Among Tibetan Texts. History and Literature of the Himalayan Plateau*, ed. by Kurtis R. Schaeffer. Boston, pp. 179-208.
Vogel, C., 1979. *Indian Lexicography. A History of Indian Literature, Vol V.*, Fasc. 4. Otto Harrassowitz, Wiesbaden.

khadrung [khashag drungyig]	bka' drung [bka' shag drung yig]; secretary to the Khashag, or council of ministers
khyugyig	'khyug yig; a variant of the Tibetan cursive script used throughout letter correspondence.
khyen	mkhyen; to acknowledge, to take to notice
guwang	gus 'bangs; formula of respect
chabshog	chab shog; hon. for khashog (bka' shog), lit. "letter of command", a type of Tibetan letter mainly bearing a political purpose, coming into fashion during the 17th century
chabshog gi rimpa	chab shog gi rim pa; collection of letters of the chabshog type.
chösrid sungdrel	the concept of religious and temporal rule united; maxim of the re-constituted Ganden Phobrang government (1651-1951).
nyanzhu	snyan zhu: written appeal (hon.); cf. zhu ba
tinyig	spring yig; a type of Tibetan letter of mainly religious purpose coming into fashion during the late 12th century
thagdam	'thag dam; small round seal, or signet used to close a letter by pressing its imprint upon the sealing wax
tho	mtho; the span between the thumb and the extended middle finger
Desi	sde srid; lay-regent
drutsa kangring	'bru tsha rkang ring; a variant of the Tibetan cursive script
Zhidö	gzhis sdod; administrator of a government estate
zhuba	zhu ba; to request, also: a written appeal
yigkur namzhag	yig bskur rnam gzhag; letter-writer
se nampa	sras rnam pa; member, or son of a noble family
sor	sor; the measure of one finger's breadth
sortse	sor rtse; the measure of a nail's tip
Sikhyong Rinpoche	srid skyong rin po che; The regent, if he belongs to the monastic branch

1 A concise and good overview of the consolidation period may be gained through
Richardson 1982, pp. 43-60, also with regard to the role outside powers such as the Qoshot and Dzungar Mongols, or Ch'ing dynasty China played in the shaping of Tibetan politics of the time. Within the present article, I am only going to deal with these political relations inasfar as they are reflected within the tradition of Tibetan epistolary theory. As for the structure of the newly formed Ganden Phobrang government cf. Petech 1973, pp. 7-21; passim; Goldstein 1989, pp. 6-16

2 This formulaic letter collection, preserved in Vol. DZA of his Collected Works bears
the title Rgya bod hor sog gi mchog dman bar pa rnams la ·phrin yig snyan ngag tu bkod pa "Rab snyan rgyud mang" zhes bya ba bzhugs so. Margin: "chab shog" [290 fols.].

Besides, so-called "samdra", i.e., wooden writing slates were in use, whose surface was chalked and then written on with a bamboo stick, but, as far as I know, only within local private, or private-official correspondence, as their surface was effaced after each use. Cf. Goldstein 1991, p. 169.

3 I.e., the heading.

4 I.e., the introductory part of a letter

5 I.e., the Tibetan khyuyig, or 'fast running' cursive script, to be employed throughout
official and private letter correspondence and also within the category of Tibetan private documents alike. The other variants of the Tibetan cursive script, e.g., the drutsa kangring, and the tshugring and tshugthung are normally reserved to fixed types of public documents e.g., edicts (rtsa tshig) and monastic decrees (bca'-yig).

6 The latter edition of 1954 also differs from the former due to a large quantity of
orthographical variants occurring therein. The text of the original blockprint edition of 1888 has been published twice in the TAR in 1987 and in 1991.

7 This is the edition of a manual of official seals, styled Gzhung zhabs rnams la nye bar
mkho ba bla dpon rim byon gyi lo rgyus tham deb Long ba'i dmigs bu. Cf. Petech 1972, p.5, who does not ascribe this work to him, but also Dieter Schuh, Grundlagen tibetischer Siegelkunde: Eine Untersuchung über tibetische Siegelaufschriften in 'Phags-pa-Schrift [MTH III/], Sankt Augustin 1981, p. 381 passim who does not affirm nor deny the authorship of Nornang.

8 Note, that the schematic disposition of Tibetan letters and of certain types Tibetan
private documents, e.g., written commitments (gan rgya) is practically identical, except for the petitio which is replaced by the dispositio, the part of the document covering the points of the settlement or ruling.

following page
Bell's entry:
"(cn) Red Hat Incarnation Lama with rosary.
His hair shows that he is not celibate."
1998.285.225 (BL.H.196)

Wealth Distribution Rituals in the Political Economy of Traditional Tibet and Bhutan

John A. Ardussi

A great deal has been learned in recent decades about the structure and operation of the traditional (pre-1950) Tibetan economic system. Much of this has come from anthropological field study and interviews. Considerably less use has been made of written Tibetan sources for such research. While economics was never a major genre of Tibetan literature, raw socio-economic data is found in documents of other types. However, the unavailability of any consistent body of such data has hampered its integration into diachronic, historical studies on Tibetan society. Even so, useful insights can be gained by studying the context in which economic data was kept and the uses to which it was put.

In this paper, I wish to bring attention to an important type of Tibetan socio-economic ritual with political implications called *manggye* (<Tib. *mang-'gyed*) meaning literally 'to divide among many,' 'to distribute,' written in many texts simply as *gye* (<Tib. *'gyed*). Although sometimes translated as 'charity,' that word misses the larger socio-economic context of what were really ceremonial distributions of wealth by individuals and institutions of authority. Typically, such events were staged at the conclusion of a larger celebration such as a religious festival, the investiture or funeral of a political or religious leader. They were characterised by the distribution of large amounts of sugar, grain, precious stones, valuable cloth, bullion, and, in later centuries, of coins. In some cases, the quantities distributed were very substantial. Entire family fortunes are recorded as having been so disposed of.

As a corollary we will briefly introduce a genre of Tibetan economic writing that has so far escaped scholarly description, namely the records of ceremonial wealth distributions. Far from being a rarity, such documents seem to have been quite commonly kept, for reasons which we shall discuss. Although only one complete example, from 18th-century Bhutan, has so far come to my attention, the existence of others is known from the literature. But abstracts of wealth distribution records are found throughout the biographies of Tibetan lay and religious figures, especially post 16th century. The collective body of these records and abstracts, over several hundred years, constitutes a fairly consistent, albeit fragmented, source of statistical data on Tibet and neighbouring Himalayan countries.

What captures our attention is the persistence of *manggye* from early monarchical times into the recent era, and their evolution in scale and scope into public rituals that transcended the structural boundaries of monastic and civil governance. A question to be addressed is their socio-economic importance. Were they merely polite adjuncts to social interaction within a Buddhist setting or, as I believe the evidence shows, a more fundamental expression of Tibetan socio-economic behaviour? A comprehensive study of this subject must be undertaken elsewhere. Here we will only survey a few *manggye* records from different centuries and contexts, and briefly address the broader questions raised.

2. Public Wealth Distributions during the Royal Dynastic Period

The earliest record of a wealth distribution in Tibetan literature occurs in connection with the consecration of Samye monastery in AD 779. Among the oldest descriptions of this event is the *Honey Essence of Flowers*, a late 12th century history by Nyang Ral Nyima Özer (1124-1192). According to Nyang Ral (p. 302), the participants included members of the royal court as well as monks and tax-paying subjects from throughout Tibet. After first honouring the chief celebrants Padmasambhava and Shantarakshita, a great festival was then staged at which a "great bestowal" of gifts (*sbyin-gtong rgya-chen-po*) was made to the assembly, followed by extensive entertainment of horse racing, games, dances, and a singing competition among the ministers and citizens. Whether this account authentically describes the actual event, or instead is based on similar festivals of his own era, Nyang Ral's description closely matches the pattern of later Tibetan public festivals at which wealth distributions were made.

3. Tibetan *Manggye* of the 15th – early 18th Centuries

Descriptions of wealth distributions during this period come from two sources, the biographies of lay rulers and important monastic figures. Each reflects a somewhat different perspective. Similarities include the expression of social hierarchy through a gradation of gifts, and the keeping of detailed donation records. Another noteworthy element is that gift recipients included ordinary citizens, in particular those who paid taxes.

3.1 The biography of Situ Rabten Kunzang Phag (1389-1442). The life of this famous king of Gyantse, founder of the great Kumbum temple, contains several detailed descriptions of public ceremonies which were the occasion of a mass distribution of food and presents. His famous proclamation of 1440 halting tax increases for three years indicates unusual regard for the welfare of tax-paying agriculturalists.[1] So it is not surprising that they would be included in any festivities. Thus, when his elder brother Chöki Gyelpo died in 1438, a large fête was held with extended religious rites. Altogether 7,600 fully ordained monks, 1,400 non-monastic men of religion (*ser tshugs 'dzin-pa*), 7,300 people (*skye-bo*), and 21,000 peasant commoners (*mi nag*) received gifts at this festival, referred to here as a 'yogurt distribution' (*zho'i 'gyed*).

The monks were given various items of gold and silver, along with tea, clothing, silk, etc., together with six *khe* (< Tib. *khal:* 1 *khal* = 15 kg) each of butter and barley. The non-monastic holy men were each given a full container (*dong*) of barley, while the lay citizens were given bridles and other such valuables worth six *khe* each. Peasant children(?) (*nag byis*) were each given one half *khe* of ground barley from Upper Nyang. The rites continued on for more than one year, following the religious calendar of local Gyantse monasteries.

3.2 The Biography of Kunkhyen Pema Karpo (1527-1592). An exceptionally detailed description of a *manggye* is found in connection with the funeral ceremonies of the famous 16th century Drukpa hierarch Pema Karpo. This elaborate wealth distribution concluded the rites held in early 1593 at his monastery of Sanga Chöling, in south-east Tibet.[3] The ceremonial protocol foreshadowed distributions sponsored during the 17th-18th centuries by the Drukpa government of Bhutan, to which we shall return. Prominent abbots were invited from the major regional monasteries, not only of the Drukpa, some of whom attended with a large contingent of monks. Each group was seated according to rank and given gifts whose value was measured in units called *gutshen* (<*Tib. dgu-tshan:* 'nine-fold'), from twelve down to five according to their ceremonial and social status. The highest luminary was Mipham Chögyal (1543-1604) abbot of Ralung monastery and head of the Drukpa sect, who came with 400 monks. Altogether, 2,800 monks and some 100 high-ranking district lamas attended, as did the local ruler or Chögyal of Bya Yul. In addition to gifts for those present, itemised quantities of tea, grain, turquoise, amber, precious metals and other gifts were sent by courier to a specific list of monasteries throughout central, eastern, and southern Tibet and parts of Bhutan. A gift was also given to each peasant household listed in the local tax-payer registries of the three surrounding districts of Gnyal, Lo, and Byar. A complete description of recipients and their gifts was recorded in a book entitled "The Large Book on the Funeral Ceremonies" (*Dgongs rdzogs bsgrubs pa'i deb chen mo*). Presumably, this document would have been kept at Sanga Chöling monastery before it was sacked during the Chinese 'Cultural Revolution.'

3.3 The installation of Karma Tenkyong as king of Tsang. In 1620 at the age of fifteen, he was installed on the regal Lion's Throne at Samdrubtse palace. After several years during which his armies defeated local and Mongol opponents, he consolidated power in central Tibet. "He now ruled the world," we are told, "and his deeds imitated the five-fold obligations of a King of Religion," the first of which was to invite all of the monks to the palace and feast them annually with a distribution of food and gifts of silver, gold, clothing, etc.[4] But his few brief years of prosperous rule were cut short by the events of 1642 and his assassination by troupes of the new yellow hat Ganden Phodrang government.

The Autobiography of the First Panchen Lama Lobzang Chökyi Gyeltsen (1567-1662).
For historical and economic reasons, both the frequency and scale of recorded wealth distributions expanded from the late 16th century, from which the Yellow Hat church and state were uniquely positioned to benefit. Competition for influence in Tibet between Mongols and Manchus resulted in increased patronage from both. From the inception of the Qing Dynasty in 1644, the emperors made generous offerings to monasteries of central Tibet, as did wealthy Mongol chieftains and their consorts.

The circumstances under which some of this wealth was redistributed at *manggye* rituals are documented in great detail in the successive biographies of the Panchen and Dalai Lamas. During the First Panchen's tour of Tsang province during 1646-47, he commented how during those times "supplies of tea and pearls from the storehouses of China were given in gift to all of the large monasteries of Tsang."[5] But, in 1647 tea was in short supply in Lhasa itself. None could be distributed during the new year Great Prayer Festival until adequate quantities were sent by Khalkha Mongol donors. The pattern became thereby set for wealthy lay patrons to step forward as sponsors of this annual event and its lavish distributions.

In 1648, we read for the first time of distributions by Gelugpa officials that included the peasantry. In that year the Panchen sponsored a distribution of tea, grain, and gold bullion in his native district of Lhan.[6] To every monastery he gave two *khe* each of tea and barley. Every large peasant (*mi-ser*) household was given one *khe*, and each small family received a half *khe*. During the winter religious services of 1648, 1,500 monk celebrants shared 500 ounces (*mgur-zho*) of gold, while the married monks received half that amount. Similar distributions were made to the other major monasteries of Tsang.

The 5th Dalai Lama's autobiography describes many such distributions from this same period, which must underlie the story told by John Marshall, English merchant in north India during 1671-2, who heard the rumour from native traders that in Lhasa the Dalai Lama was like the Pope, and that

"Many Sunosses [Sannyasis, i.e. holy men] go to [pay respects] to him, who gives them much Gold, to some 200 or 300 rupees worth."[7]

The Autobiography of the Second Panchen Lama, Lobzang Yeshe Palzangpo (1663-1737).
The 2nd Panchen Lama continued the wealth distributions of his predecessor. In 1704, he sponsored a large prayer festival in the Zhe (*Tib. Bzhad*) district of Tsang which concluded with masked dances, folk dances and horse racing, mirroring the agenda described by Nyang Ral five hundred years earlier. It culminated in gift distributions to local monasteries including a total of 1,928 *khata* scarves, 300 measures (*srang*) of silver, 100 bolts of common silk, 11 bolts of *ling* silk, and 163 squares of floral patterned cloth (*sman-rtsi*). A large distribution was also made to the villagers, peasantry and nomads totalling 5,700 *khe* of grain. Every peasant household received four *khe* while each nomad encampment got one. In 1721, a similar *manggye* was staged in neighbouring Lhan district.[8]

4. Wealth Distributions of the later 18th Century

By this time in Tibet's history her paramount position among the Himalayan Buddhist states had been long established, even as Manchu domination of Tibet was nearing its final form. These political realities had several side effects, one of which was to internationalise government wealth distributions. The 7th Dalai Lama sponsored numerous *manggye* after coming to power in 1751. But the largest of record was staged in 1757 to commemorate his death. Gifts were sent to all of the monasteries of central Tibet, the monasteries of western Tibet and for the first time to neighbouring countries with whom diplomatic relations were established, including Kusinara in Assam, Ladakh, Nepal, Sikkim and Bhutan.[9] In central Tibet, each peasant family was given grain, silver, silk scarves and other gifts, although the amount is not recorded. Clearly, in this event we have gone well beyond an institutional act of Buddhist charity into the realm of political affairs.

The same event is also described in the biography of cabinet minister Doring Pandita Gönpo Ngödrup Rabten (1721-1792), whose aristocratic family sponsored some of the distributions.[10] This text, written by Doring Tenzin Paljor (b.1760), is a mine of information on 18th century history, and shows how the upper level aristocracy sustained the tradition of wealth distribution as part of the religious calendar of their own private chapels, in addition to sponsoring both local and national public distributions. Again, many of these are documented in detail, suggesting the existence of underlying written distribution records.

5. The Great Prayer Festival of Lhasa

For the central Tibetan government, the culmination of *manggye* distributions was the *Mönlam Chenmo* or 'Great Prayer Festival' during New Year. It was really a series of religious ceremonies and public festivities with individual histories long predating the 17th century. At each of these some kind of wealth distribution was traditionally performed. The biography of Tsongkhapa (1357-1419), describes the first such prayer festival, as founded by him in 1409.[11] From the very beginning, the celebrations reflected not only a focus on religion but something of the atmosphere of Potlatch, i.e. a 'phenomenon of social structure,' a 'gathering of clans' in which giving, receiving, and reciprocation were of equal weight (Mauss 1990: 38-39).

In Richardson's recent description of the *Mönlam* (Richardson 1993: 11-58), note is made of certain unusual gift-giving rituals such as food scrambles at the Priest's New Year and at the King's Near Year. More important were distributions that accompanied performances on the 6th day of the new year. Special registers (*mang 'gyed tho sgrigs chen mo*) were kept in which the names of donors and recipients were recorded. Richardson writes from personal observation that

> "In 1946 twenty thousand monks were recorded as being present and cash to the value of six hundred thousand rupees was distributed." (*Ibid:* 26)

As shown earlier, such vast sums were not met out of government resources alone. From the 17th century, the extended *Mönlam* celebrations conceived by the 5th Dalai Lama came to depend heavily upon lay donors: the Manchu emperor, Mongol chieftains,

Tibetan aristocrats, and wealthy merchant families. Hugh Richardson describes how the British and Manchu representatives in Lhasa were expected to sponsor distributions in what reflects an almost competitive spirit. A *Mönlam* endowment fund was established by the wealthy Tibetan Angdrugtsang family of Lithang.[12] During the early 20th century, a shrewd Ladakhi monk turned businessman, Lama Tashi Upasika, became one of the richest merchants operating trading expeditions between Lhasa, British India, and the Himalayan states. Ultimately, it is said that he dedicated everything back to religion in the form of gift distributions, including one in which every monk attending the Lhasa *Mönlam* received a silver coin.[13]

6. Wealth Distributions in Bhutan

Wealth distributions were also performed in Bhutan and perhaps other Buddhist Himalayan states. In Bhutan, centralised government was founded in 1624/25 as a Drukpa monastic enterprise in which, as in Tibet, 'religion and the state were combined' (*chos srid zung 'brel*). However, the political structure of Bhutan differed from Tibet. Having a small, dispersed population and long-standing traditions of decentralised governance, the central state undertook various means, including, I would argue, wealth distributions to promote ever greater national unity.

The earliest distribution mentioned in the sources is a *manggye* of 1680 for the installation of the 4th Druk Desi or civil head of state, Tenzin Rabgye (r.1680-1694). The highpoint of this ceremony was a distribution of coins to each tax-paying household of the country. An Enumeration of Taxpayers (*dpya khral 'bul sdud kyi grangs tho*) was consulted for the gift-giving, although this record appears to be now lost. Fortunately, the record survives for a similar wealth distribution at the 1747 installation ceremony of a later head of state, *Shabdrung* Jigme Dragpa I. This unusual document is the oldest detailed census record from anywhere in the Tibetan cultural region and has been recently translated.[14] Its level of detail is sufficient to estimate the population and taxation pattern of all 140 regional administrative sub-units, and to discern other socio-economic attributes of mid 18th century Bhutan. Its chief sponsor, the civil ruler Sherab Wangchuk, went on to underwrite seven more such wealth distributions during his lifetime, the last of which, we are told, included all of his remaining possessions.

7. Conclusion: The Origin and Purpose of *Manggye*

The importance of giving is enshrined in Mahayana Buddhism as the first of the Six Perfections, namely 'Perfection of Charity.' This was clearly in the mind of the 7th Dalai Lama's biographer, who described the purpose of wealth distributions as

> "a dedication to the general happiness or welfare of all citizens, in both the centre and the outer districts."[15]

As usual with things Tibetan, however, this moral ideal was modulated by political considerations. Clearly, in Tibetan culture these festivities were treated as opportunities to celebrate and cement the social fabric. From their earliest occurrence, *manggye* were events at which the ruling power and tax-paying subjects reaffirmed a sense of community spirit and mutual commitment; to receive a gift meant having one's family registered on the tax role. As the political state grew in sophistication and became more centralised, *manggye* events of national importance became opportunities to reaffirm, and perhaps to redefine, relationships with neighbouring countries. Like the Potlatch among North American Indians, the protocols of wealth distribution became means for the celebrants to clarify their relative social and political status, through the priority of their individual participation, hierarchical seating arrangements, size of endowments and gifts received, and so forth. Viewed from a Buddhist perspective, the ceremony also offered a structured venue for aristocrats and/or wealthy individuals to gain religious merit (as well as public recognition) by re-circulating a portion of their wealth back to the monastic system and to the common citizenry. As we have seen, these sums were not always trivial and clearly had a measurable impact on the overall economy.

Societies grow in wealth through circulation and investment of capital. In Tibet, Buddhism exerted highly conservative restraints on the economy. Much of its national wealth was used to sustain the monastic system, or was tied up in religious artwork, gilt statues and temple roofs, etc. The same sources that we have already cited also describe, with great precision, the enormous quantities of gold, silver, and copper spent on such projects. Distribution rituals, on the other hand, were a form of wealth circulation and thus of potential capital growth, however small the individual monetary sums may have been. They emerge through twelve hundred years of literature as one of the few progressive elements of Tibetan socio-economic behaviour sanctioned by religious tradition.

From the late 16th century, Tibet's economy gradually shed its static, closed nature. New wealth entered from outside in the form of gifts from Mongol and Manchu patrons, and from merchant families trading to India and elsewhere. European countries began to import shawl wool and other Tibetan commodities, affecting or replacing established patterns of wealth accumulation. Some of this circulated wealth, certainly the rumour of it, made its way southward through Nepal, prompting a common belief among foreign observers in India such as Bernier, Ralph Fitch and John Marshall that Tibet was a "land of gold," perhaps ripe for exploitation. Their writings fed a mistaken hope that the southward trickle of silver and gold represented the movement of free capital characteristic of a commercial market, tempting the British to send missions northward in search of its source, which the Chinese government resisted through ever increasing political and physical intervention. Thus, the institution of *manggye* contributed indirectly to both the "opening of Tibet" and to its final absorption into the Chinese empire.

Ardussi, John & Karma Ura (2000). "Population and Governance in mid-18th Century Bhutan, as Revealed in the Enthronement Record of *Thugs-sprul* 'Jigs med grags pa I (1725-1761)," *Journal of Bhutan Studies*, vol. 2, no. 2. Thimphu, The Centre for Bhutan Studies.

Carrasco, Pedro (1959). *Land and Polity in Tibet*. Seattle: University of Washington Press.

Dalai Lama 7 = Lcang-skya Qutuqtu Rol-pa'i-rdo-rje (1717-1786), *Rgyal ba'i dbang po thams cad mkhyen gzigs rdo rje 'chang blo bzang bskal bzang rgya mtsho'i zhal snga nas kyi rnam par thar pa mdo tsam brjod pa dpag bsam rin po che'i snye ma.* (Life of the 7th Dalai Lama). Toyo Bunko xylograph #98-1070.

Dga'-bzhi-ba'i rnam-thar = Rdo-ring Bstan-'dzin dpal-'byor (b. 1760). *Dga' bzhi ba'i mi rabs kyi byung ba brjod pa zol med gtam gyi rol mo.* (1806). Lhasa: Bod ljongs mi dmangs dpe skrun khang, 1988. Biography of cabinet minister Doring Pandita Gönpo Ngödrub Rabten (1721-1792) and history of his noble family.

Goldstein, Melvyn (1973). "The Circulation of Estates in Tibet: Reincarnation, Land and Politics," *Journal of Asian Studies* vol. 32, no. 3: 445-455.

Karma Bstan-skyong = *Gtsang sde srid karma bstan skyong dbang pos bod la dbang sgyur byed skabs spel ser ba sgrig tu bcug pa'i khrims yig zhal lce bcu drug* (ca. 1630) . Contained in Tshe-ring bDe-skyid (1987): 13-76. On the rule of Karma Tenkyong, king of Gtsang.

Khan, Shafaat Ahmat (1927). *John Marshal in India, Notes and Observations in Bengal 1668-1672.* London, Oxford University Press.

Mauss, Marcel (1990). *The Gift.* New York & London, W.W. Norton. Paperback reprint of 1990 translation from the original French by W.D. Halls.

Nyang-Ral = Nyang-ral Nyi-ma 'od-zer (late 12th century), *Chos 'byung me tog snying po sbrang rtsi'i bcud.* Lhasa: Bod ljongs mi dmangs dpe skrun khang, 1988. Edited by Chab spel Tshe brtan phun tshogs, et al. (*Gangs can rig mdzod*, vol. 5).

Padma Dkar-po = Lha-rtse-ba Ngag-dbang-bzang-po (1546-1615). *Dpal 'brug-pa thams-cad mkhyen-pa chen-po'i rnam-par thar-pa rgya-mtsho lta-bu'i 'phros-cha shas tsam brjod pa dad pa'i rba rlabs.* Continuation of the biography of Pema Karpo (1527-1692), in the *Collected Works of Kun-mkhyen Padma-dkar-po. Darjeeling, 1973, vol. 4.*

Panchen Lama 1 = Blo-bzang Chos-kyi-rgyal-mtshan (1567-1662), *Chos smra ba'i dge slong blo bzang chos kyi rgyal mtshan gyi spyod tshul gsal bar ston pa nor bu'i phreng ba.* New Delhi, *Sman-rtsis Shes-rig dPe-mdzod,* 1969. Autobiography of the 1st Panchen Lama.

Panchen Lama 2 = Blo-bzang Ye-shes Dpal-bzang-po (1663-1732). *Sha2kya'i dge slong blo bzang ye shes kyi spyod tshul gsal bar byed pa 'od dkar can gyi 'phreng ba.* Autobiography of the 2nd Panchen Lama. New Delhi, 1981, vol. 1.

Rab brtan kun bzang 'phags kyi rnam thar = 'Jigs-med-grags-pa (1481). *Rgyal rtse chos rgyal gyi rnam par thar pa dad pa'i lo thog dngos grub kyi char 'bebs.* Lhasa: Bod ljongs mi dmangs dpe skrun khang, 1987. Biography of the princes of Gyantse.

Richardson, Hugh (1993).*Ceremonies of the Lhasa Year*. London: Serindia Publications.

Rizvi, Janet (1999). *Trans-Himalayan Caravans.* New Delhi: Oxford University Press.

SDE-SRID 13 = rJe Mkhan-po XIII Yon-tan-mtha'-yas (1766), *Chos rgyal chen po shes rab dbang phyug gi dge ba'i cho ga rab tu gsal ba'i gtam mu tig do shal* (Life of the 13th *Desi* Sherab Wangchuck). Reprinted in *Masterpieces of Bhutanese Biographical Literature*, New Delhi, 1970.

Shankhawa, Gyurme Sonam Tobgye (Shan kha ba 'Gyur med bsod nams stobs rgyal). *Bod gzhung gyi sngar srol chos kyi mdzad rim.* Dharamsala: LTWA, 1984. Modern study on the state protocol and celebration calendar of the former Tibetan government.

Thupten Sangay (1974). *Bod kyi dus ston.* Dharamsala: LTWA. An important Tibetan source on which Richardson 1993 is based in part.

Tshe-ring bDe-skyid, ed. (1987). *Bod kyi dus rabs rims [sic] byung gi khrims yig phyogs bsdus dwangs byed ke ta ka.* Lhasa: Bod ljongs mi dmangs dpe skrun khang. A collection of old Tibetan legal documents, including first-hand information on political protocol.

NOTES

[1] Rab brtan kun bzang 'phags kyi rnam thar: 286ff. Extracts of this text, under the name Chronicles of Gyantse were first published and translated in Tucci (1941) Indo-Tibetica vol. 4, pt. 1, and later in Tucci (1949) Tibetan Painted Scrolls vol. 2: 662-670.

[2] On various 'curd festivals' held in pre-1950 Tibet, see Richardson (1993): 99-106 and Shankhawa (1984): 89-92.

[3] Padma Dkar-po: 69.b-70.b.

[4] Karma Bstan-skyong: 20-21.

[5] Panchen Lama 1: 134.b. On the complicated political dealings between the new Yellow Hat leaders, the various Mongol tribal heads and the Qing court, see Z. Ahmad (1970). Sino-Tibetan Relations in the Seventeenth Century. Rome: IsMEO: 160ff.

[6] Panchen Lama 1: 136.b-137.b·

[7] Shafaat Ahmad Khan (1927): 169.

[8] Panchen Lama 2: 217.a-218.a; 305.b.

[9] Dalai Lama 7: 545.a-546.a.

[10] Dga' bzhi ba'i rnam thar: 61-66.

[11] Tsong-kha-pa: 45.a-48.b.

[12] Thubten Sangay (1974): 10.

[13] Janet Rizvi (1999): 156f.

[14] References and details on Bhutanese distribution rituals are to be found in John Ardussi & Karma Ura (2000). The original text is in SDE-SRID 13: 30.a-40.a.

[15] Dalai Lama 7: 270.b.

following page
Bell's entry:
"(dl) The Choten in the Palkor Chode monastery at Gyantse."
1998.285.233 (BL.H.203)

135

A Critical Assessment of the Nepal-Tibet Treaty 1856

Tirtha Prasad Mishra

The 1856 Treaty was a landmark in the history of Nepal-Tibet Relations for the next hundred years. Through this treaty, Nepal could dominate Tibet on various aspects, though she could not revive her minting rights, which she had lost in 1792. On her part, Tibet was satisfied that by making an annual payment of a small amount of money and by giving extra-territorial rights to the Nepali *Vakil*, in this manner she could well assert her independence of the Chinese domination. The objective of the paper is to analyse the main themes embodied in the treaty with historical perspectives and implementation strategies. Attempts have been made to explain some basic issues embodied in the treaty from the Nepali and Tibetan view points with the British and Chinese strategies in the background.

Background

The political and socio- religious interactions between Nepal and Tibet, the two trans-Himalayan countries, go back several centuries. Nepal-Tibet relations entered into a new phase during the mid-seventeenth century when a commercial treaty was signed for the first time between the two countries. That agreement had provided substantial and one-sided privileges to Nepal. The treaty empowered Kathmandu to open thirty two trading marts at Lhasa and to appoint its representative (*Nayak*) in Tibet. Furthermore Tibet agreed not impose any sort of duty on the goods of Newar merchants and also gave minting rights to Kathmandu.[1] This treaty was highly advantageous for Kathmandu. It not only secured a monopoly in the transit between

India and Tibet but also the Nepalese government gained a handsome profit by minting coins for Tibet. Lalitpur and Bhaktapur, the other two kingdoms of the valley, were also involved in the trade and enjoyed the same facilities. With a view to earning more profit, the later Malla rulers started sending debased coins.[2] The debased coins in due course of time proved an irritating factor in Nepal-Tibet relations.

The emergence of Prithvi Narayan Shah in the middle of the eighteenth century had changed the power structure of the valley. The Gorhkali-Kathmandu rivalry that lasted for more than two decades, produced a negative impact on the Nepal-Tibet trade. Finally, Prithvi Narayan Shah was able to conquer the Kathmandu valley in 1769. Realising the importance of Tibetan trade, the ambitious king tried to enjoy some of the privileges of his predecessors. However, the question of debased coins created a deadlock and his efforts were not crowned with success.[3] Tibet demanded that she would not accept the new coins from Nepal unless the Nepalese King took back all the debased coins at their face value. The issue could not be solved and thus all the interactions between Nepal and Tibet could not be revived. The Nepal-Tibet treaty of 1775 also could not mitigate the problem as it was never put into practice. In spite of multilateral consultations for nearly two decades, the two Himalayan kingdoms were unable to reach to an agreement.

Against this background, in 1788, Nepal assaulted Tibet on various grounds with the debased coin issue as the main factor. The Tibetans did not resist the Nepalese move and were forced to sign a dictated treaty in 1789.[4] The 1789 treaty, once again provided many privileges to Nepal. However, this treaty could not bring cordiality for long as the hostilities were renewed in 1791. Nepal was unable to cope with the situation as the Chinese army came forward to rescue the Tibetans. Nepal was rather forced to sign a humiliating treaty in 1792.[5] This treaty not only ended the century old Nepalese minting rights in Tibet but also it abrogated all the facilities enjoyed by Nepal. Nepal was forced to send a Quinquennial Mission to China.[6]

The misunderstandings between Nepal and Tibet from 1793-1853 were solved amicably through bilateral consultation and in some cases the Chinese Imperial Resident offered his good offices in solving the issues. However, Nepal was patiently waiting for an opportunity to revive her traditional assertive position in Tibet. After a lapse of six decades Nepal found a suitable atmosphere in which to realize her cherished desire.

The 1856 Treaty

Jang Bahadur Rana, the founder of family *de facto* rule in Nepal, attempted to add further peacock-feathers to his crown by reviving the historic monopoly rights in Tibet which Nepal had lost by the treaty of 1792. The early years of the 1850s were fortunate enough for Nepal in the realization of their aspirations. The Chinese were involved in the Taiping rebellion while in Tibet, the Dalai Lama was a minor and there existed no harmony between the regent and the *Kasyag*. Charging ill-treatment to the Nepalese traders in Tibet, mal-treatment of the Nepalese Quinquennial Mission on its way back home, and the Tibetan's delaying tactics in solving the boundary dispute, Jung Bahadur decided to launch a punitive attack on the land of the Lamas. Once fully prepared to move to Tibet, Jung Bahadur demanded one crore rupees by way of compensation for the ill-treatment of the Nepalese traders and cession of Kuti and Kerrung to Nepal.[7] The Tibetan only assured that the Nepalese traders would be fairly treated in future. Jung Bahadur, who was not in a mood of reconciliation, made an offensive move towards the land of the living Buddha.

Tibet was left alone in the war front as she was not aided by the Chinese and was unable to cope in the complicated situation. Consequently, Tibet was humbled down before the mighty Nepalese troops and peace talks followed. Nepal was also not in favour of the continuation of war as Jung Bahadur was primarily interested in regaining lost Nepalese prestige. Finally, the deputies of the two countries signed a treaty of peace in the Great Hall of Thapathali, in the residence of Jung Bahadur.[8]

The treaty of Thapathali was a turning point in the history of Nepal-Tibet relations and it also opened a new chapter on Nepalese hegemony in the trade with Tibet. Nepal's influence in the land of the Lamas increased drastically as both the Nepalese officials and traders occupied respectable status. Contrary to the previous treaties of 1789 and 1792, this treaty was concluded without Chinese involvement. In this process, the Chinese Ambans were merely spectators and never ventured to intervene in the interactions between Nepal and Tibet. However, the Ambans were successful in reviving one clause which obliged both Nepal and Tibet to respect the Chinese Emperor as before. It was in fact Nepal's traditional policy to appease the Chinese Emperor with an ulterior motive of seeking his support for Nepal's interest in Tibet.

The provisions of the treaty clearly show that the 1856 treaty was political as well as commercial. Nepal could dictate all terms in her favor as much as possible. Nepal hoped to extend her influence on Tibet by establishing the legation in Lhasa and granting extra-territorial rights of the Nepalese *Vakil* in Tibet. The Nepalese traders in Tibet were empowered in many ways. They were granted many privileges and administering rights by the Nepalese law not according to the law of the land. Clause 4 was included at the request of Maharaja Gulab Singh of Kashmir to rescue the Sikhs prisoners. Similarly, clause 10 was incorporated with a view to protecting those Tibetans who had helped Nepal during the period of war.

The Question of Annual Tribute

The 10 clause treaty granted many privileges and extra-territorial rights by which Nepal once again regained her power and prestige in Tibet. The first clause of the treaty clearly laid down about the annual payment of Rs. 10,000 to Nepal by Tibet. The Nepalese documents refer the amount as *Sirto*[9] (a kind of a tax). Tibet regularly paid the amount in due time and it made sure that Nepal did not encounter any sort of difficulty in receiving it. The Nepalese Maharaja, Chandra Shumsher, had considerable fears that Tibet might discontinue this system as the role of Nepal in the Anglo-Tibetan crisis was contrary to Tibetan expectations.[10] But Tibet paid the tribute as usual.

During his visit to Nepal in 1924, the Tibetan Commander-in-Chief, *Chharung Kazi*, had requested the Nepalese Maharaja to accept the total amount in one payment, which could earn Rs. 10,000 interest per annum. But the humble request was not accepted by Nepal.[11] Nepal had already been drained of a substantial amount of money in the war but the Rs. 10,000 per annum was not being claimed to cover the war expenses. Nepal insisted on this payment only to elevate her status and national pride. In this connection, Rose remarked:[12]

> The first clause of the treaty was the face–saving provision so far as Nepal was concerned, for it made Tibet into a "tributary" state in Kathmandu's interpretation of the terminology. The annual payment was far less than Jung Bahadur had hoped to wring from Lhasa , and did not even begin to compensate Nepal for the heavy expenses of the war, Rs. 2,683,568, according to one source. The Durbar's insistence upon this arrangement should not be viewed in economics terms, however, but rather from the standpoint of the traditional Nepali comprehension of the intrinsic character of interstate relations.

Even after the occupation of Tibet by China, the system of sending annual tribute to Nepal continued. It is thus clear that the inclusion of this clause was made only with a view to upgrade the status of Nepal. This provision reinforced Nepal's claim on Tibet as a tributary state to Nepal. Nepal, up to the 1930s, was trying to dominate Tibet on bilateral issues by using the power of the treaty.

The second clause of the 1856 treaty placed Nepal as a guardian or protector of Tibet. This clause made it obligatory for Nepal to help Tibet in case of attack by any third power. Both Nepal and Tibet had their respective interest in this clause being included in the treaty. To quote Rose again:[13]

> Indeed, Jung Bahadur told the British Resident that he had agreed to this clause because he assumed that one of the first acts of Kalon Shatra would be to play false with the Umbah (Amban) and to call upon the Gorkhas to assist the Tibetans in throwing off the Chinese Yoke, Nepal would then be in position to subvert the authority of the Amban and replace it with that of Nepalese envoy in Lhasa.

Nepal, on the other hand, had a grand design to upgrade her status by this clause and also to show the obligation of Nepal in return for the privileges and extra-territorialities enjoyed in Tibet. There were also similar provisions in the Sino-Nepalese treaty of 1972, by which China would come to assist Nepal in the event of an attack by a foreign power. Nepal, imitating the Chinese attitude and policy in the Anglo-Gorkha war (1814-16), never helped Tibet when she was invaded by a third power.

This provision of the treaty in due course of time, proved to be one of the most irritating factors in Nepal-Tibet relations. In accordance with this clause, Nepal was to help Tibet in the event of attack by a third power. Tibet most humbly solicited Nepal's help during the Anglo-Nepal dispute of 1903-04[14] and Sino-Tibetan conflict of 1908-12.[15] Nepal, however, did not bother to involve itself in this issue and professed her neutrality. Nepal actively supported British policy to Tibet and helped them with men and materials. The Tibetan government sharply reacted to Nepal's attitude and charged it for not complying with the treaty. In addition to this, Nepal repeatedly advised Tibet to come to terms with the British and even threatened to move into Tibet if the Nepalese were harmed there. The same was the case in the Sino-Tibetan conflict of 1908-12. Nepal politely refused to provide any assistance in the conflict, but forced Tibet to pay a handsome amount of money as compensation for the loss of Nepalese property in the turmoil. In both of these crises Nepal's mediatory role gained success. It is true that in the 1903-4 crisis, Nepal's attitude and action was contrary to the spirit of 1856 treaty, but her role was favourable to national interest. Both Nepal and Tibet began to interpret the terms of the treaty to suit their own national interests. In this context Tibet also did not hesitate to annihilate the provisions of the treaty. Consequently, different issues dominated in the relations between the two countries.

Privileges to Nepalese Businessmen

Out of the 10 clauses of the 1856 treaty, the third, sixth, seventh and the ninth clauses were directly related to the benefit of the Nepalese business community. These clauses were advantageous to the Nepalese traders residing in Tibet, granting them the right to trade in all types of commodities, and bestowing on the Nepali *Vakil* extra-territorial rights in Tibet.

The Nepalese traders throughout Tibet were exempted from the burden of taxes. There seemed to be no serious friction regarding the implementation of this clause between the two countries up to the year 1904. However, after the conclusion of the Lhasa Convention in 1904, the Nepalese could not enjoy this privilege. The Chumbi valley trade route was opened legally after 1904, and this route was the shortest to Calcutta. As the Nepalese traders had the upper hand in both the internal and external trades of Tibet, they naturally wanted to benefit by also carrying trade through this route. After the opening of the Phari trade route, the Nepalese merchants had transferred their centre of operation from Kathmandu to Kalimpong (India).[16] However, the Nepalese merchants' desire to benefit from the newly opened route met an adverse result due to the attitude and policy of the Tibetan government. The Tibetan government adopted a two-fold policy to discourage the Nepalese traders: firstly they tried to impose duties on the goods passing through Nepal and prohibited all the Nepalese merchants from carrying trade through the Chumbi valley route. This new development posed a serious threat to the Nepalese trading interest and the Nepalese government took this issue promptly and seriously. The Nepalese government charged Tibet with violating the "sacred treaty" by preventing the Nepalese merchants from enjoying the right of extra-territoriality.[17] The Tibetans asserted that the Nepalese *Vakil* had no jurisdiction over the Phari route as the route was not discovered in 1856. The Nepalese government reacted in the following way:[18]

> Not only the Newar half-breeds (Khacharas) but no one also
> had travelled and undertaken their trade through the recently
> opened trade route of Phari (Chumbi valley).... Therefore, it is
> unfair and unjustifiable to mention that the Newar half-breeds
> do not have the custom and usage to use this trade route. The
> agreement of 912 B.S. (1856) has permitted our businessmen
> to conduct trade and commerce throughout the kingdom of
> Bhot (Tibet). If the Newar half-breed traders are not allowed
> to carry trade through this route, a conflict will be flared up

between the two neighbours cordially living together……..
The loss sustained by the Nepalese traders of wool and furs
should also be duly compensated ….. If these things are not
agreed upon, the Gorkha would initiate any desirable step for
the sake of justice.

The Nepalese protest received partial success. They were permitted to carry trade through Phari route but not exempted from the taxes. This was the beginning of the curtailment of Nepalese extraterritorial rights.

The treaty of Thapathali, as noted earlier, provided many facilities to the Nepalese merchants so that they could enjoy a most favourable atmosphere in which to expand and promote their business. The other merchant communities thus could not compete with the Nepalese. Consequently, all the merchants were jealous of the Nepalese and they mostly attempted to defame and place obstacles in the way of the Nepalese traders. With a view to creating harmony among the traders of Tibet in 1866[19] an understanding was made between the Nepalese and the Tibetans traders. This understanding empowered the Nepalese merchants to sell jewelry along with tent and garments while the Tibetans were to sell only grains. However, this arrangement also could not produce desired results as both the Nepalese and Tibetans traders charged each other with violating the treaty.

In 1876 another attempt was made by the Nepalese agent to erase the differences between the two merchant communities. However, these ample endeavours also could not mitigate the misunderstanding between them. The Nepalese merchants charged their Tibetan counterpart with trading in commodities contrary to the agreement and also asserted that the Tibetan officials harassed them. The Tibetan authorities on their part claimed that the unnecessary interference of the Nepalese agents in favour of their traders was the root cause of the misunderstanding. Such confusing situation was primarily responsible for the origin of the crisis in 1883-84, which virtually led both powers to war.[20] The two governments also involved themselves in an endless dispute over the rice and salt trade. These are some of the instances. Such incidents, however, repeatedly appeared up to 1930. The root cause of such frictions was the privileges of the Nepalese traders granted by the treaty of 1856. Despite all these factors, the Nepalese traders were able to monopolise the Tibetan trade up to the closing years of the 19th century.

Nepalese Extra-territorial Rights

The 1856 treaty had granted Nepal the right to appoint its envoy to Tibet, but according to Charles Bell[21], it was not permitted to appoint its envoy from the Newar community. Within a period from 1856 to 1956, twenty Nepalese agents assumed their offices in Lhasa and none were Newars. Prior to 1856 there was a tradition of appointing a *Nayak* who was generally the top Nepali merchant in Tibet. The *Nayak* being a representative of the traders always used to advocate the case of the Nepalese traders. So it was assumed that if the envoys were appointed from the Newar community they would be biased towards these traders. The Nepalese *Vakil* played a pivotal role in shaping Nepal's policy towards Tibet and China. The Nepalese government was free to appoint any official, but unofficial approval was needed from the Chinese Amban. The Tibetan had no say in this matter. To quote one example in 1901, the Tibetan Kazis requested Nepal to continue using Indra Dhoj Pandey, but, ignoring the request, Nepal replaced him by Jit Bahadur K.C.[22]

The Nepalese agents were entrusted with several formal and informal duties. The Nepalese Prime Minister also exported a large quantity of contraband goods and the *Vakils* were entrusted to sell these commodities. One of the letters even indicates that Jung Bahadur had ordered the sale of a girl named Naina Shova in Tibet for a handsome amount.[23]

The Tibetan government received the Nepalese agents as unwanted guests and was not often responsive towards them. The Tibetan Tsepons on many occasions tacitly refused to give audience to the Nepalese *Vakils*. The contemporary records indicate that the Tibetans Kazis once refused to initiate talk with Mahabir Gadtaula, considering him as a low official.[24] Likewise, in 1873 the Nepalese officiating *Vakil* was insulted and even assaulted at a public function of Tibet. After sanguine protest Nepal withdrew her representative and even threatened to attack Tibet with a view to obtaining the rights of 1856 treaty. Upon the powerful protest of the Nepalese, the Tibetan authorities begged apology and promised to treat the Nepalese *Vakil* fairly. Nepal was satisfied and the Nepalese *Vakil* was sent back to Lhasa.[25] The Tibetan government even charged one of the *Vakils*, Jit Bahadur K.C with having taken bribes from them. In addition to this, the Nepalese agents were charged with backing Nepalese traders and unnecessarily protecting them in their illegal undertakings.[26]

The relations between the Nepalese *Vakils* and Tibetan agents were also marked by cordiality. There are many instances where the Tibetan authorities appreciated the Nepalese envoys' endeavours. The Nepalese *Vakils* Jit Bahadur and Lal Bahadur played a vital role in terminating the Indo-Tibetan deadlock of 1903-04 and Sino-Tibetan conflict of 1908-12 respectively. The *Vakils* were duly respected in public functions and there was a tradition of visiting Tibetan Kazis in the office of Nepalese representative.[27] From 1856 to 1956 the Nepalese agents worked as link persons between Nepal and Tibet.

The Nepalese in Tibet were to be administered according to the Nepalese law and not according to the law of the land. Cases between the Nepalese and the Tibetans were to be decided by a joint court comprising the representatives of the respective governments. The Nepalese agent had exercised his judicial power and the Lhasa court was installed during the period of Bir Shumsher (1885-1901).[28] There are several instances of protests from the Nepalese *Vakils* and of the Nepalese government charging Tibet with not acting according to the spirit of the treaty. The Tibetan government interfered in the cases where Nepalese and Tibetans were involved. However, the Chinese officials decided many cases where only the Nepalese were involved. The Chinese Ambans never respected the 1856 treaty as they maintained that the said treaty was not applicable to the Chinese Emperor and his employees.[29] In the nationality case of Gyalpo, the Tibetans' attitude brought both countries to the brink of war.[30] After 1930 no serious problem appeared as Nepal no longer had such vital interests in Tibet as before.

The Nepalese also acted unilaterally in many cases. The Nepalese government forced the Tibetans to extradite a Tibetan national to Nepal and then inflicted capital punishment on him. The Nepalese agent was accused of wanting to inflict harsh

143

punishment in cases where Tibetans were proved culprits and advocating lenient punishment to Nepalese culprits.[31]

Abrogation of the Treaty

The power structure in the Trans-Himalayan regions drastically changed during the period 1947-55. The British gave complete independence to India. In Nepal the 104 years old family oligarchy of the Rana came to an end and a democratic set-up was initiated. In 1951, China occupied Tibet and declared it an integral part of China. All these recent developments forced the change of the traditional patterns of foreign policy in the whole region. It is interesting to note that even in this changed context both Nepal and Tibet were anxious to maintain their traditional relations. Tibet paid the tribute regularly and was prepared to fulfill the treaty obligation with a view to underscoring their independent status. The government of Nepal also reiterated that changes which had occurred in Tibet since 1950 had not in any way affected its age-old relations with that country. The republic of China was, however, interested in a new arrangement with Nepal regarding Tibet. The government of Nepal formed after 1951 was often blamed for dancing to the tune of the Indian government. The inter ference of the Indian Ambassador in the external and internal policies of Nepal was allegedly manifest in many instances.

The emergence of the King Mahendra in Nepalese politics produced a new turn in the foreign policy of Nepal. The new King was very eager to modify Nepal's foreign policy with a view to restraining the growing Indian influence on Nepal. In this context, the Nepalese Prime Minister asserted that his government's determination to modify Nepal's special relations with India in the direction of equal friendship with all countries was necessary. He also gave indication regarding the amendments of the 1950 Indo-Nepal treaty in order to establish trade relations with other countries.[32] The Chinese government responded to the statement as a positive gesture and the Chinese ambassador visited Nepal and discussed for a new treaty. Finally, a treaty between Nepal and China was signed in September 1956,[33] abrogating all the past agreements between Nepal and Tibet. In order to restrain growing Indian influence, Nepal was in fact compelled to sign this treaty even at the cost of compromising her paramount interest in Tibet.

Conclusion

To sum up, the 1856 treaty opened a new chapter in the diplomatic relations between the two countries. The terms of the treaty were dictated and Tibet was forced to them accept under compulsion. The treaty, if analysed in a historical perspective, produced more animosities than cordiality between the two governments. The agreement became a source of endless dispute and friction. The Nepalese had gained superior status over Tibet by force and always tried to maintain it in the same manner, even in the changed context of later events. However, up to the end of 19th century, Nepal was successful in dominating Tibet and was able to enjoy the good taste of the treaty. Nepal and China were in many cases united, and forced Tibet to dance to their tune, whereas the main objective of Tibet in these years was to create friction between

Nepal and China so as to assert its' independent status. Nepal tried to dominate Tibetan affairs by keeping the Chinese in good humour. She never opposed or even questioned the suzerainty of China over Tibet. After 1891 Nepal was eager to end the Chinese domination over Tibet and so mediated in the Sino-Tibetan conflict. Tibet was not in favour of a close link between Nepal and China and always wanted to create a gulf between Nepal and China so as to assert its independence. The root cause of the outburst of the Tibetans towards the Nepalese trader in 1883 was the desire to break the close relations between Nepal and Tibet, which were viewed as a threat to Tibet's virtually complete autonomy. By the opening of the 20th century, China was no longer powerful in Tibetan affairs. The British appeared as a political power in the Trans–Himalayan politics which posed a serious threat to Nepal's monopoly. The Nepal government was forced to change her policy towards Tibet and was compelled to help the British Mission to Tibet in 1903-04. Nepal was restrained by the British to pursue its own course of action in the Sino-Tibetan dispute and had to accept British mediation in the crisis of 1928-29. It was the British policy towards Tibet which instigated the Tibetans to challenge Nepalese rights. In the Gyalpo case, Britain played the role of 'witch doctor' for a problem which she herself 'bewitched'. Now, both Nepal and Tibet began to interpret the obligations of the treaty to suit their national interests. Nepal did not hesitate to violate the treaty by rendering assistance to the British Mission in 1903-04, whereas Tibet prevented the Nepalese traders from carrying out trade without paying duties.

Until the end Tibet wanted the treaty to be retained in order to demonstrate her political status. However, after 1951 China realised that the treaty had become an obstacle to establishing her domination over Tibet. Hence, China pressed Nepal to abrogate the treaty. Nepal, on the other hand, in order to prevent the growing Indian influence in Nepal entered into a new treaty with China in 1956. The 1956 treaty between Nepal and China finally abolished the 1856 treaty, which became of interest only to historians.

NOTES

[1] Chitaranjan Nepali, Nepal Ra Tibet Ko Sambandha (Nepali-Relations between Nepal and Tibet) Pragati, No.10,2014 B.S(1957), pp.105-106

[2] N. Rhodes, Development of Currency in Tibet in Michal Aris and Aung Sam Sun Kyi (editors) Tibetan studies in Honour of Hugh Richardson (New Delhi-1980), p.265.

[3] Tirtha Prasad Mishra, The Taming of Tibet: A Historical Account of Compromise and Confrontation in Nepal Tibet Relations 1900-1930 (Delhi –1991), pp. 34-35.

[4] Yogi Narahari Nath, Itihas Prakash (Nepali- Light on History) Vol. 1, (Kathmandu 1955-56). p. 20, For the Tibetan version, see Tsepon W.D. Shakabpa, Tibet: A Political History (London-1967), p. 25, and for the Chinese version, see Leo. E. Rose, Nepal: Strategy for Survival, (Delhi- 1973) p. 43.

[5] There is no documentary evidence of the treaty. However, it is fairly certain that the clauses of the treaty were drawn from the correspondence between Chinese general and Nepalese King, See Mishra, op.cit. f.n. 3 pp. 38-39.

[6] For the origin of Quinquennial Missions see Tri Ratna Manandhar and Tirtha Prasad Mishra- Nepal Quinquennial Missions to China, (Kathmandu- 1986).

[7] Padma Jung Rana, Life of Maharaja Sir Jung Bahadur Rana of Nepal, (Kathmandu- 1974) (Reprint) pp. 200-203.

[8] For the text of the treaty, see Prem R. Uprety, Nepal -Tibet Relations 1850-1930 (Kathmandu: 1980),

pp. 213-214 in translated version from Nepali and translation from Tibetan version see Charles Bell, Tibet: Past and Present (Delhi-1997, Reprint) pp. 278-280. There are some minor differences in the Tibetan and Nepalese version.

9 Sirto was a tax levied to the local King during the process of unification. The local Kings, acknowledging the sovereignty of Nepal, used to pay this tax and they were granted some administrative rights.

10 Chandra Shumshere to Revenshaw, 25 January 1905, Foreign Department, Ext. B., June 1905, National Archives of India, New Delhi.

11 Tirtha Prasad Mishra, Bhot Ka Pradhan Senapati Ko Nepal Yatra (Nepali: The visit of Tibetan Commander-in-chief to Nepal) Garima No. 50, p. 33.

12 Leo E.Rose, Nepal: Strategy for Survival (Delhi-1973), p. 115.

13 Ibid. p. 116.

14 The role of Nepal in the Anglo-Tibet dispute is discussed in Tirtha Prasad Mishra, Angrej Bhot Bibadma Nepal Ko Bhumika 1903-04 (Nepali- The role of Nepal in the Anglo-Tibetan dispute of 1903-04) (Kathmandu: 1997).

15 Uprety- op.cit. f. n. 8, 127-141.

16 Rose, op.cit. f.n.12, p. 154.

17 Mishra, op.cit f.n. 3, p. 235.

18 Chandra Shumshere to Four Kazis of Tibet, 1971 B.S., Jestha 26 (June 2914), Poka no. 90 Foreign Ministry Archives of Nepal.

19 Tri Ratna Manadhar, Nepal: The Years of Trouble 1877-85, (Kathmandu: 1986) pp. 143-144.

20 In April 1883 a Nepalese merchant Ratna Man and two Tibetan women picked up a quarrel on the price of a coral. Within a few hours of this incident most of the Nepalese traders' were looted, their property was ransacked and burnt. Tri Ratna Manadhar, Nepal Bhot Bibad 1883-84 (Nepali: Crisis between Nepal and Tibet), (Kathmandu- B.S. 2041) pp. 12-13.

21 Bell, op.cit., f.n. 8, 279. Bell has translated the Tibetan text in which it is mentioned in Clause 5 that henceforth the Gorkha Government would keep a high officer, who was not a Newar, to hold charge at Lhasa.

22 Tri Ratna Manandhar, Some Aspects of Rana Rule in Nepal, (Kathmandu-1983), p. 8.

23 Ibid, p. 23.

24 Ibid, p. 24.

25 Ibid p.25-27

26 Tirtha Prasad Mishra- Jeet Bahadur Ek Upecchit Nepali Kutnitigya (Nepali: A dishonoured Nepalese Diplomat Jeet Bahadur) Ancient Nepal, Vol 123-25, April- September, 1991, pp. 16-22.

27 Lhasa ko Dastur Kitap (usages Book of Lhasa), Foreign Ministry Archives of Nepal.

28 Rewati Raman Khanal, Nepali Kannoni Itihas Ma Lhasa Adalat (Nepali- Lhasa Court in the legal History of Nepal) Nepal No. 65, p. 4.

29 Mishra, op.cit, f.n.3, p. 136.
In the nationality case of Gyalpo, both Nepal and Tibet were virtually prepared for a war. However, the British goverment offered mediation and the war was avoided. For detail see- Tirtha Prasad Mishra- Nepal – Bhot Sambandhama Gyalbu Kanda (Nepali: The Gyablu case and Nepal-Tibet Relations) (Kathmandu: 2053 B.S.)

30 Tirtha Prasad Mishra, Bhot Ma Nepali Khachara (Nepali: Nepalese half-breeds at Tibet) Ancient Nepal, No. 119, pp. 7-8.

31 Jagadish Sharma, Nepal: Struggle for Existence, (Kathmandu: 1986), pp. 106-11.

32 For the treaty see, Yogi Narahari Nath, Itihas Prakash ma Sandhi Patra Sangraha (Nepali: The collections of the treaties in the light of History) (Kathmandu- B.S. 2022), p. 161.

following pages
Bell's entry:
"(j) A room in the Dalai Lama's A.D.C.'s (Tsen-dron's) house.
His younger brother and two monk friends drinking tea and talking.
The brother is on the right.
Between the two cups of tea on the table is a Tibetan inkpot."
1998.286.42 (BL.Q.33)

Political, economic and religious relations between Mongolia and Tibet

L. Chuluunbaatar

From early times Mongolia has had political, economic and religio-cultural connections with the lands of China, Tibet, Russia, Manchuria, Korea and the countries of Central Asia. The Mongols have had ancient and deep connections with Tibet, the "Country of the Snows", dating back to the 1st century A.D. In the historical record we have some evidence of this. The chiefs of ancient Mongol tribes, such as Tamachi and Horicher mergen, are known to have invited Tibetan monks to worship with them.

The beginnings of deep relationships date back to Chingis khaan's time; during Khubilai Khaan's reign these were consolidated. In 1212 the Tanguts repealed their concordat not to attack each other; they started to assist the Mongols from 1213.[1] Then, when the Mongols attacked the Tangut Xi-xia state, they never touched the Tibetan monasteries and monks who were part of this Xi-xia state.[2] Concerning this matter, Rinchen Lhamo has commented that probably the racial affinity of Mongols and Tibetan contributed to this. Very likely there were Tibetans among the Mongol hosts. And the religious connection might perhaps, even at this early time, have already commenced.[3]

During the XIII century AD, when he was living in Khokhnuur, Lord Goodon, a son of Guyug Khaan, invited Saja bandida Gungaajaltsan to join him; Gungaajaltsan composed a new grammar for written Mongol script, which was very important in the formation of the Mongol written language.[4] At that time Gungaajaltsan's nephew Lodoijaltsan, who was 10 years old, accompanied him. In 1260 Pagva lama was invited to the court of Khubilai Khaan and given the title of state teacher. The Mongols decided to adopt Buddhism as state religion. By order of Kubilai Khaan, Pagva lama devised a new script in square characters; the shape was akin to Tibetan, while the writing style was like Mongol script. Tibetans called it *hor-yig*. Pagva lama played an important role in establishing the two ruling systems of religion and state.

During the Mongol Empire, Tibetan monks had powerful rights; they could travel by relay services as state delegations. Khubilai Khan, eclectic in religion and sensitive, like the Roman magistracy, to the use of the Church in temporal affairs, invited the then leading priest of Tibetan Buddhism, the abbot of the great Sakya monastery, to his Court to give the blessing of the greatest Church in Asia to the widest Empire then known to man. By this time the development of the church in that country into a temporal power had progressed so far that the clerical princes were as numerous and as powerful as the lay, and the Sakya hierarch was himself the most important individual prince in the country.[5] When the Mongol Empire collapsed, relations between Mongol kings and lords and Tibetan monks were almost severed. This time was called "The nadir of religion" in the historical sources. So it is likely that the relations between the Mongol and Tibetan countries were not extensive. However, beginning once more in the XVIth century and lasting until the beginning of the XVIII century, there was once again a flowering of relations whose extent and depth had very important consequences in the history of the two countries.

By the beginning of the XVI century, Mongolia had undergone political disintegration and was divided into fragments-Khalkh Mongolia, Inner Mongolia and Oirad Mongolia. The Mongol aristocracy desired this separation. China, Russia, Manchuria, Tibet and Central Asian neighbours likewise counted them as three different countries, and formally referred to them as the "Oirad State, Khalkh State" etc. It was also clear that some powerful neighboring countries were keen to maintain and endeavoured to exploit this situation for their political advantage.

Of course the transmission of Buddhism to Mongolia was directly from Tibet; there was no need to receive it from other countries. Tibet was the heartland of the Buddhist religion, the holy place to which all believers naturally gravitated. Thus the Mongol aristocracy supported Tibetan Buddhism, while by doing so they increased their prestige in both countries. They maintained this as a policy which enabled them to play a leading role in Central Asian relations. Hence it was a matter of historical necessity that relations between Tibet and Mongolia should be restored.

By the start of the XVI century, in Tibet a political and religious crisis had arisen as a result of conflict between the many sects. This had its ultimate origin in the conflict between the new Gelugpa sect founded by Tsongkapa (1357-1419) and the old established sects. At that time the Pagro held the reins of state power in Tibet. This politico-religious group crushed the power of the Sakyapa in 1354 and from that time hence ruled for over 260 years.[6] So other groups were pressing to unseat them from government. Out of all Tibet's religious and political groupings, only the new Gelugpa sect founded by Tsongkapa supported the Pagro government. The Gelugpa sect was opposed by three other sects; the Garjudva of Karmapa, the Garjudva of Beriganga, and a powerful politico-religious body grouped around Zambaa Khaan, the then ruler of Southern Tibet. Monkh Khaan, the ruler of Mongolia, bestowed the Black Hat on the Karmapa who was of the second generation of the Black Hat Garjudva sect. Meanwhile, a *khutugtu* of the Karmapa's Garjudva sect was bestowed with a red hat with a golden rim by the Yuan dynasty monarch. Thenceforth they were known as the Red Hats; gradually their power increased and they developed into a distinct sect in their own right.

Together, the Black and Red Hat sects made contact with Zamba Khaan, the leader of the influential group in Southern Tibet, and they formed a single entity that led all the separate groups which opposed the Gelugpa sect. In this struggle they sought a powerful outside ally. Such an ally was to be found in the Mongol aristocracy, with whom traditional ties, dating from the Yuan period, had never been fully broken and indeed were beginning to revive. The Mongols were experienced in war; both sides had an interest in reviving relations, they were comparable in size and had the same lifestyle and aspirations, as a result of which it was possible for them to become of one accord. Some scholars have noted that certain Tibetans wished to pre-empt attack from Mongolia; they were exhausted by many years of warfare, and hoped that they would be able to derive economic advantage from Mongolia, which held them in such reverence.[7]

To put this clearly, by the second half of the XVI century it was possible for Tibet and Mongolia to re-establish relations on the basis of historical necessities. At the start of this century, Altan Gegeen Khaan (also named Ananda) (1502-1582), one of the lords of Mongolia, who was head of the Tumed tribe, established for the first time a contact with Tibet and with the Yellow sects. Both Altan Khaan's foreign and domestic policies were directed at enhancing his own political influence and personal reputation. Altan Khaan combated the efforts of the Ming dynasty to block off trade and other ties between Mongolia and China. He supported border trade that was mutually advantageous. He and the rest of the Mongol lords considered that if they had consolidated relations with Tibet and the countries of Central Asia they would be able to make friends with the Ming on a more equal basis and would no longer be so subject to Ming economic domination.

Altan Khaan established relations with China. In addition he attacked Khukhnuur, Tibet and Central Asian countries, and levied taxes from them. When he first made contact with the monks of the Yellow sect who were working in the palaces of State of the Ming, he invited them to his court and received texts and sutras. Thereupon he adopted the precepts of the Yellow sect. His attempt to worship in this way was not merely an act of devotion; it was politically motivated. Altan Khaan was better able than other Mongol lords to promote Buddhism in Mongolia and to increase his power in so doing. His territory bordered directly on Tibet after he annexed Khokhnuur at the start of the XVII century. Khukhnuur was a strategic region between several lands, a well-favoured spot for the massing of herds, and the crossroads for several races-the Mongols, Tibetans, Khoton and Uighur among them. Altan Khaan was thus in a strategic position to develop the Mongol-Tibetan relationship.

In addition, the leaders of Tibet, who were looking for outside allies, had an interest in establishing relations with Altan Khaan, whose troops had already penetrated Tibet's borders. When for the first time the high lamas of the Gelugpa sect made contact with Altan Khaan when he captured Khukhnuur in 1566, the Khutagtai Setsen Khun Taiji of the Ordos attacked North-east Tibet at Altan Khaan's orders. The Taiji told the Tibetans that if they allied themselves to him, his people would adopt their religion. The Tibetans discussed his suggestion and sent delegations led by the Darkhan Lama who held negotiations at the triple river junction at Shilimj. This was the first official meeting between Mongols and Tibetans in the course of the XVI century.[8] When the Taiji returned from Tibet, he took several monks back with him to Mongolia and bestowed titles on them. In one source it is recorded that 1570 Altan

Khaan attacked Tibet, fighting with many merchants and saving the lives of many monks.[9] In 1571 he conveyed Ashin, Gummu sokho and many other monks of the Gelugpa sect to Mongolia. This Ashin Lama was one of the first to teach the Yellow sect's religion in Mongolia.[10] He also informed Altan Khaan clearly about Sodnamjamts, the head lama of the Baraivan Temple in Tibet, and suggested that it would be useful to establish relations with him.

In 1574 Altan Khaan sent Taglin Nanso, Uizeen Zaisan, Dain Khia and Bonbo Sandig to pass an invitation to Sodnamjamts, head of the Gelugpa sect. After travelling for ten months they reached Tibet where they gave presents to three Gelugpa monasteries, (Galdan, Sera and Baraivan), and also gave gifts of food and money to the monks while explaining their purpose. The high lamas of the Gelugpa sect and the local lords who supported them met in secret to discuss this invitation. They decided to accept. Then Sodnamjamts explained to the delegation that he wished to meet Altan Khaan near the Mongol-Tibet border; the timing of the meeting would be for further discussion.

Altan Khaan also discussed the matter with lords of the Baruun Tumen; they chose a place called Tsavchaal in Khukhnuur. At Altan Khaan's order, the Tegchenchoinkhorlin Monastery was built in that place.

In 1577 Altan Khaan went to Tsavchaal and appointed three delegations who each in their turn would meet the Tibetan delegation. The first meeting was to take place in Ulaan Murun in the south of Khukhnuur. Yunshiobugiin Barhuu Daichin grandson of Bujidara Otgon Taiji, a younger brother of Altan Khaan, and Khatanbaatar of the Ordos, with Magachin Bagshi of the Tumed, led the first delegation; they gave treasures, gifts, camels and oxen to Sodnamjamts. At the second meeting Chinbaatar of the Ordos and Zorigt Tumen Noyon of the Tumed headed the delegation; they also gave many gifts. On the third occasion the Khutagtai Setsen Khun Taiji of the Ordos and, Dayan Noyon of the Tumed headed the delegation. They gave many treasures, gifts of gold and silver, fine knives, bear's gallbladders, camels with fine silk trappings and horses with golden saddles and bridles to Sodnamjamts.

Sodnamjamts came to the Tegchenchoinkhorlin Monastery on 15 May 1578. Altan Khaan met him accompanied by his wife and lords, wearing a white robe and riding a white horse. In some sources it is said that Sodnamjamts came to Khukhnuur in 1577, but Yu. N. Roerich worked out from Tibetan sources that in fact he had left Lhasa in the autumn of 1577, but reached Khukhnuur in 1578. In the Monastery, over 10,000 Mongol, Chinese, Tibetans and Uighur monks and lay people crowded together. At that meeting the two sides discussed Khubilai Khaan's law called the "White History of the Ten Sacred Texts" (*arvan buyant nomiyn tsagaan tuukh*) edited by the Setsen khun Taiji. On the basis of this law the Mongol side formally vowed to adopt the Buddhist faith. At the meeting Altan Khaan bestowed the title of "Dalai Lama" on Sodnamjamts, and gave him the same freedom to travel as had been enjoyed by the Pagva Lama, State Teacher to Khubilai Khaan.

Concerning this matter, Zava Damdin Gavch in his work the Golden Book (Altan devter) records that Altan Khaan gave to Sodnamjamts a golden seal with Mongol inscriptions, pearls, an outer robe made of ermine and a sable sleeveless jacket, a sitting mat made of felted birds' down and other treasures, as well as livestock. At the same time the Khaan bestowed titles and gifts on the other monks who accompanied Sodnamjamts. Then Sodnamjamts, Manzushri and Maidar Khutugtu gave to Altan

Khaan ritual scarves tied five-fold in a special charm and one precious bowl full of medicinal pills; they bestowed on him the title of Powerful Chakravartin King of the Dharma, as well as presenting a silver seal. They gave presents to his wife and the other lords in Altan Khaan's entourage.

The meaning of the word "Dalai" is an assemblage of many waters collected in a mass. There was a reason for Altan Khaan to choose it. The idea was that it would imply that Sodnamjamts was to be the single leader of all the disparate Tibetan sects. He wished in this way to pursue his political aims through Sodnamjamts. Since this time until the Manchu occupation of Mongolia aristocracy, there can be no discussion of Central Asian relations that does not take account of the figure of the Dalai Lama.

When Altan Khaan held his meeting with the new Dalai Lama in Khukhnuur, he handed over to be students 108 children who were sons of Bayagud Taiji and other nobles. The aim was both to create a cadre of monks and to guarantee that the lords would support the religion. The lords of Baruun Tumen gave different kinds of rich gifts to Sodnamjamts including 1,000 livestock. Sodnamjamts's reason for going to the meeting was to halt Altan Khaan's attack on Tibet and on the Ming. The Ming had asked him to persuade Altan Khaan to withdraw his forces. Sodnamjamts acted to resolve this grave issue, and thereby his name and reputation became greatly enhanced.

The relationship thus established between Altan Khaan and Sodnamjamts did much to consolidate the influence of the Gelugspa sect and to cement relations between Tibet and Mongolia.

Among the Mongol aristocracy there were some who did not welcome the establishment of ties between Mongolia and Tibet. Altan Khaan and Manzushri Khutugtu collected the lords of twelve *tumen* and together with the Setsen Khun Taiji, obliged them to abjure resistance to the monks. Then they passed an additional law to further legitimise the formal adoption of Buddhism. The new (but also formally Third) Dalai Lama did not go back directly to Lhasa; he made visits to the local lords in Amdo, Ningxia, and Khukhnuur. This was because there was a great crisis in Tibet and power rested with the Garjidva sects of the Karmapa.

Also, at this time (1581) Altan Khaan died suddenly, and it was vital to reinforce relations. In the next generation, Altan Khaan's son Sengeduuren adhered to his father's policy. In 1582 he sent information to the Dalai Lama (who was then at the Kumbum Monastery) reporting his father's death and asking him to perform an obsequy. The Dalai Lama came in 1586. He was the figure who established the relationship between Tibet and Mongolia through aristocracy of the Baruun Tumen and through Altan Khaan.

During the XVII century an important development in the history of Tibeto-Mongol relations was the fact that the next, the Fourth Lama, was from Mongolia. In 1589, some students of Sodnamjamts chose a Mongolian boy to be his successor in the next generation. From the three main temples, delegations were sent to check the incarnation in 1592. They accepted it. This was vital to the development of Mongolia's relations with Tibet, and for the development of Buddhism on Mongol soil.

The Fourth Dalai Lama, Yondonjamts, (1588-1616) lived in Mongolia until he was 14, when he was invited to Tibet to receive teaching from the high-ranked monks. Among believers, the reputation of the Mongol Dalai Lama became high, and the power of the Gelugpa sect grew greatly. Opponent sects were active against this.

In 1660, at the age of 47, Yondonjamts suddenly died. As a consequence of his death a conflict began in Tibet between the Red and Yellow sects, at which time 2000 Mongol soldiers moved to defend the Dalai Lama; they fought the soldiers of the Zamba Khaan, and were victorious.

From the beginning of the XVII century, relations between the states of Central Asia and the northern region of modern west and east China were in turmoil, with short-lived federations arising and fighting each other. In 1604, Ligden Khaan of the Tsakhar became ruler of Mongolia. He wanted to unite the Mongols by peaceful means, through the use of religion, and so made contact with the lamas of Tibet. By his orders many temples were built. Between 1628 and 1639 he assembled 30 translators who started work on a great project-the 108 volume Ganjur. Some chieftains of Mongol tribes sided with the Manchus. Danger from the Manchu was acute at this time. Danzanbamba, the Tibetan Zamba Khaan, sent a delegation to Ligden Khaan suggesting that they might fight together against the Yellow sect. Ligden agreed and lent his support to the Red sect; he also invited Tsogt Khun Taiji of the Khalkha, Donyed of Beri aimag in Kham and others who set up a new resistance against the Yellow sect. In 1634 Tsogt Taiji captured Khukhnuur and Amdo. Ligden Khaan died in that same year.

Another important figure is Avtai Sain Khaan. He met with Sodnamjamts in 1585 and gave him many gifts. When he returned to his homeland he had the great temple of Erdene Zuu built. After him, relations between Tibet and Mongolia expanded greatly.

Another key figure is the first Javzundamba, Zanabazar. In 1639 a ceremony was held to award this title. From Tibet, Yonsa Khutugtu Luvsandanzanjamts attended. He was one of Zanabazar's first religious tutors. The Fifth Dalai Lama sent lamas to Zanabazar to teach him. Between 1649 and 1651, Zanabazar visited Tibet and learned much from the Dalai Lama and from the Panchen Lama.

The lords of the Dorbon Oirad ("Four Oirad") from the XV century had invited Tibetan monks to their entourage, as is recorded in the Ming History. Therefore relations were very close between the Oirad and Tibet. During the reign of the Oirad ruler Baibagas, official relations were established. In 1636, Turbaikh of the Khoshuud people, with a great army defeated Tsogt Taiji when he was in Khukhnuur. Then he captured the whole of Tibet. Turbaikh assumed state and military control over Khukhnuur and Tibet, leaving religious control in the hands of the Fifth Dalai Lama and the Panchen Lama. Thus the Fifth Dalai Lama and the Gelugpa sect made contact with Turbaikh and the Khoshuud lords, and they unified the whole of Tibet after many centuries of regional in-fighting; they created a strong, centralised religion in the heart of Asia. Later, Lavzan Khaan, himself of Khoshuud origin, supported the Red sect and Sanjaajamts sought to drive him out of Tibet; he fought but was defeated and killed. A well-known figure in Tibetan history Sanjaajamts died tragically young, fighting for his nation. In 1770, Tserendondov of Zuun Gar (Dzungaria) captured the Potala Palace; he ended the power of the Khoshuud that had lasted for more than 70 years. Then Mongolia and Tibet were both taken by the Manchus and remained under Manchu control until 1911. After the Nationalist revolution, in 1914 Mongolia and Tibet formally agreed to recognise each other's independence, but at this time, the international context made it impossible for this to be accepted by all other world states. Since the time of the Third Bogd Gegeen Javzundamba all Bogds have been born in Tibet, but they have contributed greatly to Mongolia's culture and relations.

They developed the corpus of Oriental science and knowledge. Nowadays in Mongolia the Mongol people honour Tibetans as persons living in the heartland of Buddha's faith.

BIBLIOGRAPHY

Sh.Bira, "Khutagtai Setsen khun taijiin zokhioson negen huuliin tukhai" *(One law by Khutagtai Setsen khun taij)*, Ulaanbaatar, 1970, No. 3

BNMAU-iin tüükh *(History of MPR.,)* Ulaanbaatar, 1966, Vol.I

D.Dashbadrah, "Altan Khan Tübdtei haritsaj baisan ni" *(Altan Khan had relationship with Tibet)*, Historical Study, Vol.22, Ulaanbaatar

D.Dashbadrakh "Mongol Tubdiin uls tör, shashnuii kharitsaanii tuukh" *(History of political and cultural relationships between Mongolia and Tibet)*, Ulaanbaatar, 1998

Zaba Damdin "Umar zugiin Mongol orond deedsiin nom erdene garsan altan devter hemeegdekh oroshivo" *(Golden book which showed how to develop Buddhist teaching in North Mongolia)* Library of Historical branch of Mongolian Sciences, Translated from Tibetan by Prof.D.Dorj

Jamba, "Ligden khutagt khaanii tuukhen bair suuri" *(Historical view of Ligden Hutagt Khan)*, Social Science of Inner Mongolia, 1991, No.6

Rinchen Lhamo, "We Tibetans", New York City, 1985

Yu.N.Rerih, "Mongoloy Tibetskii otnosheniy v XVI i nachale XVII v", Mongoliskii sbornik (economy, history, archaeology) (Reletionship Mongolia and Tibet in XVI and in the beginning of XVII centuries), Moscow, 1959

S.Purevjab, "Mongol dakhi shariin shashnii khuraangui tuukh" *(Brief history of Yellow Sect of Buddhism in Mongolia)*, Ulaanbaatar, 1978

S.Purevjab, "Khubisgaliin ömnökh Ikh Khuree"*(Ikh Khuree before the revolution)*, Ulaanbaatar, 1961

Sagan Setsen, "Erdeniin tovch" *(Erdeniin Tovch)*, Edited by Ts.Nasanbaljir, Ulaanbaatar, 1960

L.Chuluunbaatar, "Mongoliin ard tumnii useg bichig, tuunii tuukh soyoliin ach kholbogdol" *(Mongolian Script, its historical-cultural importances)*, Dissertation, 2000

"Erdeni tunamal hert sudar orshivoi" *(Sutra Clear Treasure)*, Edited by Zurenga, National Publishing House, Beijing, 1984

Ya Khani Chjan, "Dalai lamiin namtar" *(Biography of Dalai Lama)*, National Publishing House, Beijing, 1992

Ya Khani Chjan, "Banchin Erdeniin namtar" *(Biography of Banchin Erdene)* People's Publishing House of Inner Mongolia, Hoh Hot, 1990.

NOTES
[1] BNMAU-iin tüükh, Ulaanbaatar, 1966, Vol.I, p.229
[2] ibid.
[3] Rinchen Lhamo, *We Tibetans*, New York City, 1985, p.21
[4] L.Chuluunbaatar, "Mongoliin ard tumnii useg bichig, tuunii tuukh soyoliin ach kholbogdol", 2000, p.53
[5] Rinchen Lhamo, *We Tibetans*, New York City, 1985, p.20
[6] Ya Khani Chjan, "Dalai lamiin namtar", National Publishing House, Beijing, 1992, p.24
[7] S.Purevjab, "Khubisgaliin ömnökh Ikh Khuree", Ulaanbaatar, 1961, p.15
[8] Sagan Setsen, "Erdeniin tovch", Edited by Ts.Nasanbaljir, Ulaanbaatar, 1960, p.222.
[9] Ibid
[10] Zaba Damdin "Umar zugiin Mongol orond deedsiin nom erdene garsan altan devter hemeegdekh oroshivo" Library of Historical branch of Mongolian Sciences, Translated from Tibetan by Prof.D.Dorj, p.32.

following page
Bell's entry: "(g) King Kesar's brother (right) and Minister."
1998.285.255 (BL.H.230)

The conceptual framework of the dGa'-ldan's war based on the *beye dailame wargi amargi babe necihiyeme toktobuha bodogon i bithe,* 'Buddhist Government' in the Tibet-Mongol and Manchu relationship

Ishihama Yumiko

In 1688 dGa'-ldan's attack upon Tüsiyetü QaGγan of the Qalqa Mongol tribe led to the JegunGar-Qalqa war. Soon after Qalqa had fled to the Qing's territory, dGa'-ldan attacked the Qing dynasty, resulting in dGa'-ldan's defeat and the Qalqa's subordination to the Qing empire. This series of events have long been a major focus of research.[1] Previous study[2] has provided the view that the term "Buddhist Government", that refers to the symbiotic relationship between religion and state, was a common idea between the Tibetans, Mongolians and Manchus from the latter half of the 16th to the middle of the 17th century. "Buddhist Government" was the translation used for *chos srid, lugs gnyis* or *lugs zung* in Tibetan, *törü shasin* in Mongolian and *doro shajin* in Manchu, whose literal rendering is "State and Religion". Its interpretation later changed into the "Government following the Dalai Lama's teaching" or "Government following the Yellow Hat sect's teaching" owing to the successful propagation of the fifth Dalai Lama.

   This essay suggests that "Buddhist Government" was still common among all sides during the war caused by dGa'-ldan during 1688-1697 and provided the framework of this war.

We have two basic sources on dGa'-ldan war. One source is the original documents included in the 8th volume of the *Gongzhong-dang Kangxi-chao zouzhe* (hereafter KZ), a collection of the original extant documents. The other is *An authorized record on the north-western frontier's pacification* (hereafter WA), compiled by imperial order in the 47th year of Emperor Kangxi's reign. The former covers only the very end of the war, while the latter covers the whole process of the war and is thus required to obtain a total picture of it. *An authorized record* has Manchu, Chinese and Mongolian versions.[3] Among these trilingual texts, the Manchu one can be considered most useful on the grounds that that version has no translation-time variable, because the important documents were originally written in Manchurian, the royal language during the Qing period. Incidentally, the Mongol text (hereafter OU) is an obvious translation from the Manchu text[4], not to mention the Chinese one (hereafter Shuo-mo).

But *An authorized record* is not an original but a compiled source. Thus it is necessary to examine the validity of the Manchu text, the regent Sangs-rgyas-rgya-mtsho's letter to the Emperor Kangxi for example. This letter consisted of 29 pages in fifteen lines to a regular page and was received by the Qing on 24 February, Kangxi reign year 36. In it, Sangs-rgyas denied the Qing's demands and we may demonstrate that Sangs-rgyas-rgya-mtsho's letter in WA is almost an exact citation of the corresponding original texts in KZ except for some minor deletions and abbreviation. Although it is dangerous to generalize on the basis of a single example, we may conclude that WA should be given a high value.

Next we may point out a fault of the Chinese text. Despite its popularity, the Chinese text departs in manifold ways from the original text. For example, if we turn the spotlight onto a single term, *doro shajin*, we find in the Shuomo that it was rendered in so many ways[5] that we cannot even identify the original word, much less perceive the nuances of meaning held by *doro shajin* in the Tibetan Buddhist world. It is obvious that this has been due to the Chinese translator's ignorance of Tibetan Buddhism terminology. In short, Shuomo is less valuable than WA[6], because of its inaccurate translation of Tibetan Buddhism terminology.

The usage of "Buddhist Government" during the War (1686-1697)

Based on this valuation of WA, this section will reveal how the political theory of "Buddhist Government" (*doro shajin*) affected the war. We know that the term *doro shajin* was referred to not only by dGa'-ldan but also by Kangxi on many occasions from the Kulen-belciger conference in 1686 up to the UlaGyan-botong battle in 1690, when a dialogue between the two parties still existed. Before we get into details of a specific case, we should note the first half of dGa' ldan's life.

He was born in the royal lineage of JegunGyar in 1645 and recognized as the reincarnated lama of dBen-sa-srpul-sku. In his adolescence he studied in Tibet under the Panchen Lama until he went back to his homeland. This career made dGa'-ldan an enthusiastic follower of the Dalai Lama's teaching. Inevitably he often referred to Tibetan Buddhism during the whole process of the war.

Events prior to the Kulen-belciger conference

It was an event that had occurred at the Kulen-belciger conference to mediate the conflict between the Right and Left Wings of the Qalqas that triggered an open break between Tüsiyetü QaGyan and dGa'-ldan. Before the opening of this conference, Kangxi had appealed to the Dalai Lama to send an emissary as an intermediary:

> The QaGyans and Beises of Qalqa tribe making offering to you, rely on your religion (*shajin* / *jiao*) and esteem your teaching on state (*doro* / *dao-fa*). You send me tribute steadily. They [the Qalqa] show their good faith to me and are Patron to you. Why could we look on their destruction idly ? (Iron-mouse day February Kangxi 23, WA, vol. 3, 3b/Shuomo, vol. 3, 2ab)

When difficulties arose in Inner Asia, it was an usual practice for the Manchu-Chinese Emperor to appeal to the Dalai Lama to act as the intermediary.[7] Considering the overwhelming influence of *doro shajin* theory in Inner Asia, this action could also be interpreted as the Kangxi's demonstration of following the Dalai Lama's teaching (*doro shajin*). When the Dalai Lama sent an emissary Sems-dpa'-chen-po QutuGytu response to this appeal, Kangxi stated as follows: "you sent [Sems-dpa'-chen-po] QutuGytu thinking of Buddhist Government (*doro shajin* / *li-fa*)" (WA, vol. 3, 8b-9a/ Shuomo, vol. 3, 6b-7a).

From this statement, we can know that the Dalai Lama's co-operation was regarded by Kangxi as a benefit of "Buddhist Government" (*doro shajin*). Eventually the conference was held at Kulen-belciger in August, Kangxi year 25. Shangshu Alani from the Qing court and the head lama of dGa'-ldan monastery, the most prestigious monastery of the Yellow Hat sect in Tibet, were sent as the intermediaries. The author of the biography of rJe-btsun-dam-pa summed up this conference as follows:

> This autumn, when Seven-Banners of Qalqa were assembled at Kulen-belciger in the presence of Ngag-dbang-blo-gros-rgya-mthso, a representative of Supreme Victorious King (Dalai Lama) and Alani, a representative of Kangxi, Acitu-chos-rje, an embassy sent by Kangxi, invited this lord (rJe-btsun-dam-pa) as a protector of this conference by edict. This lord and the head lama of dGa'-ldan monastery got together and had a talk with each other [while] sitting on the same height of throne...... Mergen-pandita Rab-'byams-pa and royal grandson dGa'-ldan-rdo-rje were sent to Peking to inform Kangxi of the issues of controversy at this conference contributing to the state and religion (*gzhung bstan pa*) (BTM, 68a1-b1).

Thus Zaya-pandita, the author of this biography, also regarded the issue of this conference as "Buddhist Government" (state and religion). This accords with the Emperor's recognition. According to WA, the conference was closed after both wings of QaGyans swore before the Buddha's statue that they would make efforts toward peace.

Next new year (Kangxi 26), both wings of Qalqa's QaGyans offered to confer titles on Kangxi. Though this offer was rejected by Kangxi for some reason, it is noteworthy that this action is related to Buddhist Government, *doro shajin*. They stated that "thanks to [the] Kangxi Emperor and the Dalai Lama, Many sentient beings got benefit and comfort. State (*doro* / *dao*) [was] pacified and Buddhism (*shajin* / *fa*) developed".(WA, vol. 4, 2a / Shuomo, vol. 4, 1b)

Moreover, in the same month Tüsiyetü qaGyan also stated: "When I had gone to Tibet and had audience with the Dalai Lama before, the Dalai Lama deigned to give me the teaching on "Buddhist Government" (*doro shajin / dao-fa*) and to confer title and honor on me.(WA, vol. 4, 4a / Shuomo, vol. 4, 3a) Therefore, this time if you confer title and honor on me, I will be very appreciative".

In these two offers, Qalqa's QaGyan juxtaposed Kangxi with the Dalai Lama in the context of praising Kangxi. This reveals that there was a common notion between Qalqa and Qing that Kangxi, at least officially, should be delighted with the juxtaposition to the Dalai Lama.

From the dGa'-ldan's Invasion to the DoluGyan NaGyur conference

The temporary peace brought about by the Kulen biliciger conference was broken by Ga'-ldan's letter sent to Alani in April. In this letter dGa'-ldan accused rJe-btsun-dam-pa of meeting a representative of the Dalai Lama while seated on the same height of throne.[8] Dorgi Ambans said

> "As for religion the Yellow Hat Sect is best. As for lama, the Dalai Lama is best" So you, ministers should carry out what seems to be good for the Yellow Hat Sect's teaching. As I am a patron of the Yellow Hat Sect, I wrote to ministers based on verbatim report. Please give me a clear answer to do all that you can do for Buddhist Government (doro shajin / dao-fa). (WA, vol. 4, 7b-8ab / Shuomo, vol. 4, 5b-6a)

Obviously in this statement, dGa'-ldan regarded rJe-btsun-dam-pa's discourtesy to the head lama as insulting to the Dalai Lama and as profaning the Buddhist Government (*doro shajin*). Thereupon in May, rJe-btsun-dam-pa sent the letter to Kangxi, reporting dGa'-ldan's accusation to him. The fact that the same information was immediately shared between Kangxi, the Qalqa's princes and dGa'-ldan, shows us that there is common diplomatic ground between these three parties through Tibetan Buddhism.

During the initial phase of the war, despite dGa'-ldan and rJe-btsun-dam-pa's reports, Kangxi observed developments calmly. However conditions were getting worse and it was reported to Kangxi that dGa'-ldan had invaded Qalqa and destroyed the Erdeni-Joo temple on Iron-monkey day, June, Kangxi reign year 27. The article of WA dated Wood-dog day July Kangxi 27, conveyed dGa'-ldan's words as follows:

> rJe-btsun-dam-pa and Tüsiyetü qaGyan betrayed the Dalai Lama's teaching and did not esteem the head lama. I admonished them what is good for Buddhist Government (*doro shajin / li-fa*), but they rejected [this admonishment]. Then I went to Qalqa and destroyed their residence under the name of the Dalai Lama (WA, vol. 4, 32ab / Shuomo, vol. 4, 22b-23a).

Responding to these words, Kangxi made an appeal to dGa'-ldan on the same day:

> You, Oyirad and Qalqa, have been following Buddhist Government (*doro s hajin / dao-fa*) preached by the Dalai Lama. The Dalai Lama instructed you to benefit all sentient beings, namely, to nourish and to cheer up and not to perish and not to destroy them. (WA, vol. 4, 33b / Shuomo, vol. 4, 24b)

To sum up the matter, dGa'-ldan invaded Qalqa because Qalqa disturbed Buddhist Government (*doro shajin*), whereas Kangxi remonstrated with dGa'-ldan referring to Buddhist Government. In dGa'-ldan's context, observing *doro shajin* meant to attack Tüsiyetü QaGyan, the enemy of *doro shajin*, whereas in Kangxi's context it meant for everybody to live peacefully. *Doro shajin* no longer functioned as the grounds for friendly relations between the two parties, though it still provided the framework for the diplomatic ground. This state of the war was becoming chronic despite Kangxi's attempts at mediation and eventually Tüsiyetü QaGyan and rJe-btsun-dam-pa, leading a great number of subjects, sought shelter in Qing territory.

Counterattack by the Qing

In the following new year (Kangxi 29), Kangxi informed the Dalai Lama of his protection of Qalqa and requested him to send an ambassador in order to make peace between Qalqa's princes and dGa'-ldan. In response to this, the head lama of Byams-pa-gling monastery was sent as an ambassador in December with the Dalai Lama's statement demanding that Kangxi yield up Tüsiyetü QaGyan and rJe-btsun-dam-pa. The words were, in fact, given by the regent Sangs-rgyas-rgya-mtsho, who, as is well known, concealed the Dalai Lama's death for many years.

Kangxi wrote his reply rejecting this demand on the same day, saying "I cannot believe that these are the words of the Dalai Lama who benefits sentient beings". This – rather ironically, was of course the truth. But what is significant is that Kangxi did not reject the Dalai Lama's word, but only rejected the words that did not seems to be the Dalai Lama's. In other words, Kangxi committed himself to not violating the Dalai Lama's commands. In this connection, a few years later, after Sangs-rgyas-rgya-mtsho made the Dalai Lama's death public, Kangxi accused Sangs-rgyas of fabricating the fifth Dalai Lama's words, whereas Sangs-rgyas claimed that he was right because the Dalai Lama had instructed him that after his death he (the Regent) should follow his shaman's words and divinations as if they were the Dalai Lama's words.[9]

This argument also shows that dGa'-ldan and Kangxi shared the common notion that the Dalai Lama's words should be observed.

In March Kangxi 29, Kangxi assembled both wings of Qalqa at DoluGyan naGyur and made them swear to be subordinates of the Qing dynasty. As a result, dGa'-ldan had to invade Qing's territory to pursue Tüsiyetü QaGyan. In June he eventually invaded Ujumucin within Qing's territory and Kangxi immediately prepared to go to war. In July, Kangxi appointed imperial prince Heshuo Yu Wuyuan Jiangjun (Far Consoling General) and imperial prince Heshuo Gong Anbei Jiangjun (North Pacifying General).

It is important to note that the Qing insisted officially that their advance would not be to put down dGa'-ldan, but to discuss Buddhist Government (*doro shajin*), as evidenced by these two general's frequent statements[10], e.g., "to discuss for the benefit of Buddhist Government" (*doro shajin i jalin gisureme*; WA, vol. 8, 6a: "jiangli-xiuhao"; Shumo vol. 8, 4b6), "to pacify to be good for Buddhist Government" (*doro shajin acara be toktobuki*; WA, vol. 8, 15a: "ding li hao", Shumo vol. 8, 11a2)

The following passage reveals the cause of advance:

The Holy King especially sent the Imperial Prince Yu and the Prince Royal to discuss Buddhist Government (*doro shajin / li-fa*) and to establish everlasting peace.

In past years, our vast army, you know, moved to [the] frontier to sign a peace treaty with Russia and returned [to the] homeland without any collision (Earth-dog day, July Kangxi 29, WA, vol. 7, 22ab / Shuomo, vol. 7, 16b-17a).

As this statement shows, Kangxi implied that as long as dGa'-ldan refrained from hostile acts, he would not resort to force. In such a highly volatile political situation, both parties, officially avoiding military conflict, were trying to achieve their end under the name of Buddhist Government: one to capture Tüsiyetü QaGyan and the other to drive dGa'-ldan's army out of its territory.

Moreover, it is noteworthy that the Prince Royal referred to *doro shajin* not in the public appeals in which the official position was shown, but in the internal reports sent from the frontier. This indicates that the purpose of the advance was regarded both in rhetoric and in intent, not as the punitive expedition to punish a traitor, but as the pacification of Buddhist Government.

The time of the UlaGyan-bodong war

On 1 August, following a conflict between the Qing army and dGa'-ldan's force at UlaGyan-bodong, the latter was defeated and forced to swear an oath not to intrude into the Qing's domain before rJe-drung QutuGytu, who had been sent by the Dalai Lama and who acted in concert with dGa'-ldan:

> "All knowing Dalai Lama sent rJe-drung-Erdeni to benefit Buddhist Government (*doro shajin / li-fa*). Now I (dGa'-ldan) [will] never invade Qalqa by Kangxi's favor. Faithfully I offer you this sealed letter" (Water-hare day August Kangxi 29, WA, vol. 8, 16b / Shuomo, vol. 8, 12a).

After this statement, dGa'-ldan came out from the Great Wall. Three months later, the Dalai Lama sent a letter in which he proposed conferring a title on Kangxi in honor of his contribution to the cease-fire. The title "Compassing All Sentient Beings, Pacifying All Conflicts and Propagating Virtue, Holy Bodhisattva Manjusri East King (WA, vol. 8, 46b / Shuomo, vol. 8, 23a)" is very interesting from the perspective of Buddhist Government.

The Manchu word "*dergi\/*" has two meanings, namely, "upper" and "east". Though Shuomo took the former interpretation, we might suggest the latter interpretation. This would be supported by the fact that the Dalai Lama's title conferred by Kangxi contained the word "West"[11] and that Kangxi was juxtaposed to the Dalai Lama by the Mongol princes as mentioned above. Kangxi actually rejected this title, stating that it was not the appropriate time for accepting it. But the reason for rejecting it was not because he regarded this title as one forced upon him by an alien group. For in May Kangxi 30, Tüsiyetü Qinwang Shajin from Qorcin tribe, leading Forty-Nine-Banners from Inner Mongolia that had already been subordinate to the Qing dynasty, tried to offer him a similar title "All Bowing Civilizing Power, Buddhist Government (*doro shajin / dao-fa*) Shining like the Sun, Lord of Speech and East Pacified Holy King"(WA, vol. 10, 26ab / Shuomo, vol. 10, 17b-18a). This praises Kangxi as the Glory of Buddhist Government, and, in terming him "Lord of speech", identifies him with the Bodhisattva Manjushri (*ngag gi dbang phyug*). In short, these two titles obviously have almost the same contents. Moreover, it appears that the Dalai Lama (in fact, Sangs-rgyas-rgya-mtsho), dGa'-ldan, the Princes of Inner Mongolia and perhaps the potential honoree Kangxi, all had the same notion that it was honorable to be praised as the advocator of Buddhist Government, in other words, as a Bodhisattva King.

In September Kangxi 31, Tidu (commander) Sun-si-ke reported to the Qing court that Yuanwailang Madi had been killed by dGa'-ldan's subordinate (Shuomo, vol. 12, 19a-20a). At the same time, dGa'-ldan renewed his request to Kangxi to yield up Tüsiyetü QaGyan and rJe-btsun-dam-pa. Kangxi got angry and sent dGa'-ldan the letter in which he brought dGa'-ldan to account for his breach of promise and queried whether this was the result of following the Dalai Lama's teaching.[12]

In November, as soon as Kangxi had heard that dGa'-ldan was agitating in Inner Mongolia saying "follow the teaching of Tsong-kha-pa (the founder of the Yellow Hat sect)", he sent Erdeni-chos-rje to inner Mongolia. The latter explained how Kangxi had contributed to Tsong-kha-pa's teaching, namely, the Yellow Hat sect, by enumerating three instances. Firstly, the Manchu-China Emperor had invited the fifth Dalai Lama to Peking, secondly, following the Dalai Lama's request, he had forced Phag-mo-grub-pa, the ex-regent of Tibet to make restitution of his official seal to the Qing court in Kangxi 8, and, thirdly, following the fifth Dalai Lama's instruction, he had banned the rNying-ma sect from practicing in Peking.

In the end, Kangxi's claim ended with the following passage:

> Across the generations I have acted according to Tsong-kha-pa and the
> Dalai Lama's teaching. What I am doing here and now is also Tsong-kha-pa and
> the Dalai Lama's teaching. All monks wear Yellow Hat and read the Dalai Lama's
> scripture. Thus I have esteemed Tsong-kha-pa and the
> Dalai Lama's teaching. Did not you, Qalqa and Oyirad, esteem Tsong-kha-pa and
> the Dalai Lama's teaching? ...... You should know that I have brought together
> State and Religion (*doro shajin* / *dao-fa*) together with the Dalai Lama for a long
> time (Fire-hare day November Kangxi 31, WA, vol. 12,
> 59a-60a / Shuomo, vol. 12, 38a-39a).

Kangxi's stress on his contribution to the Yellow Hat sect shows that he was enraged – not at the default of dGa'-ldan – but at the implication that Kangxi was the real enemy of the Yellow Hat sect. In this claim Kangxi entirely drifted into the logic of the Tibetan Buddhism world. Thereupon, the Qing launched an all-out offensive and the exchange with the delegate came to a standstill. This war ended with dGa'-ldan's suicide in 1697, after his cause had been damaged by three imperial expeditions.

Conclusion

It may be concluded that, on the ideological level, Kangxi and dGa'-ldan shared common ground in their understanding of "Buddhist Government" (*doro shajin*) as the path to be followed throughout the whole process of the war. When dGa'-ldan attacked the Qalqa, invaded China and offered to confer a title on Kangxi, he always invoked the Buddhist theory of Government as the justification for his claims. On the other hand, when Qing Kangxi offered a cease-fire and talks, he justified his action by also referring to the Buddhist Government theory. To sum up, the concept of Buddhist Government provided Tibet, Mongol and Manchu figures with common diplomatic ground not only in peace time, as my former paper has stated, but also in wartime.

BIBLIOGRAPHY

[WA] *beye dailame wargi amargi babe necihiyeme toktobuha bodogon i bithe*. Kyoto University Faculty of Literature Library.
[Shuomo] qinzheng pingding shuomo fanglue. Qingchu xijian fanglue sizhong yibian, vols. 2-3. Quangguo tushu wenxian guan suowei fuzhi zhongxin, 1993.
[OU] Beye ber dayilaju orun-e umar-a yin Gyajar i tubsidken toGytaGyaGysan bodulGy-a yin bicig. Neimenggu wenhua chubansha, 1992.
[BTM] sh'akya'i btsun pa blo bzang 'phrin las kyi zab pa dang rgya che ba'i dam pa'i chos kyi thob yig gsal ba'i me long las glegs bam bzhi pa, 62b-78b3.
Collected works of Jaya-Pandita blo-bzang-'phrin-las, vol. 4. Sata-pitaka series, vol. 281. New Delhi, 1981.
Gongzhong-dang Kangxi-chao zouzhe di ba ji. Taiwan guoli gugong bowuguan, 1977.
Shizu Shilu. Zhonghua shujiao, 1985.Mengwen laodang. No.1 Historical Library at Beijing, No.243 (2-117).
Ahmad, Z. (1970). Sino-Tibetan Relations in the 17th century. Roma.
Jaqa Cimeddorji (1991). Die Briefe des K'ang-hsi-kaisers aus den Jahren 1696-97 an den Kronprinzen in-ch'eng aus mandschurischen Geheimdokumenten. Otto Harrassowitz, Wiesbaden.
Zlatkin, I.Y. (1983). Istoriya Jungarskobo qanstva (1635-1758). Moskva.
Fuchs (1940). "Zur mandjurisch-chinesischen Ausgabe des Shuo-mo fang-luch von Walter Fuchs". Toyoshi-Kenkyu, 5-3, pp.1-5.
Ishihama Yumiko (2001). Tibeto Bukkyo Sekai no Rekisiteki Kenkyu. Toho Shoten.
Okada Hidehiro (1979). Kokitei no tegami. Chuko Sinsho.
Wakamatsu Hiroshi (1974), "dGa'-ldan shiretu-QutuGytu Kou". Toyoshi kenkyu, 33-2, pp.1-33.-
(1978). "Jirung Katsubutsu Shoden". Bukkyo Shigaku, 21-1, pp.19-45.

[1] Zlatkin (1983) provided an overview of this war based on the Russian Translation of WA. Okada (1979), (1983) and Cimeddorji (1991) detail the Imperial Expedition based on the imperial letters from the frontier to his son. Ahmad (1970) ch.8 discussed the Sino-Tibetan relationship based on Tibetan source and Shilu. Regarding the High priest sent from Tibet as intermediary, see Wakamatsu (1978).

[2] See, Ishihama (2001) ch.7. This English translation will be published in the proceeding of the Lumbini conference 2000.

[3] To my knowledge there are few studies on these trilingual texts except Fuchs (1940).

[4] Translation by DacungGya, the Qaracin's educationist, in Dao-guang 9 (OU, pp.3a-4a).

[5] As *daofa* (passim), *lifa* (passim), *liyi* (e.g. WA, vol. 37, 20b etc.), fajiao (e.g. WA, vol. 26, 3a etc.), *guidao* (passim) and *shengjiao* (e.g. WA, vol. 2, 43a etc.).There are numerous other such examples. Cf. note 10.

[6] But Shuomo can not be completely denied, because the words deleted in WA are found in Shuomo. For example, the passage that is carelessly omitted in WA (number 7) exists in Shuomo.

[7] Ahmad, 1970, pp.148-150

[8] According to Zaya Pandita, dGa'-ldan also got angry because rJe-btsun-dam-pa did not ask the head lama for initiation (*phyag dbang*) (BTM, 69a1).

[9] Ahmad, 1970, pp.44-50.

[10] There are many more examples apart from the ones cited in the body of this paper, e.g. :"to pacify Buddhist Government" (*doro shajin toktobume gisure-*) WA, vol. 7, 53ab, 58b, 59a: "jangxin xiu-li" (Shuomo, vol. 7, 39a), "he-hao" (Shuomo 42b7), "xiu-hao" (Shuomo 43a5).

[11] *Xitian dashan zizai-fu suoling tianxia shijiao putong wachiladala dalai lama* (on Fire-snake day April Shunchi 10, Shizu Shilu, vol. 74, 12ab).

[12] On Earth-dragon day September Kangxi 31 WA, vol. 12, 43a, Shuomo vol. 12, 29a.

following page
The Thirteenth Dalai Lama (1876-1933) seated on a throne
on an ornately carved and painted dias in the Norbulinka Palace.
This is the throne used by the Dalai Lama on important occasions.
Bell describes this occasion in detail:
"I am to take the Dalai Lama's photograph again...
the first time that anyone has photographed him in the Holy City (Lhasa)...
The arrangement of the throne-room is not ready. I watch them arranging it.
The throne is built up of two or three wooden pieces;
the nine silk scrolls, representing the Buddha in the earth-pressing attitude,
are already placed on the wall behind and above the throne...
Below these scrolls red silk brocade covers the wall.
The throne is four feet high, a seat without a low balustrade
of beautifully carved woodwork running around it.
Hanging down in front of the throne is a cloth of rich white silk,
handsomely embroidered in gold, with crossed thunderbolts
(symbol of equilibrium, immutability and almighty power)...
Crysanthemums, marigolds and other flowers are arranged round the dais."
1998.285.86 (BL.H.76B)

The Tsar's Generals and Tibet. Apropos of some 'white spots' in the history of Russo-Tibetan relations

Alexandre Andreyev

As is well-known, the Tsarist Russian government entered into political relations with Tibet at the turn of the XXth century, as a result of persistent mediation work by the 13th Dalai Lama's emissary, Agvan Lobzang Dorzhiev (1854-1938)[1]. A Buryat by birth and a Russian subject, Dorzhiev was educated in Lhasa, and then, after being attached as a *tsan-shav* or debating partner, to the youthful ruler of Tibet in 1889, he quickly rose to eminence at the Potala. The profound erudition of the Buryat monk-scholar coupled with the obvious charm of his personal qualities helped him win the good graces of his august pupil and Dorzhiev eventually become one the leading figures on the Lhasan political scene. It was owing to his counseling that the Dalai Lama adopted a pro-Russian orientation, which had such dramatic consequences for his country in the long run. Seeking to counter British encroachments upon Tibet, the Buryat prompted his patron towards what seemed then to be the best solution: since China, the formal suzerain of Tibet, was very feeble and could not provide adequate protection for her, so Tibet should turn to a more powerful state, namely the northern potentate of the White Tsar. Russia, Dorzhiev argued, was known for her tolerant policies towards her Buddhist inhabitants, the Transbaikal Buryats and Lower Volga and Don Kalmyks; and, being remote from Tibet's frontiers, would pose no threat to the Land of Snows, but, on the contrary, would surely stand up for Tibet, due to its age-long rivalry with the British in Central Asia.

Dorzhiev's shuttle diplomacy on his three visits to St Petersburg (in 1898, 1900 and 1901), turned out to be relatively successful, bringing about a Russo-Tibetan rapprochement. The Russian imperial policy makers, although they were disinterested in the reclusive Tibetan theocracy at first, could not fail to respond to the overtures of the Dalai Lama's "roving ambassador". What Dorzhiev was primarily after was, firstly, a protectorate treaty with the Russians or a formal agreement that would secure Tibet against any potential aggressor, and, secondly, Russian military aid (arms and instructors to modernize the Tibetan army). However, these two objectives were not so easy to accomplish. The Tsarist diplomats, despite the severe Anglo-Russian antagonism and the declining Manchu rule in China, were not prepared to go as far as to declare Tibet a Russian protectorate. Such a bold step would no doubt have lead to a serious confrontation with both London and Peking, and Russia did not want to be entangled in any power conflict in Central Asia at a time when the menace of Japan was looming in the Far East. Besides, this action could be taken by Western powers as a signal for the beginning of partition of the Chinese Empire, and Petersburg did not want that either. So the Tsar's response to the Dalai Lama's petition, as expressed in the official letter he handed over to Dorzhiev in July 1901, was evasive and non-committal. He merely voiced Russia's moral support for the far-off land by expressing his strong hope that, "under the friendly and benevolent favour of Russia no harm may come to Tibet"[2]. At the same time the Ministry for Foreign Affairs agreed to establish a Russian consulate "for maintaining direct and regular intercourse between the Imperial Government and the supreme Buddhist authorities of Tibet"[3]. The consulate was set up in Tachienlu (Darchendo or Kandin) in Szechuan Province, close to the Tibetan border, and it existed for about one year, between September 1903 and September/October 1904, under the direction of Dorzhiev's associate, Buddha Rabdanov. The consulate was basically used by the Russians as a listening post to monitor the British and French activities in the south-eastern part of Asia.

The history of Russo-Tibetan relations "along the diplomatic line" has been fairly well researched, mainly by Russian scholars[4]. At the same time the military aspect of these relations have completely escaped scholarly attention[5], probably because of the *apriori* belief that this was only a marginal issue, with almost no impact on the nature of the St.Petersburg-Lhasa political dialogue. However the available military records show that Russian generals played quite an active part in that dialogue, especially at its initial stage.

As has been already pointed out, the question of Russian military aid to Tibet was high on Dorzhiev's agenda during his parleys in St Petersburg. The Buryat was most persistent in his attempts to win the cooperation of the Russian top brass – the War Minister, A.N. Kuropatkin, and head of the Main Staff (of the War Ministry), V.V. Sakharov. According to one document, Kuropatkin, as early as 1898, "expressed his readiness to lend military instructors, as well as ammunition to Tibet"[6]. Furthermore, he permitted Dorzhiev to privately approach the Kalmyk officers of the Don Cossack troops on the subject, and it is known that the Tibetan envoy travelled to the Kalmyk steppes for that purpose later that year. In 1900, Dorzhiev had further discussions with Kuropatkin, this time in Yalta. These seem to have been even more successful, as the general agreed to grant the Tibetans "the cannons of the latest make", which had been captured by Russian troops during the suppression of the Boxer Rebellion (in which they participated together with other European powers in July-August 1900). The cannons were most likely the Krupp guns which had been purchased earlier by China from Germany. This was a "beau geste" on the part of the Russian general, but it must have also been a good bargain for the Russians, who could thus rid themselves of an embarrassing war trophy, one that made them uncomfortable due to their friendship with Peking. Still, the transportation of this weaponry to Tibet presented a serious problem, which at first led Dorzhiev to decline Kuropatkin's generous offer, although on second thoughts he agreed to accept it. "Now, after some consideration", he wrote to Kuropatkin on 11 October, "I think that if it proves to be difficult to deliver the cannons to Central Tibet, they nonetheless will be of great help for the defence and prestige of that country"[7]. Dorzhiev probably wanted to bring the cannons to Eastern Tibet (Kham), where they could be used for the defence of the Tibetan frontier, but it seems most unlikely that he was able to realize these plans. Still, there is another highly intriguing aspect to this story. Dorzhiev's letter was annotated with Kuropatkin's curt resolution: "To go to a special Tibet file. To be kept in my office". But any such secret Tibetan dossier of the War Minister, with perhaps other important documents that could throw light on Dorzhiev's covert dealings with the Russian military, is not to be found in the military archives in Moscow (the Russian Archives of Military History, RGVIA). It has simply vanished without a trace from Kuropatkin's personal collection there!

A year later (in July 1901) when Dorzhiev, assisted by Lozang Kainchok, brought another Tibetan embassy to Russia, styled as an "extraordinary mission", the War Ministry attached a special officer to it in the capacity of an interpreter. This was a person already known to Dorzhiev, a Kalmyk subaltern of the Ist Don Cossack Regiment named Naran Ulanov. There were more discussions with Kuropatkin and Sakharov at Terioki (today's Zelenogorsk), held at Kuropatkin's dacha, and then at his private apartment in St Petersburg. The Tibetan envoy presented the war minister with some gifts and a rather cryptic message from the Dalai Lama which read as follows:

> "To the Tibetan state, remaining in the lap of the Buddhist teachings, the English foreigners are enemies and oppressors. For this reason we, trying to eradicate the bane of our people, dispatched these two emissaries, having given them precise and secret instructions. Please report kindly of these circumstances to His Majesty so as to promote our mutual well-being"[8].

Dorzhiev was no doubt pressing for Russian military aid again. According to Ulanov, the war minister reiterated, as he had three years previously, his willingness to provide the Tibetan army with Russian instructors and ammunition (though not with Russian firearms). It was agreed then that Dorzhiev would bring another mission to St Petersburg the following spring that would seek a final solution to the military issue. It could be that Kuropatkin needed a formal petition from the Dalai Lama to provide a pretext for sending Russian instructors to Tibet[9]. (The instructors, of course, were to be selected from the among the Buryat and Kalmyk Cossacks). However this arrangement collapsed for some unknown reason, and the question remained unresolved. In the meantime, Ulanov volunteered to go to Tibet as an instructor, for which purpose he was allowed by his superiors (with Kuropatkin's and Sakharov's due approval) to undergo special training, first at the Officer's Cavalry School and then at the Academy of General Staff.

Judging by the above cited facts, the Russian generals had clearly begun to take some interest in Tibet by 1901. This does not mean, of course, that they were lured by Dorzhiev's "fantastic plans", which he made no secret of and which implied, in the words of the Russian diplomat, I.Ya. Korostovets, "the Russian advance across the

Himalayas to liberate the oppressed people"[10]. Yet at the same time Kuropatkin and Sakharov must have been seriously alarmed by whatever evidence they had of the aggressive designs of Britain on Tibet. Something had to be done to prevent the British from annexation of that country, and the best they could do under the circumstances was to help the Tibetans strengthen their rather primitive military potential[11].

And here we come to the biggest riddle in the history of Russo-Tibetan relations, the issue of Russian arms in Tibet. Our main source of information is the Japanese monk, Ekai Kawaguchi, who then resided in Lhasa. According to Kawaguchi, weaponry was delivered by two large caravans from Russia, about two months after return of Dorzhiev's Mission to Lhasa (though not of Dorzhiev himself, who had remained in Russia), which must have been some time in spring 1902. Kawaguchi obtained this information confidentially from one Tibetan officer who "was quite elated with the weapons, saying that now for the first time Tibet was sufficiently armed to resist any attack which England might undertake against her". The Japanese had a chance to inspect one of the "Russian guns" and this is how he described it:

> "It was apparently one of modern pattern but it did not impress me as possessing any long range nor seem to be quite fit for active service. The stock bore an inscription attesting that it was made in the US of America. The Tibetans being ignorant of Roman letters and English firmly believed that all the weapons were made in Russia. It seems that about one half of the load of the 500 camels consisted of small arms and ammunition"[12].

The arms referred to were probably Berdan rifles, as these are also mentioned in British sources. Kawaguchi's curious evidence, however, has been given little credit by scholars and dismissed as unreliable. But, in my opinion, given what we already know about Dorzhiev's secret dealings with Koropatkin and other generals, it does not look so incredible at all. It will be recalled at this point that the Berdan rifles were then being replaced in the Russian army by the more sophisticated Mosin 7.62 mm magazine rifles (the so-called "triokhlineika" of the 1891 model). Being out of use, the outdated weaponry was stocked in large quantities at the arsenals. Much of it was then either sold abroad or simply scrapped. So Kuropatkin could easily grant Dorzhiev something which he did not need and which did not cost him a penny. As for the arms transportation to Tibet, this again, as in the case with the German cannons, would be entirely Dorzhiev's concern, as the War Ministry certainly did not want to be implicated in the shady transaction.

One last remark regarding the marking of the arms. The Berdan rifles, as is known, were American rifles. The first quantity of these, some 30,000 pieces, were originally purchased by Russia in 1868 directly from the US manufacturer. The entire stock, made after the design of the Russian engineer A.P. Gorlov, were a slightly modified version of the standard Berdan model, and bore an inscription in Russian: "The Colts arms factory. Hartford. America", followed by a serial number. Two years later, this model was further improved by the same Gorlov, after which it was finally adopted by the Russian Army. The modified 4.2 mm Berdan-Gorlov rifles (known as Berdan II rifles) were manufactured mainly at three Russian armouries (in Tula, Sestroretsk and Izhevsk), and bore their names, inscribed naturally in Russian. So theoretically it does not seem impossible for at least some of these presumably

"Russian rifles" spoken of by Kawaguchi to bear the inscription "America". However, the arms, even if they did come from Russia, were of little help for Lhasa during the British invasion of Tibet in 1904. Francis Younghusband, the British mission leader, for example, believed that the condition of the rifles had been so neglected that the Tibetans were only able to use a very few of them against the British[13]. But, of course, there could be other explanations as well.

A few words on the Russian War Minister. Aleksei Nikolaevich Kuropatkin had an excellent military record, having participated in all the major Russian campaigns in Central Asia in the latter half of the 19th century. Being appointed to his post in 1898, he became one of the chief promoters of the expansionist "Big Asiatic Programme" of Tsar Nicholas II. His focus was mainly on the Far Eastern region (Manchuria, Korea and Kwantung Peninsular), though some attention was also given to the Central Asian area, that being the traditional playground for the Russian and British "Great Gamers". However, even in the absence of Kuropatkin's mysterious Tibet File, there is hardly any reason to believe that the general had any aggressive designs on Tibet. The War Minister was known to be an advocate of the delimitation of the spheres of influence between the two rival powers in Asia through an amicable agreement, and this seems to have been his solution to the Tibetan problem. Still, Tibet, despite its remoteness from the Russian frontiers, was something he would not readily agree to yield to the British, who, had they established themselves in Lhasa, would have been able to exercise a pernicious influence on the Buryat and Kalmyk populace in Russia through the Tibetan Buddhist leaders. It was probably this consideration that made Kuropatkin take some steps to counteract the British "Forward policy" vis-à-vis Tibet. He agreed to grant the German cannons to the Tibetans in 1900 and I see no reason why he could not have also granted them some Berdan rifles a year later. This move after all, looks like no more than a little anti-British intrigue by the War Minister, one which was especially timely - the bulk of the British Indian troops, including the Gurkha force, were then fighting against the Boers in South Africa and thus could not be employed against the Tibetans. In addition, the Dalai Lama's overtures to St Petersburg were certainly a temptation for the Russian general, one hard to resist. But this, of course, is only my conjecture.

Tibet came into the spotlight of the Russian generals once again at the end of 1903, after the beginning of Younghusband's military expedition to Lhasa. Kuropatkin, of course, could not remain indifferent to this serious breach of the "status quo" by the British. It is known that in January 1904 he secretly dispatched, with the Tsar's approval, a reconnaissance mission to Lhasa under Naran Ulanov. The Kalmyk officer was instructed to gather intelligence on the British in Tibet and, as a sideline, to explore and charter a new route to Lhasa, one leading across the Russian Turkestan via Baku, Krasnovodsk, Tashkent and Kulja[14].

There was yet another, much more sinister project that was considered by Kuropatkin at that time. Around mid-November 1903, the well-known traveller and officer of the General Staff, Petr Kozlov, came up with a plan for sending "an expeditionary force" to Tibet "to counter the steps of the British-Indian government"[15]. The Russian mission was to incline the Tibetan government, following the British example,

171

to open their country to Russian pilgrims and goods, by resorting to either diplomatic negotiations, or, if need be, to "appropriate" military action. The reaction of Kozlov's superiors to his proposal was neatly expressed by the 2nd Quartermaster General, Ya.G. Zhilinsky, in his brief note, recently discovered in the military archives:

> "The guiding idea for the expedition: it must try to secure the same privileges for the Russians which the British are seeking by their expedition, however it should avoid, by all means possible, any clash with the British"[16].

Kuropatkin, however, decided not to hurry events and dispatched Ulanov's reconnaissance party to Tibet first. But then, in February 1904, the Russo-Japanese war suddenly broke out, and the Russian generals had to give up on any Tibetan designs. In the meantime the Ulanov Mission, despite the fact that its leader died of altitude sickness en route, still made it to Lhasa. The Kalmyk party headed by Ulanov's aide, a monk, Baksi Dambo Ulianov, reached the Tibetan capital in May 1905. However, they did not find there either the Dalai Lama, who had by then fled to Mongolia with a small retinue, nor the British, who, having forced a humiliating treaty upon the Tibetans on 7 September 1904, had withdrawn to India. Still, the mission's journey was not altogether in vain. While in Lhasa, Ulianov contacted high Tibetan officials, including the Regent, Ganden Tri Rimpoche, Lozang Gyaltsen Lamoshar, to whom he submitted a special report. In this he sought, *inter alia*, to prove, by referring to an ancient Buddhist prophesy, that the Buddha's teachings would flourish in the future primarily in Russia and China, so Tibet should seek protection of only these two powers and not of England, a country they claimed was profoundly hostile to Buddhism[17].

Dorzhiev resumed his contacts with the War Ministry in early 1906 after he had settled down permanently in St Petersburg. His highest priority then was to arrange a Buryat Cossack escort which the Russian government promised to provide to the Dalai Lama to safeguard his return to Lhasa. The new War Minister, A.F. Rediger, responded positively to a number of Dorzhiev's petitions to this end, including his request for additional 100 Mosin rifles to arm the Lama's retinue. However the Foreign Ministry objected to the latter request as "undesirable" for political reasons[18]. But in 1912 Dorzhiev eventually succeeded in bringing Russian military instructors to Tibet. These were three Buryat Cossacks from the Transbaikal Cossack Army who had escorted Dorzhiev to Lhasa due to the Sino-Tibetan hostilities, and they were later hired by the Dalai Lama to drill Tibetan troops. But this again was entirely Dorzhiev's own initiative, and subsequently, upon his return to Russia, he reported this to the War Ministry as a *fait accomplie* [19].

CONCLUSION

In conclusion I would like to emphasize that the Russian generals played a much more active part in Russia's dialogue with Lhasa in early 1900s than is generally believed by scholars. There is evidence that the War Minister, A.N. Kuropatkin, agreed to give some military aid to the Tibetans in response to the petitions of the Dalai Lama's envoy, Agvan Dorzhiev. At the same time he did not want Russia to be directly involved in Tibetan affairs, given the Anglo-Russian rivalry in Central Asia. However the British invasion of Tibet in 1903 persuaded the general to take some measures to protect the Russian interests in these regions. Kuropatkun dispatched a secret reconnaissance mission to Lhasa under Naran Ulanov in January 1904, and he also considered the possibility of sending a Russian military expedition there headed by P.K. Kozlov, with the aim of restoring the disturbed balance of power in Tibet.

NOTES

[1] Re Agvan Dorzhiev, see A.I. Andreyev, *The Buddhist shrine of Petrograd* (Ulan Ude, 1992); John Snelling, *Buddhism in Russia: The Story of Agvan Dorzhiev, Lhasa's Emissary to the Tsar* (Shaftesbury, Dorset, 1993).

[2] Letter of Nicholas II to the Dalai Lama, 4 July 1901, Archive of the Foreign Policy of the Russian Federation (AVPRF), f. Kitaiskii stol, d.1448, l.100.

[3] Ibid., d.1449, l.1.

[4] The most recent publications are Nikolai S. Kuleshov, *Russia's Tibet File: The unknown pages in the history of Tibet's independence* (Dharamsala, 1996); Tatiana Shaumian, *The Great Game and Tsarist Russia* (New Delhi, 2000).

[5] The only scholar who has showed interest in this subject is D.H. Schimmelpenninck van der Oye from Brock University in Canada. See his paper "Tsarist Intelligence and the Younghusband Expedition of 1904", presented at the Symposium on Intelligence and International Relations at Yale University, 3 May 1996.

[6] Memo of subaltern of the 1st Cossack Regiment, Naran Ulanov, to the head of the Military Academic Committee (VUK) of the Main Staff, 14 July 1901, the Russian State Archive of Military History (RGVIA), f.401, op.5/929, d.158, l.124.

[7] RGVIA, f.165 (Kuropatkin Collection), op.1, d.5304a, l.7 and 7ob.

[8] Ibid., l.15. The military archives have only a Russian translation of that letter but not its Tibetan original.

[9] RGVIA, f.401, op.5/929, d.158, l.124.

[10] I.Y. Korostovets, *Von Chhingis Khan zur Sowjetsrepublik* (Berlin, 1926), p.207.

[11] A special Memo on Tibet and its armed forces was drawn up by the Main Staff on 24 November 1901 (RGVIA, ibid., ll.53-54ob). Most of the facts it contained obviously came from Dorzhiev. According to this document, the Tibetan troops "in the time of peace" included some 3000 militia men, 200 men of the Dalai Lama's bodyguard, and 4500 Chinese troops "of the green banner".

[12] Ekai Kawaguchi, *Three Years in Tibet* (Benares-London, 1909), p.506.

[13] F. Younghusband, *India and Tibet* (London 1910), p.320.

[14] A draft of Ulanov's project for a scientific expedition to Tibet, dated 30 May 1903, was discovered by the present author in the Archive of the Russian Academy of Sciences in St Petersburg, f.208, op.1, d.151, ll.1-10ob (Proekt Zapiski ob Ekspeditsii v Tibet).

[15] Draft of Kozlov's Memo to the head of the Military Academic Committee of the Main Staff (undated), Archive of the Russian Geographical Society, f.18, op.1, d.40, l.1-4.

[16] RGVIA, f.447, op.1, d.53, l.93ob. The quotation comes from what seem to be the guidelines for the memo of the Statistical Section to be submitted to the head of the Main Staff, specially drafted by Zhilinsky.

[17] For more details on the Ulanov and Kozlov Missions see A.I. Andreyev, *From Lake Baikal to Sacred Lhasa: New materials on the Russia expeditions to Central Asia (Buryatia, Mongolia, and Tibet) in the 1st half of the XXth century*, St Petersburg-Samara-Prague, 1997, pp.9-60.

[18] Archive of the Museum of Military History, St Petersburg (AVIMAIV & VS), f.6, d.149, ll.26, 39-41.

[19] Dorzhiev's report to the Russian military administration of the Transbaikal Region from Troitskosavsk, 5 January 1913, RGVIA, f.2000, op.1, d.7668, ll.58-58ob.

DISCUSSION

TSARIST RUSSIAN ARMS SUPPLIES TO TIBET?

In discussion following this paper, the main question concerned the existence or otherwise of Russian arms in Tibet; none having been found by the Younghusband mission in 1904, although their alleged existence was a factor behind that British-Indian mission's invasion of Tibet. It was noted that concealment of these weapons was a possibility. In the 1930s, for example, the Tibetans had used artillery the source of which is not known, and which had apparently been concealed for some time. It was also noted that Russian arms would have come into Tibet from the north, while Younghusband's mission ventured no further north than Lhasa.

The weapons would, in any case, have had to pass through areas outside of central control and dominated by war-lords and bandits. Thus they could also have been siphoned off, sold, or plundered by soldiers in the north east, a region in which at that time there were considerable amounts of weapons available from a variety of sources. The question of whether Tsarist Russian arms were actually supplied to Tibet thus remains open.

following pages
Bell's entry:
"(an) Street in Lhasa. Chorten in background.
Some Nepalese in middle distance, on right."
1998.285.293 (BL.H.267)

From Conflict to Conciliation: Tibetan Polity Re-visited

Parshotam Mehra

An earlier monograph had sought to broadly map out the principal contours of the relationship between the 13th Dalai Lama and his near contemporary, the 9th Panchen Lama. Both, sadly, were unreconciled to the very end of their days. For by the time the 13th Dalai Lama breathed his last in December 1937 or, as the Tibetans would have it, retired to the Heavenly Fields, the issues that divided them had remained unresolved. The two representatives the absentee Panchen Lama had designated, on the Dalai Lama's initiative, to negotiate on his behalf did indeed arrive in Lhasa in June 1933 and engaged in long confabulations with the Tsongdu, but the talks had led nowhere in particular. For even though the Dalai Lama himself is said to have been keen on a settlement, the failure of the mission was rightly or wrongly laid at the door of two of his closest advisors, Kunpel La (Dechen Chodren) and Lungshar (Dorje Tsegyal). It may bear mention in this context that in Tibetan tradition, the Dalai Lama or the Panchen Lama for that matter, are blameless; the real guilt for harbouring any unpleasant thoughts or committing evil deeds is not theirs and must, by definition, be visited on the heads of their advisors.

The four years that were to elapse before the death of the 9th Panchen Lama in December 1937 were witness to any number of attempts by the authorities in Lhasa, the Lama himself and, not unoften, by the KMT regime in Nanking to bring the Panchen back. Nor was Whitehall entirely unconcerned. As a matter of fact, it made no end of effort both by pressurising the government of the Regent into accepting the Panchen Lama's reasonable demands and at the same time persuading the latter to be more realistic about the ground situation and climb down a notch or two from his near-precarious perch and opt for a compromise of sorts. Both the British Political Officers, F.W.Williamson, who died in Lhasa itself in November 1934 while helping to knock a settlement into shape, and later Basil Gould – and his successor Hugh Richardson – were deeply involved in bringing the two sides closer.

Try as they might, however, two stumbling blocks seemed insurmountable. One, the Panchen Lama's stubborn insistence that he would return only with an armed escort of 300-500 well-accoutered soldiers. Nor was the Nanking regime any the less keen that the Lama should be accompanied by such an escort.

Even as the Panchen Lama and his political supporters, the KMT regime in Nanking, appeared to have set their heart on an armed escort, for the authorities in Lhasa it was the one demand they were not prepared to concede. Nor must we go far to seek their reasoning. Having had an earlier brush with Chao Erh-feng's levies, which had poured into Lhasa in the wake of the return of the 13th Dalai Lama from his first exile, in December 1909, they were now doubly circumspect. For however innocuous it might appear to be on the surface, the armed escort's presence in Tibet would be enough to subvert the authority of the government and thereby endanger Tibet's independence.

Sadly for Lhasa, the post-December 1933 scenario did not inspire much confidence. As was not unusual, the pro-monk faction in the Tsongdu, even though it may not have been pronouncedly pro-Chinese, was prepared for all sorts of compromises. One, that from Nagchuka the Panchen Lama with his escort proceed direct to Shigatse, thereby bypassing Lhasa. Another, that the escort should beat a retreat as soon as it could- perhaps within six months of its arrival. It was also suggested that a third party (read Great Britain) guarantee the return of the escort, preferably by way of India, and by sea.

As in Lhasa, so also in New Delhi- and Whitehall- there were sharp differences of opinion. Broadly, the hawks suggested that Britain mediate in the dispute between the Lamas and guarantee a settlement; the doves, that while it may help bring the two sides closer, the Raj should refrain from playing an active role and the parleys resume only when the Panchen Lama returned home to Tashilhunpo. Once in Tibet, it was argued, the Panchen Lama would be amenable to reason, the outright Chinese support that made his stance rigid and intractable having been removed. In other words, a mutually satisfactory solution might be easier to work out once the extraneous Chinese factor did not weigh in the balance.

All through the four years that separated the deaths of the two Lamas, the Chinese position seemed to be unambiguously clear. They did their best to exploit to its maximum advantage the gulf that separated the Panchen Lama from the post-Dalai Lama regime in Lhasa. For his part, the Panchen made no bones about the fact that the Nanking government was keen that he take the escort. Nor for that matter was the Nationalist regime any the less insistent, if also enthusiastic. It had over the years wooed the Lama right and left - with generous, sizeable subsidies for himself and his large retinue. Moreover it had conferred on him high-sounding titles and, to underline his importance, given him a personal escort. Nor was the Lama found wanting in paying back for all the attention, and largesse, he had received. Thus he acted as Nanking's unofficial ambassador both in Inner Mongolia and the predominantly ethnic Tibetan provinces of Qinghai (Amdo) and Xining (Kham). He had also sought funds from an almost financially bankrupt government for the education of his people, both in Tibetan and Chinese, and for a major highway construction linking Tibet, so as to forge closer links with the motherland.

To its credit, the KMT regime rejected numerous British protests on Tibet's behalf and refused to entertain any concessions on the issue of an escort for the Panchen Lama. And overall, it was prepared to go the extra mile to help the Lama regain his lost position and status. The end game was clear, on the coat-tails of the Panchen Lama, China might yet reclaim its role as the ultimate arbiter in Tibet's affairs.

Sadly for it, in the final count, in September 1937, Chiang's China did yield ground to British protests - and Lhasa's obduracy. But only because of the compulsion of events beyond its control. Unashamedly, the Japanese had launched a frontal assault on the mainland and the most sensitive parts of the government in and around the Chinese capital. And for a regime driven to such sore straits, British support, moral as well as material, had become crucial. In the event, Nanking halted the Panchen Lama in his tracks and deferred his proposed march into Tibet. Even though the Lama was sorely disappointed, the Tibetan government heaved a sigh of relief. And the tension that had built over the past year or two happily dissipated.

II

For Tibet though, it proved to be a temporary, short-lived reprieve, largely because China did not give up its long-term interests, nor yet relent its pressure on the post 13th Dalai Lama regime in Lhasa. Two developments are of some significance in this context. One, the Nationalist regime's desperate efforts in the early 1940s to obtain supplies via a Trans-Tibet route designed to link up the plains of Assam with south-western Sichuan and all that was left of Guomindang China. This had become the more urgent after the Japanese had choked all coastal ingress and egress and the fall of Rangoon (March 1942) dried up the trickle of supplies that had poured through the Burma-Yunnan road. Sadly for Chiang and his men, despite the intense pressures to which they were exposed both by the British and the US, the Tibetans stood their ground and denied both transport of any military hardware and at the same time sternly refused to build any roads through their territory. In material terms, Lhasa may not have added up much to Chiang's war effort even if it had been more forth-coming. The important thing though was that the Chinese were unrelenting and invoked the urgency of the war and that the Tibetans were equally unwilling to be browbeaten into submission.

On the issue of the new incarnations of the Dalai Lama and the Panchen Lama, the battle lines remained firmly drawn. Happily for Lhasa, the new incarnation of Chenrezi, the incumbent 14th Dalai Lama discovered in Qinghai had escaped the Chinese dragnet and was safely installed in the Potala without any major hiccup. Conscious that it had not been able to achieve its objective of having a say in his selection, Guomindang China went through the motions attendant upon the choice of the new incarnation and its traditional enthronement. A high level delegation was readied to repair to Lhasa, via Calcutta and Sikkim, to be around during the celebrations and despite firm and categorical denials by eyewitnesses as well as the government in Lhasa that it had any special role to play, either in the choice or enthronement of the Dalai Lama, insisted that, in fact, it did. For the KMT government in Chungking claimed that its representative had, to start with, put his stamp of approval on the new incarnation - after an examination, and scrutiny, of his credentials and later invested him with the authority it alone could, as the sovereign state, bestow. Whatever the merits of its claims, China's aura over the new Tibetan ruler was at best shadowy and notional, if not almost non-existent.

The reverse was the case when it came to the new Panchen Lama. His discovery is shrouded in some mystery and is said to have been made by the leftover entourage that had remained steadfastly loyal to their master the 9th Panchen's memory and had been handsomely rewarded by the KMT authorities through their long years of exile and homelessness. Thanks to their high stakes and legitimately possessive instincts, they had shied away from sending him to Lhasa when Tibet's government desired that he take his place, alongside other prospective candidates, for the new incarnation. In sum, they now stoutly resisted Lhasa's likely use of the Golden Urn to settle conflicting claims, fearing that should their candidate lose they would face certain disaster. Meanwhile events in China itself moved thick and fast with a raging civil strife between Mao's men and the incumbent KMT regime, with the latter fast losing ground. They were soon driven into a corner, not only figuratively, but also literally.

One of Chiang's last desperate acts before he fled the mainland in the face of relentless pressure from the advancing Red armies was to accord recognition to the boy lama (June 1949) that the late Panchen's entourage had discovered, in the face of Lhasa's known dissent. For its part, the KMT regime had hoped to groom him for fighting afresh its battles with the Tibetan authorities in which the 9th Panchen had not exactly succeeded. Sadly, it had not quite calculated that its own days were so severely numbered. For within a few weeks of the installation of the new Panchen at Kumbum (August 1949), Xining fell into the hands of the advance guards of the PLA, who presently drove Chiang across the Taiwan Strait.

Happily for the new Panchen, his entourage lost no time in switching loyalties and pledging support to China's new rulers. The boy Lama affirmed his faith in Mao and his men beseeching them inter alia to "liberate" his land from the stranglehold of an unfriendly Lhasa regime and its alleged imperialist lackeys. Not that the great helmsman needed such persuasion, for Tibet's "liberation" had from the very outset been high on the PLA's agenda. And unlike their predecessors, China's new rulers were men of determination who possessed the requisite wherewithal to realise their plans.

When, after a flurry of loud protests and exchange of messages, the youthful Dalai Lama's representatives reached Beijing to negotiate a deal, the principal sticking point was the issue of the Panchen Lama. At one stage the Chinese threatened to call off the parleys unless the matter was sorted out to their satisfaction and after some preliminary shadowboxing, the Lhasa delegation was convinced that there was no alternative but to yield ground. Their first major concession was to recognise the credentials of the Kumbum-based Panchen Lama as the genuine reincarnation of his predecessor. Again, the two principal clauses of the 21 May (1951) Agreement related to Lhasa's affirmation of the new Panchen Lama, his return and due installation at Tashilhunpo and the restoration of all the powers and privileges the 9th Panchen enjoyed before he left home in the early 1920s.

Not long thereafter, the Panchen Lama accompanied by an impressive escort of 2,000 PLA soldiers arrived in the Tibetan capital (March 1952). A few months later he was duly installed, with all pomp and pageantry, at his traditional seat of authority in Tashilhunpo.

Relations between the two Lamas though superficially cordial, were not exactly free from strain and this to no small extent was inherent in the situation. For to no one's surprise, the Panchen and his entourage leaned heavily on the Chinese, a fact that made them natural suspects in the eyes of the average Tibetan, who significantly enough referred to him as the 'Chinese Lama.' As a matter of fact, both the Lama as well as his entourage appeared to be integral parts of the new Beijing rulers with whom they shared a common one-point agenda; namely that Tashilhunpo must be raised to the status which the Potala enjoyed, and its head, the Panchen Lama, must rank as the equal of the Dalai Lama - by no means his second in command, much less his under-study. It followed that such pre-eminence as the master of the Potala had hitherto enjoyed in the polity must be a thing of the past. In sum, to raise Tashilhunpo and build up its status, and importance, it was incumbent upon Tibet's new rulers to cut the Dalai Lama and his government to size.

With the Chinese now solidly arrayed behind Tashilhunpo, Lhasa's once powerful clout seemed to diminish with every passing day. So that in the final count, it was a battle between two unequals, the Panchen Lama backed to the hilt as it were by Tibet's new Chinese masters, steadily if surely gaining ground and the Dalai Lama, almost forlorn, equally clearly losing his former status and position. As if to make things doubly sure, the administrative structure which the Chinese presently introduced in the shape of the Preparatory Committee for the Tibetan Autonomous Region (1956) institutionalised the new power equation.

Clear if equally unambiguous pointers to the new relationship between the Lamas could be discerned on the two occasions they travelled together. At first, during their year-long sojourn in China (1954-5) and later in the course of their visit to India to participate in the celebrations of the Mahaparinirvana of the Buddha (1956-7), Beijing had been keen to demonstrate its new-gained position, both nationally and internationally and reasoned that the Lamas should see the mainland for themselves, its vast resources, and even greater potential, both in men and material wealth and its immense active and disciplined manpower on the land and its new factories, busy ports. Above all, Chairman Mao harangued them, individually and collectively, to forget their past rivalries and jealousies and start afresh in rediscovering themselves – and embracing the motherland.

However well the Chinese may have managed their own part – and there is little on public record to show any major discords – the Lamas' Indian sojourn embarrassed the Beijing regime no end. To start with, the media rightly or wrongly viewed the Panchen Lama as a Chinese protégé and therefore with an inherent, in-built prejudice. In sharp contrast to the robustly independent Dalai Lama, the Panchen was the "Chinese Lama". Again, true to tradition, New Delhi treated the Dalai Lama, to the great chagrin of the Panchen, and his masters in Beijing, as the ruler of Tibet entitled to the protocol, and courtesies, of a virtual head of state.

As the weeks sped by, the reported decision of the Dalai Lama and his entourage not to return home invested him with a little more than ordinary importance. The Chinese Prime Minister, Zhou Enlai sought him out more than once in the course of two brief visits to India in less than a month and pledged his word of honour to attend to the Dalai Lama's principal concern: loosening the rigours of Chinese rule and slowing down the pace of reform. Above all, he pledged not to play the Lamas off against each other, to the grave disadvantage of the master of the Potala. The Indian Prime Minister for his part, tried to allay the worst fears of the Dalai Lama concerning

China and impressed upon him the urgent need to return home. For his rightful place, Nehru stressed, was among his own people. All in all, the Dalai Lama received far more attention than the Panchen did. No wonder then, that the latter returned to Tashilhunpo ahead of the Dalai Lama - in a big sulk and in high dudgeon. This was more than evident in the denial of courtesies to which the master of the Potala was entitled when he passed through Shigatse on his return journey to Lhasa.

By the time, early in 1957, that the Lamas were home, a major new development had raised its ugly head. This was the Khampa rebellion complicating, and precipitating, matters no end. While the rebellion as such does not have a direct bearing on the evolving relationship between the two Lamas, its importance to the events as they unfolded themselves is crucial. A slight digression may not therefore be out of place.

To start with, the Khampas' principal preoccupation was the firm conviction that the Beijing government constituted a threat to the life and safety of the Dalai Lama and, by implication, to Tibet and the Tibetan way of life. Hence there could be no question of a compromise with it, much less its policies and programmes. Since their land had been in the vanguard of the Chinese assault, the Khampas had ever since the "liberation" been exposed to all that the Chinese revolution meant; they had experienced it at first hand.

It bears mention that the bulk of the Khampa influx was in central Tibet, in the province of U; in, and around, Lhasa. The numbers that had poured into Tsang and the Panchen Lama's estate, around Tashilhunpo, were small. They made no major impact. It should follow that the principal thrust of the revolt was confined to the domain of the Tibetan government and that the Panchen Lama and his estate were, by and large, free from the "contagion".

With the Khampa rebels pouring in sizeable numbers, the resultant situation was confused at best; at worst, well nigh chaotic. To start with, the Dalai Lama and his ministers, the Kashag, were in an unenviable position, in the thick of the battle with the unruly – and almost uncontrollable – mass of Khampas. Their near-helplessness, evident even to the purblind, came as a godsend to the Chinese authorities stationed in the Tibetan capital. And knowing only too well how very impossible the situation was, they increasingly impressed upon the Dalai Lama and his ministers that it was part of their duty to maintain peace in the capital by containing the Khampa insurrection.

That was easier said than done. Unruly at the best of times and notorious for their reputation as uncouth "bandits" who looted from villagers and were prone to violence, the Khampas were in no mood to listen to exhortations for peace and harmony. The more so for their honest conviction that the Kashag was hand in glove with the Chinese and would barter the Dalai Lama away for a petty mess of potage. As noticed, they believed that Beijing for its part was determined to kidnap the Dalai Lama and whisk him away to the far away motherland. And with the Dalai Lama gone, Tibet's cause - and its identity - would be completely lost

The third leg of the tripod in the Tibetan capital was the Chinese. Not only the inveterate hostility of the Khampas but the near rebellion of the mass of Tibetans in Lhasa itself was an eye-opener to them. And while both the Dalai Lama and the Kashag were straining every nerve to bring about some semblance of law and order, the Chinese were half-suspicious that the Lama's ministers - if not indeed the Lama himself - were lending countenance to the rebels and buttressing the cause of the revolt. As if that were not confusing enough, the Khampas, while professing to protect the Dalai Lama from the Chinese had, wittingly or otherwise, made him into a virtual prisoner, so that he was for all practical purposes, no longer a free agent.

III

With the Dalai Lama's escape from the Norbulingka, the situation in Tibet in general, and Lhasa in particular, underwent a complete metamorphosis. The Chinese, who had hitherto held their hand to bring about some semblance of order to an almost chaotic state of affairs, swung into action. No longer did they have any constraints operating on them. It is worth recalling that within forty-eight hours of the Dalai Lama's flight they had used their superior firepower and armed might to bombard the summer palace and had, unmindful of the loss to life and property, managed to contain the revolt in Lhasa and its immediate neighbourhood.

It is to this period one has to turn to delineate the principal strands in the relationship between the two Lamas. With the Chinese stranglehold in Lhasa tightening its grip with every passing day, especially after the induction of the PCTAR, the Dalai Lama and the Kashag were no longer able to escape the mounting pressures. These were now tangible, almost palpable. It may be interesting to recall in this context that nearly three months before he took the final plunge, the Dalai Lama had played with the idea of effecting an escape from the well-nigh-intolerable situation in which he now found himself. He seriously considered establishing a government of his own in the southern part of the country reportedly under the sway of the rebels and negotiating with the Chinese *de novo*. Just about the same time, the Panchen Lama is said to have written to the master of the Potala laying bare his own disillusionment with Beijing's rule: "with the situation deteriorating throughout the country", the Panchen confided, "we needed to formulate a strategy for the future." "This was the first indication", the Dalai Lama was to note later, that the Panchen had given of "being no longer in thrall of our Chinese masters."

On the very eve of leaving Tibet to cross over into India as a refugee, the Dalai Lama proclaimed his own and his country's independence from Beijing and denounced the May 1951 Agreement on Tibet's "liberation". He was prepared to negotiate with the Chinese afresh and even named a new Prime Minister, a monk official whom the Chinese had earlier insisted on sacking for his stubborn resistance to their rule. More importantly, he wrote to the Panchen Lama informing him of his decision to flee and inviting him (the Panchen Lama) to join him, "if he could".

There is no knowing whether the Panchen Lama received the above communication from the master of the Potala, much less as to what his reaction was. What is known is that he did not join the Dalai Lama, perhaps because he was not able to.

There was no one-to-one meeting between the Lamas and hardly any exchange of messages during the decades that followed. The only exception being some telephonic conversations when the Panchen Lama managed briefly to escape his protectors' vigilant gaze. There were three such exchanges, twice while the Lama was in Beijing and once when he was in Australia and the Dalai Lama in Germany.

In all this, two things stand out clearly. One, that even though he towed the Beijing line in denouncing the March rebellion and the Dalai Lama's flight, the Panchen did at no stage upbraid, much less censure, the conduct of the master of the

Potala. To the contrary, even during the worst days of *thamzing* ('struggle sessions'), when such a denunciation could have earned him rich political dividends, the Panchen refused to rise to the bait. More, in 1964, in the heart of Lhasa during the one-day Monlam festival, he had the courage to assert that the Dalai Lama was the true leader of his people, reiterating his "firm belief" that he "will return to the golden throne" and praying for the Dalai Lama's long life. The price the Panchen paid for this seeming bravado was pretty high but, to all appearances, he stood his ground and did not flinch, much less falter.

Beijing's unqualified denunciation of the Panchen Lama in the wake of his 70,000-character 'petition' to the 'respected' Prime Minister Zhou Enlai earned him no end of humiliation - and ultimately a 14-year term of solitary imprisonment and, in the bargain, a long lease of forced exile from his beloved Tashilhunpo. By the time he was released (1978) and rehabilitated (1981 onwards), the Tibetan scenario had undergone a sea change. For one, the all-powerful Chairman no longer bestrode the political stage as a colossus; for another, the worst days of the Great Proletarian Cultural Revolution belonged to a forgettable past. The new supreme leader, Deng Xiaoping, was prepared for compromises. In the event, the Panchen Lama was permitted a measure of freedom to revisit his land and his people. The enthusiasm of the crowds that greeted him on his return home came as an eye-opener, even perhaps a rude shock to the Chinese. So also the warmth and affection, and fervour, with which the three delegations of the exiled Dalai Lama were received by his people. There could be no clearer, if also perhaps convincing evidence that despite decades of Chinese rule, the two Lamas were still very relevant to the Tibetan polity.

How had the relationship between the two Lamas evolved between 1952, when the youthful Panchen Lama returned home, and his sad even tragic – and mysterious – death 37 odd years later? To start with, the two Lamas and their entourages were clearly on the warpath. The Panchen and his men enjoying unqualified support from Tibet's new rulers who were only too keen to rebuild Tashilhunpo as a rival power-centre and restore its lost power and prestige. In the process, nothing was left undone to cut the Dalai Lama to size and reduce the importance, and relevance, of the government at Lhasa. Here was an open challenge to his traditional preeminence and the Chinese rendered no small help with the new institutional framework of the PCTAR launched in 1956 and tailor-made, as it were, to the purpose. For the Dalai Lama's 'Local Government of Tibet' was only one of the three regional authorities into which Tibet was split, the other two being the Panchen Lama's "Council of Khenpos" and the People's Liberation Committee of the Chamdo Area.

It did not take the Lamas long to see through the Chinese gameplan. By end-1958 it should be obvious, both Lhasa as well as Shigatse had shown their complete disillusionment. The Dalai Lama was planning to flee and establish a government inside Tibet that would re-negotiate the 17-Point Agreement which, as he saw it, the Chinese had torn into tatters. The Panchen too had expressed his disenchantment with the way things were going. It would thus appear that the Abbot of Tashilhunpo had drawn closer to the master of the Potala. This is further reinforced by the Dalai Lama's invitation to the Panchen to join him in his exile, so that they could perhaps face the future together.

Even though there is no concrete evidence, all the pointers indicate that in the decades that followed the March 1959 rebellion, the personal rapport between the Lamas had grown and slowly but surely, they were drawing closer. The Dalai Lama was convinced that 'under the most difficult circumstances' the Panchen Lama 'tried his best' for his people, for the preservation of 'their culture and language.' His last political testament that while there 'certainly' had been 'development' in Tibet, the price paid for it 'has been greater than the gains', the Dalai Lama held, made up for all that the Panchen had ever said in praise of Mao and Chinese communist rule. The fact is that the Lamas' petty jealousies and rivalries were now shadowy memories of a forgotten past. These had in fact lost all meaning, being no more than empty, lifeless shells. Both were now exiles, strangers to their country – and both had been kept far, far away from their hearths and homes; their land and its people.

BIBLIOGRAPHY

Charles Alfred Bell,	*Portrait of the Dalai Lama*, Collins, London, 1946.
Dalai Lama, H.H. The 14th,	*Freedom in Exile*, 2nd edition, Rupa Paperback, New Delhi, 1991.
Melvyn C Goldstein,	*A History of Modern Tibet, 1913-1951*, Indian edition, Munshiram Manoharlal, New Delhi, 1993.
Isabel Hilton,	*The Search for the Panchen Lama*, Penguin Books, London, 1999.
Parshotam Mehra,	*Tibetan Polity, 1904-37*, Otto Harraassowitz, Wiesbaden, 1976.

following page
Bell's entry:
"Picnic party near Lhasa. Playing a dice game (sho) in the foreground.
Note the pad – (shoden) – dice cushion) in foreground with cowries round it.
The cowries are used for calculation."
1998.286.128.1 (BL.Q.118)

The Ernst-Schaefer-Tibet-Expedition (1938-1939): New Light on the Political History of Tibet in the First Half of the 20ᵗʰ century

Isrun Engelhardt

"When the Russians entered Berlin, they found among the corpses a thousand volunteers for death in German uniform without any papers or badges, of Himalayan origin. As soon as the [Nazi] movement began to acquire extensive funds, it organised a number of expeditions to Tibet, which succeeded one another practically without interruption until 1943[1]." "The German expeditions to Tibet in 1937 and 1943 had as their mission the discovery of a connection between lost Atlantis and the first civilisation of Central Asia[2]." "Schaefer believed that Tibet was the cradle of mankind, a refuge of an 'Aryan root race', where a caste of priests had created a mysterious empire of knowledge, called 'Shambhala', adorned with the Buddhist symbol of the wheel of life, swastika[3]." These SS-men "were the warrior elite of a new civilisation, immeasurably superior to the old, the high priesthood of the New Age, the standard bearer of the coming Superman. Their leaders were magicians, who had formed alliances with the mystic Tibetan cities of Agarthi and Schamballah and had mastered the forces of the living universe[4]." They had "to measure Tibetan head sizes and ascertain that the Tibetans were not Jews but true Aryans. Hitler even is reputed to have brought a group of monks back to Germany, instructing them to perform special chants to alter weather patterns in preparation for his ill-fated Russian invasion[5]."

What do all these statements have in common? They are all false.

These quotations refer to one of the most controversial expeditions to Tibet during the 20th century, the so-called Schaefer expedition of 1938/39, carried out by the German scientist Ernst Schaefer. Because the members of the expedition all belonged to the SS, a great deal of Nazi ideology, esotericism and occultism has been attributed to it. Because Schaefer's accounts of this expedition have never been translated into English, public opinion in the English-speaking world has been mainly formed by the available sources in the India Office in London. This may account for the doubtful legacy of the expedition in the English-speaking world. In Germany this mission has nearly been forgotten. Also forgotten is the fact that the Schaefer expedition collected an amazing amount of scientific material about Tibet, material that continues to be of great value even today.

What little is recalled concerns the potential political, ideological, esoteric and occultistic aspects of the expedition. With my paper I hope to contribute to the demystification of this expedition[6]. My primary sources are the voluminous hand-written expedition diaries of Schaefer, the records of the interrogations of Schaefer, the SS Ahnenerbe files, as well as Tibetan documents. I have also examined, for comparative purposes, the British sources, consisting mainly of confidential reports and letters of British officials.

First I will give a short summary of Schaefer's life up to the eve of 1938, the year of the expedition. Second I will provide a short description of the expedition. Third, I will focus on the person of the Regent, Reting Rinpoche, and the picture we receive of him from Schaefer's diaries. That a relationship was successfully established between Reting Rinpoche and the members of the German expedition in Lhasa is quite well known, but information hitherto available as to the nature of this relationship ultimately led to the distorted view of German-Tibetan relations in the 1940s. Today's Neo Nazi propaganda, however, still relies on the alleged "Nazi friendliness" of the Tibetans. Therefore one particular purpose of my paper is to correct this distorted view.

Schaefer – a brilliant, ambitious, energetic and impulsive man – was born in 1910 in Cologne. After he had graduated in 1929 from high school in Mannheim, he studied zoology and geology in Goettingen, Hannover and Philadelphia. In 1930 Brooke Dolan, a rich young American, came to Germany to recruit scientists for his zoological expedition. Schaefer participated in this first Brooke-Dolan expedition to West China and Tibet, despite being only twenty years old at the time. In 1932 he returned to Germany to resume his studies. In 1934 he followed the advice of the Lord Major of Goettingen to enter the SS. From 1934-1936 he took part in another scientific expedition with Brooke Dolan to Eastern Tibet and China.

Schaefer returned with Dolan to the United States in January 1936. In Philadelphia he received a telegram from the German government congratulating him on his successes and indicating that his return to Germany was desired. Shortly thereafter, a second cable arrived, informing him that in recognition of the success of his expedition he had been nominated SS Untersturmfuehrer (SS Second Lt.).

The short obituary of Schaefer in 1992 of the Academy of Natural Sciences, Philadelphia, mentions that Schaefer and Dolan "collected scientific data and specimens of the region's birds and mammals that have never been equalled in size and importance. In recognition of his many scientific contributions Dr. Schafer was elected to life membership in the Academy in 1932."

After his return to Germany, Schaefer continued his studies in Berlin and received his doctoral degree in zoology in 1937. The "Reichsfuehrer-SS" Himmler was at that time already trying to avail himself of Schaefer's reputation for Nazi propaganda purposes and he was summoned by Himmler, who inquired about his future plans. Schaefer told him of his wish to lead yet a further expedition to Tibet. Himmler, who believed in Karma and who was fascinated by somewhat crude and fantastic ideas about Asian mysticism, was immediately keen on sending this expedition to Tibet under the auspices of the "SS Ahnenerbe" (SS Ancestral Heritage Society). He wanted Schaefer also to carry out research based on the so-called "Glacial Cosmogony" theory of Hoerbiger. While Himmler intended to use the expedition as a tool for those esoteric pseudo-sciences which the "Ahnenerbe" wanted to promote, Schaefer, as a scientist, had more legitimate scientific purposes in mind and he declined to include Edmund Kiss, a representative of this doctrine, on his team.

Thus Schaefer, in order to obtain the scientific freedom he needed, asked for the acceptance of twelve conditions, all of which were granted by Himmler himself. However, Sievers, the head of the "Ahnenerbe", declared in January 1938, "The task of the expedition in the meantime had diverged too far from the targets of the Reichsfuehrer-SS and does not serve his ideas of cultural studies." Thus, in the end, the expedition was *not* sponsored by the "Ahnenerbe". Himmler, nevertheless, only gave his consent to the expedition on the condition that all of its members join the SS. Schaefer understood that in order for the expedition to succeed, he needed Himmler's support to obtain foreign currency (extremely difficult during the Nazi period). He therefore had to compromise on some points. In preparation for the expedition he had "Schaefer Expedition 1938/39" letterhead printed and applied for sponsorship from businessmen. The expedition's name, however, had to be changed on the order of the "Ahnenerbe" to "German Tibet-Expedition Ernst Schaefer (in big letters), under the patronage of the Reichsfuehrer-SS Himmler and in connection with the Ahnenerbe" (in small letters). This letter head caused him considerable difficulties with the British authorities after his arrival in India.

Schaefer actually raised the funds of his expedition by himself. 80% of the cost of the expedition was financed by the "Werberat der deutschen Wirtschaft" (Public Relations and Advertising Council of German Business) together with large German business enterprises, Deutsche Forschungsgemeinschaft (the Reich Research Council) and Brooke Dolan. The rest was provided by minor contributions. Only the flight back to Germany was sponsored by Himmler's circle of friends.

The expedition began in the spring 1938, going first to Calcutta. When Schaefer arrived there he must have noticed an article about himself in the "Voelkischer Beobachter" (the Nazi propaganda newspaper) which stated that he was undertaking a further expedition on behalf of the SS. An article in the international press was even headlined "A Gestapo agent in India." These articles caused him considerable troubles in negotiating with the British authorities. Later he received a telegram from the Consul General in Calcutta informing him that the government of Tibet refused to permit the entry of the expedition. However, some months later, Schaefer and his crew were admitted to Lhasa, which was considered a great achievement in Germany. How then Schaefer did manage to get the permission to travel to Lhasa?

When Schaefer learnt that the entry into Tibet was still forbidden after having already spent several months in Sikkim, he somehow tricked the British, following the personal advice of Francis Younghusband, "to sneak over the border". He successfully crossed into Tibetan territory for a short time and established friendly contact with local Tibetan officials, who forwarded an application directly to the Tibetan government. In this he referred to his personal acquaintance with the former Panchen Lama, and asked for permission to be the first Germans to enter Lhasa. Some weeks later they received an official letter of invitation with five seals from the Kashag, which stated:

"To the German Doctor Saheb Sha-phar:

Thank for your letter of the 17ᵗʰ day of the 9ᵗʰ of the English month together with two boxes containing a gramophone, records and two pair of binoculars.

Concerning you and the other Germans, Doctor Wienert, Mr. Krause, Mr. Beger, and Mr. Geer (altogether no more than five persons) who want to visit Lhasa and the holy Tibetan monasteries, please understand that no foreigners whatsoever are allowed to enter Tibet.

Although we know if we allow you to enter, others might come the next time, it nevertheless appears from your letter that you intend only friendship and to see the holy land and its religious institutions.

Acknowledging this, we deign to give you permission to go to Lhasa and to stay there for two weeks, on condition that you oblige yourself not to harm the Tibetan people and consent to not hunt any birds or game, which would deeply hurt the feelings of the Tibetan people, both clergy and lay. Please kindly keep this in mind.

Sent from the Tibetan Kashag on the auspicious 3ʳᵈ day of the 10ᵗʰ month of the earth-tiger year."

Schaefer considered this letter from the Kashag a minor sensation, as it was the first official invitation for a German mission to Tibet. It also certainly demonstrated some Tibetan independence from the British. We therefore have to see the German-Tibetan relations of the 1930s in the broader geopolitical context of the rather complicated and ambiguous relations between Britain and Tibet.

The expedition included five members altogether: Schaefer as mammologist and ornithologist, Ernst Krause, entomologist and photographer and movie-operator, and ethnologist, Karl Wienert, geophysicist, and Edmund Geer, technical caravan leader. Some words about Bruno Beger, the anthropologist: he was one of the two true Nazis on the expedition and was strongly influenced by the then leading racist anthropology of Nazi ideology. However, his actions in Tibet in regard to measuring people's skulls and taking masks of their faces was actually within the bounds of international scientific practice at that time. But his later actions in Auschwitz, where he carried out experiments on prisoners, discredited the expedition and contributed to its controversial image today. The actual purpose of the expedition can actually be characterised, in Schaefer's own words: "The expedition might be called a complete natural history expedition, comprising studies of terrestial magnetism, ethnology, anthropology, ornithology, mammology and partly botanics and of course geography.

While in Lhasa, Schaefer successfully extended the mission's stay several times, so that they were able to stay a full two months in Lhasa, instead of two weeks.

Schaefer witnessed the Mönlam festival and gave a most vivid and extensive description of it. The members of the expedition established official contact with the Kashag ministers and the Reting Regent. They also made contact with many aristocratic families. The person who fascinated them most was Dzasa Tsarong, whom they thought to be the only true politician. They valued him as highly as the British representative Hugh Richardson did. And their Tibetan interpreters even had a short biography of him composed, having interviewed him for that purpose. But their most valuable informant, with whom they met almost every day, was Möndro, a high monk official, who had been one of the four boys who had been sent to Rugby school in England in 1913. Möndro was responsible for the police force, but he had been degraded from the 4th to the 7th rank after his motorbike caused a Kashag minister's horse to shy and throw him off.

Upon the completion of the expedition Lord Linlithgow, the Viceroy of India, received Schaefer in a private audience in Simla during the first days of August 1939, just before Schaefer´s return to Germany. Lord Linlithgow congratulated Schaefer on his great success. Moreover, referring to Schaefer's political skills, he told Schaefer that he himself at the same age would have acted just as Schaefer had done. He then revealed to him what Schaefer had suspected for a long time: Hugh Richardson had been sent to Lhasa in order to prevent the expedition's advance there.

This act by the British needs to be understood in light of the ever increasing tensions between Nazi Germany and Britain. The Viceroy explained the British view to Schaefer in a very frank manner and asked him to transmit a personal message to Hitler. Shortly after his return Schaefer tried to see Hitler, but Himmler prevented him from doing so. When Schaefer turned to Canaris (chief of German intelligence) in order to deliver his message, Himmler soon learned of it and was upset. Schaefer was given a severe two-month education in the "SS-Leibstandarte" to break his "behaviour like a general" and to make him obedient.

* * *

The German expedition to Tibet turned out to be highly successful in terms of the scientific material collected as well as in terms of the improvement of the political relations between Germany and Tibet. What were then the reasons for this success?

Firstly, all the members of the expedition tried to learn Tibetan etiquette before they entered Tibet; they took with them to Tibet for this purpose a Sikkimese aristocrat, who also served as one of their interpreters. Schaefer was also clever enough to create the idea of a shared collective identity of Germans and Tibetans by the use of the Swastika, with his motto of a meeting of the Eastern and Western Swastika. Thus a link between the two nations was drawn even on the symbolic level.

Secondly, Schaefer must have been an excellent negotiator. As is clear from his diaries he proved to be successful even when he complained about ill-treatment by the Tibetans. He also seemed to have been very much concerned about his honour, which he often connected with that of Germany. Thirdly, Bruno Beger, the anthropologist of the expedition, had undergone brief medical training that enabled him to treat members of the Tibetan aristocracy successfully. Every morning people queued in front of the government guesthouse where Schaefer and the other men were staying. Thus the expedition members were frequently invited into the houses of the nobility.

For medical treatment of the famous Pha-lha family, they were even given a complete copy of the Lhasa Kanjur (Tibetan Buddhist scriptures).

Finally, the Tibetans simply seemed to have liked and enjoyed the Germans' cheerfulness. According to Schaefer's diaries they were fond of the expedition members singing German songs. It is quite amusing to read about parties in the house of Tsarong. One can imagine the Germans linking arms with the Tibetans and swinging from side to side, singing the most popular songs from the Munich "Octoberfest".

* * *

Although the Schaefer expedition seemed to be very successful, its outcome proved to be tragic. Soon after the return of its members to Germany World War II broke out, and Schaefer was prohibited from publishing his results and giving lectures because of political considerations. On the one hand, he was lionized, his expedition having been the first German mission to reach the "Forbidden City" of Lhasa. On the other hand, Schaefer was considered politically suspect and thought to be some kind of a rebel. In 1941 he was sent to join the "Waffen SS" in Finland, with the order "to be forgotten" there, as he learned later.

Because the "political myths" surrounding the alleged aims of the expedition have contributed greatly to the current notion of Tibet's "pro- Nazi attitude", I want to focus on this specific aspect of the Schaefer expedition.

German-Tibetan relations can best be analysed when we look at the picture Schaefer draws of the Tibetan Regent, Reting Rinpoche, and of Reting's attitude towards the members of the expedition, especially towards Schaefer. In his diaries Schaefer gives a lively and detailed account of his meetings with the Regent. He tells us that, although it was the rule that one had to request an audience at least three days in advance, and that even the prime minister had to wait a long time, Schaefer himself was soon able to have an audience whenever he liked. Though Richardson and various Tibetans told Schaefer that Reting Rinpoche would only grant "ten minutes audiences", Schaefer succeeded in staying with the Regent for more than three hours.

During the German's visits the Regent would be sitting on his throne bed together with his favourite dog. There was always a young boy present, the son of the new Kashag minister, whom he called his favourite. Reting was dressed in a yellow suede coat, with many German pistols and two golden Belgian pistols hanging above him. According to Schaefer he knew little about the outside world, and also little about Buddhism. Schaefer was very keen to learn more about Buddhism and was rather disappointed that Reting could not, or did not like to, respond to his curiosity.

In the beginning Schaefer seemed to be impressed by the personality of the Regent. Schaefer invited him to Germany and they seriously discussed plans for the journey, while several other aristocratic young men also wanted to travel there. Reting wanted to be picked up by a German plane in Calcutta and flown to Germany, but apprently the Kashag would not give consent to the trip. Gradually, however, Schaefer's initial impression changed and his judgement of the Regent became increasingly negative, as the Reting Rinpoche was apparently always seeking some benefit from their contact.

Reting must also have been very fond of Bruno Beger, whom he wanted to engage as a bodyguard and it was rather difficult for Beger to get out of this situation without offending the Regent. Reting suggested that Beger stay in Tibet and that a Geshe ("Doctor of Divinity") go to Germany in exchange, in order to introduce Buddhism there. This might have been the first official attempt by the Tibetans to spread Buddhism in Europe.

Perhaps the most famous outcome of the expedition is the letter the Regent wrote to Hitler. It has played a key role in the legacy of the expedition and the resulting judgement of German-Tibetan relations. Schaefer convinced the Reting Regent to write a letter to Hitler, although Reting probably had little sense of who Hitler was. The address on the envelope of one letter reads:

> "To his Majesty Herr Hitler, Berlin, Germany
> *'Jar man rgyal po har hi ti lar mchog la 'bul*
> *rgyu bod kyi rgyal tshab srid skyong rwa greng ho thog thus*
> *sa yos bod zla chig 1 tshes 18 bzang bor phul'*

The letter in the original translation, (which omits something at the beginning) reads:

> "To his Majesty Fuhrer Adolph, Hitler, Berlin,
> <u>Germany</u>.
>
> From.
>   The Regent of Tibet.
> On the 18ᵗʰ day of the first month of Sand-Hare Year.
>
> Your Majesty,
> I trust your Highness is in best of health and in every progress with your goodly affairs.
> Here I am well and doing my best in our religious and Government affairs.
> I have the pleasure to let Your Majesty know that Dr. Schaefer and his party, who are the first Germans to visit Tibet have been permitted without any objection, and every necessary assistance is rendered on their arrival. Further, I am in desirous to do anything that will help to improve the friendly tie of relationship between the two Nations, and I trust your Majesty will also consider it essential as before.
> Please take care of Your good self, and let me know if Your Majesty desire anything.
> I am sending under separate parcel a Tibetan silver lid and saucer with a red designed tea cup, and a native dog as a small remembrance.
>
>   Sincerely Yours,
>   Reding Ho-Thok-Thu."

Tibetan diplomatic correspondence follows strict rules and upon visual inspection, this letter seems to have been written rather hastily. The lines run too close to the margin. There are no adorning attributes for Hitler and no seal on the letter itself, only on the envelope. There is no space of respect between inscriptio and introduction formula. The space between the lines is too big. According to Loden Sherab Dagyab

Rinpoche it is not a letter to an equal but from someone slightly superior to an inferior. And *phul* is missing at the end in this letter. The letter is a typical example of polite Tibetan correspondence, nothing more.

Many have regarded this letter as proof of the Tibetans' friendly attitude towards Nazi Germany. Reinhard Greve in 1995 published a translation by Johannes Schubert, instead of the much more accurate one made by Helmut Hoffmann. Schubert was a Tibetologist from Leipzig who had sought in vain to enter the Sven-Hedin-Institute in the early forties and he might have thought it advantageous to try to translate this letter in Nazi terms. Thus he may have falsified the translation deliberately as a mean of propaganda for Nazi Germany. But his translation is simply wrong. He also added remarks that are not found in the original document. The most egregious interpolation is: "At present you [Hitler] are making all efforts in creating a lasting empire in peaceful prosperity based on a racial foundation," instead of translating correctly the usual Tibetan phrase: "Here I [Reting] am well and doing my best in our religious and Government affairs." Schubert's translation is relied upon by Neo-Nazis as propaganda for their cause, as they seek to demonstrate Tibetan sympathy for racist ideas. At the same time the left-wing parties of Germany tend to ascribe to the Tibetans an uncritical friendship toward the Nazis.

Conclusion:

For years, professional and amateur scholars have imagined that the Schaefer expedition was steeped in occult Nazi ideology, and this fantasy has been deployed from both ends of the political spectrum. Some recent German publications on Tibet refer explicitly to the expedition, drawing a direct line from Blavatsky's Theosophy to Nazi occultism, citing the Schaefer expedition as evidence. They argue that since the late 1930s there have been occult and esoteric connections between Tibet and Nazi groups, leading to a direct influence on the Dalai Lama by Nazi ideology.

Let me stress here that it is not my purpose to rehabilitate Schaefer or to claim that he was not a Nazi or was not influenced by Nazi ideology. But it is clear that in the preparations and undertaking of the expedition, he approached this expedition as a scientist, seeking to collect scientific materials on Tibet. The goals of the expedition were not political, esoteric or occult. Unfortunately, due to constant misinformation, the fantasy of a "Nazi-Tibet-connection" among certain authors only adds to the already existing "myth" of Tibet, only this time stressing its dark sides. We encounter here what Donald Lopez called the "logic of opposites", in which a highly idealised image of Tibet transforms itself into its darker and equally distorted opposite.

NOTES

[1]Pauwels, Louis – Bergier, Jaques: *The Morning of the Magicians*, New York: Stein and Day 1964, p. 198.
[2]Angebert, Jean-Michel: *The Occult and the Third Reich*, New York: MacMillan 1974, p.71.
[3]"Der Spiegel", No. 16 (1998), p. 111.
[4]Suster, Gerald: *Hitler, the occult Messiah*, New York, St. Martin's 1981, pp. 191-192.
[5]Feigon, Lee: *Demystifying Tibet*, Chicago: Elephant Paperbacks 1996, p. 15.
[6]Recently Martin Brauen did this in a somewhat different way in his excellent "Traumwelt Tibet", Berne (Switz.) 2000, pp.53-81.

UNPUBLISHED SOURCES

Ernst Schaefer: Tagebuecher (diaries), Berlin Bundesarchiv, R135/38-40.
SS-Ahnenerbe, Berlin Bundesarchiv, NS 21/682.
German Captured Records, Washington National Archives, RG 238, M-1270/R27; M-1019/R62 .

PUBLISHED SOURCES:
Bruno Beger: *Mit der deutschen Tibetexpedition Ernst Schaefer 1938/39 nach Lhasa*, Wiesbaden: Schwarz 1998.
Ernst Schaefer: *Fest der weissen Schleier*, Braunschweig: Vieweg 1949.
Ernst Schaefer: *Geheimnis Tibet*, Munich: Bruckmann 1943.

SUGGESTED READINGS:
Martin Brauen: *Traumwelt Tibet*, Bern: Haupt 2000; [English translation forthcoming, 2003, Weatherhill, U.K.]
Reinhard Greve: *Tibetforschung im SS-Ahnenerbe*, in: Thomas Hauschild (Ed.): Lebenslust und Fremdenfurcht, Frankfurt: Suhrkamp 1995, pp. 168-199.
Mark J. Rogers: *The SS-Ahnenerbe and the 1938/39 German-Tibet Expedition*, Atlanta: Georgia State University, M.A. Thesis 2000. (This mainly contains a retelling of the above mentioned "Geheimnis Tibet").

DISCUSSION

A NAZI MISSION?
In discussion the question was raised as to the extent to which the popular under-standing of the Schaeffer mission as a 'Nazi mission' was accurate. One factor that needed to be taken into account was the implacable hostility displayed towards the mission by Hugh Richardson, the then British representative in Lhasa, who clearly saw it in those terms. His judgement had been largely accepted, but the author's research suggested the need for a more nuanced analysis of the motivations of those involved.
In regard to the scientific results of the Schaeffer mission it was noted that they brought back to Germany about 2,500 ethnological objects, mainly those concerned with daily material culture. While some items had been destroyed in the war, the remainder was captured by the Americans in 1945 but eventually returned to Ethnological Museum of Munich, where it remains.

following page
Portrait of an aristocratic woman of Lhasa
wearing typical Central Tibetan coral and pearl headdress,
turquoise ear-rings, a 'gau' (amulet box) at her neck,
and the married woman's striped apron.
The pose and setting, with the European furniture and textiles
of a wealthy Lhasa family is carefully arranged
in the style of Indian studio photography.
1998.285.134 (BL.H.117)

A Brief Survey of Tibetan Relations with the United States

A. Tom Grunfeld

While unofficial contacts between Americans and Tibetans can be traced back to the earliest years of the 20th Century, it was not until the second world war that there was to be any official contact.

In search of a reliable land route for war supplies from India to western China, the U.S. government authorized a mission to cross Tibet in 1942-43, ostensibly to ascertain the viability of such a route. The expedition produced nothing of substance and its true intent remains in dispute.

Wartime exigencies aside, Tibet played no role in U.S. foreign policy interests and the first official U.S. statement on the status of Tibet, in 1943, declared:

> For its part, the Government of the United States has borne in mind the fact that the Chinese Government has long claimed suzerainty over Tibet and the Chinese Constitution lists Tibet among areas constituting the territory of the Republic of China. This Government has at no time raised a question regarding either of these claims

The next official contact came three years later when Tibet, neutral in World War II but determined to end a centuries old policy of isolation, dispatched a "goodwill" mission to congratulate the allies on their victory. However, because the Nationalist (Guomindang, GMD) government of China considered Tibet a part of the Chinese state, the Tibetan delegates were denied visas and remained in India where they presented their congratulations to the foreign embassies.

197

The Lhasa government's next gesture was to send a "Tibetan Trade Mission" to several nations, including the United States, in 1947. Trade was vital to Tibet's economy and there were difficulties. Delegation leader, W.D. Shakabpa, claimed the expedition was designed to ease Indian restrictions on Tibetan trade, expand trade, purchase gold bullion to support the Tibetan currency, and "to demonstrate Tibet's independence and sovereign status." Anglo-Indian officials believed the group's purposes was the enrichment of the participants.

The Tibetans travelled on the first official passports issued by the government in Lhasa. Visas, however, were issued under circumstances which allowed each nation to permit travel but not to accord recognition to the passports. Ultimately the mission failed to enhance Tibet's trade, end Tibet's isolation, or bring international recognition.

Lhasa also tried inviting American journalists to visit the once forbidden land in an attempt to garner some favorable publicity. In that regard the visits were momentarily successful but they changed nothing of significance.

Ultimately, China ended Tibet's isolation. On 1 October 1949 Mao Zedong proclaimed the establishment of the People's Republic of China (PRC) and promised the "liberation" of Tibet from western "imperialism" was imminent.

The communist victory in China made Tibet a greater priority for the United States. U.S. diplomats in the region urged relations with Lhasa to counter communism. But there were two problems; the U.S. alliance with the GMD who insisted that all relations with Tibetans be conducted only through the government on Taiwan and the reluctance of India to act against the PRC. Indian concurrence was considered essential, since India, in the words of the U.S. Ambassador in New Delhi, had a "practical monopoly on Tibet's foreign relations."

Nevertheless, in 1949, American diplomats and Tibetan officials met in India. Tibetans were advised the United States was sympathetic to their predicament although it could not publicly demonstrate concern or involvement. Secret talks continued throughout 1952 but available documentation gives no hint of any aid being provided.

Just about this time an unusual pamphlet surfaced in India. Entitled "Armed Forces Talk No. 348: Tibet—Roof of the World", it was published by the United States Department of Defense and "intended as a lesson plan for military unit commanders or their representatives to use in conducting troop education and information programs," and, was a "part of a continuing program on international awareness." All documentation concerning the pamphlet has either been lost or destroyed, according to the U.S. government.

In the summer of 1950, after the outbreak of the Korean War, Washington began "to initiate psychological warfare and paramilitary operations against the Chinese Communist regime," to, in the words of a government memo, "foster and support anticommunist elements both outside and within China with a view to developing and expanding resistance in China to the Peiping [Beijing] regime's control..."

> Consequently, the U.S. "...[was] now in [a] position [to] give assurances [to the] Tibetans re U.S. aid to Tibet," and that it was "ready to assist procurement and financing;" but only with Indian concurrence.

At Washington's urging, and with its financial support, the Tibetans turned to the United Nations using a public relations firm and an international lawyer. But this also failed as the UN voted to indefinitely postpone the vote.

The main concern of U.S. policymakers was never Tibetan independence. "Historically, the United State Government has recognized a continuing claim by the Government of China to suzerainty over Tibet...," according to a government report. Yet at the same time, "the United States Government believes that Tibet should not be compelled by duress to accept violation of its autonomy and that the Tibetan people should enjoy the rights of self-determination..." The obvious contradiction in this policy was never clarified because Tibetan independence was always secondary to other goals.

When the communist People's Liberation Army (PLA) reached the Tibetan border at Qamdo a battle of several days duration ensued in which the Chinese overcame Tibetan resistence. Several weeks later the Dalai Lama fled Lhasa for the town of Yadong, where U.S. diplomats implored him to cross over into India.

Ultimately the Dalai Lama returned to Lhasa which prompted negotiations with Beijing resulting in the "Agreement of the Central People's Government and the Local Government of Tibet" (Seventeen-Point Agreement). Ironically, Chinese insistence on such a pact demonstrated that Beijing understood that Tibet was not a Chinese province but an entity outside of China's boundaries that required official incorporation.

Washington continued to pursue the Dalai Lama laying out terms in a secret 1951 letter. In return for a "disavowal" of the Seventeen Point Agreement and a public appeal for United Nations and U.S. aid, Washington would totally fund: his exile to another country; the organization and supply of a resistance movement (sending, "...light arms through India"); his brother, Thubten Norbu's travel to the U. S. under the auspices of the American Committee for Free Asia, a Central Intelligence Agency (CIA) -funded anti-communist organization; a propaganda campaign and a personal yearly allowance. The Pontiff rejected all U.S. offers.

While these negotiations were in progress, another of the Dalai Lama's brothers, Gyalo Thondup, began conferring with GMD officials in Taiwan.

Secret U.S.-Tibet talks lasted until 1952 when the U.S. Department of State gave up its efforts to enlist the Dalai Lama into Washington's anti-communist crusade. While State may have given up on Tibet, the CIA was just getting interested.

THE CENTRAL INTELLIGENCE AGENCY

No aspect of Tibetan-United States relations is more controversial than the role of the Central Intelligence Agency. For years the Dalai Lama and his followers denied the relationship existed. Chinese accusations of outside aid were met by the Dalai Lama with retorts that the reports were "completely baseless." In 1961 he was quoted as saying, "the only weapons that the rebels possess are those they've managed to capture from the Chinese. They have guns but they've even been using slingshots, spears, knives, and swords." In 1974 he was unequivocal: "The accusation of CIA aid has no truth behind it. My flight [in 1959] was conditioned by circumstances developing in Lhasa because of Chinese atrocities...."

When Thubten Norbu, was asked by US News and World Report, "Are you getting any weapons to resist the Chinese?" he replied, "There is nothing at all coming in from the outside." In fact, Gyalo Thondup had been receiving arms from the GMD since 1952 and from the CIA in 1956.

In keeping with long-held U.S. policy, the impetus for CIA involvement was not an independent Tibet but rather "...to keep the Communists off balance in Asia."

By 1956 Chinese policies in the Tibetan areas of western Sichuan (Kham) had led to such severe alienation of the local population that a major revolt broke out against Chinese rule. The CIA saw the revolt as an opportunity by which it could escalate its covert harassment of the PRC.

Gyalo Thondup became the Tibetan liaison to the CIA arranging the first training missions. The first group was dropped back into Tibet in the autumn of 1957, from a plane flown by an American pilot. Their mission was to contact rebel forces and to urge the Dalai Lama to publicly appeal for U.S. assistance; only then could Washington publicly support him.

The Dalai Lama's government was split; some supported the rebels while others elected to work with the Chinese. How much the Dalai Lama knew about the rebels' activities remains a mystery. Within Tibet proper the Chinese had promised that traditional Tibetan society would remain intact and it was, to a large degree, until March 1959. Consequently many of the Lhasan aristocracy was more intent on preserving their privileged lifestyles through compromise with the Chinese.

Despite their inability to get the Dalai Lama to join their cause, the CIA went ahead with training and equipping Tibetans rebels. The CIA's proprietary airline, Civil Air Transport, began flying from Thailand using Polish and Czech mercenaries as pilots. Some 25-30 missions dropped some 250-400 Tons of equipment into Tibet from 1957 to 1961: arms, ammunition, radios, medical supplies, hand-operated printing presses and more. By 1958 the U.S. had established a training base at Camp Hale, Colorado and over the next 6 years some 170 guerrillas were trained there.

In March 1959 the Dalai Lama fled Lhasa in a revolt whose origins remain unknown. By 1961 the last of the guerrillas were dropped into Tibet; a total of 49 men since 1957 of whom only 10 made it back out of Tibet; 1 surrendered, 1 had been captured, and the remaining 37 killed.

In 1960 the rebels, with CIA assistence, established a guerrilla base in Mustang, a small semi-autonomous feudal principality in Nepal. By early 1964 the Indian and American governments initiated a Combined Operations Center, funded by Washington, to oversee the Mustang operation. The U.S. supplied materiel and aid, the Tibetans manpower, while India "controlled the territory and therefore the operations." From 1964-1967, 25 teams were sent into Tibet little success. Their activities were confined to ambushes of Chinese military convoys, sabotage of communication lines and the mining of roads and bridges. One foray did bring out some valuable Chinese government documents.

In the realm of propaganda the U.S. created supposedly popular organizations such as the American Emergency Committee for Tibetan Refugees, prodded its clandestinely funded "human rights" organizations (eg., International Commission of Jurists) to prepare "official" report attacking China (some of the Tibetan aid groups were CIA-created fronts, others legitimate organizations penetrated by CIA agents who pushed the Tibetan human rights cause), arranged for press tours for Thubten

Norbu, paid for Tibetan delegations to travel to Geneva to press their case before international organizations and subsidized the establishment of offices in Geneva and New York to allegedly promote Tibetan handicrafts and to publicize the Tibetan cause but really to establish quasi-diplomatic offices for the Dalai Lama. Tibet House in New Delhi was CIA funded. Money also went to Cornell University ($45,000 a year) to educate several Tibetans to prepare them for bureaucratic careers in Dharamsala, the seat of the Dalai Lama's administration in India. There were also direct subsides to the Dalai Lama himself ; from 1959-1974, US$180,000 a year for his personal use.

At this point the Indian government established, with U.S. support, a Tibetan military unit called the Special Frontier Force. Eventually 12,000 Tibetans were trained by U.S. Special Forces (Green Berets) to operate from bases along the Kashmir frontier where they crossed into Tibet planting electronic listening devices.

By 1969 with very little to show, the CIA decided to end the Mustang operation. It lingered until Henry Kissinger's secret visit to Beijing in 1971 when all covert operations in that theater ended. After almost 15 years the guerrillas had been unable to create a sustainable, independent military force, nor a beachhead inside Tibet. When the U.S. prop was pulled out, the whole operation collapsed; the Tibetans in Mustang were left to fend for themselves.

The first phase of the U.S.-Tibetan relationship ended in a betrayal of the dissident Tibetans. For all the money expended, there was never any intention of supporting a military force sufficient to achieve Tibetan independence; the military efforts, the propaganda, the phoney organizations were only intended to harass the government in Beijing.

RECENT TIMES

Meanwhile China underwent momentous changes. In 1971 Lin Biao, Mao Zedong's designated heir, died mysteriously followed in 1976 by Mao himself, leading to a purge of a leadership group dubbed "the gang of four."

Chinese policies changed dramatically; admitting past practices in Tibet were harmful, allowing tourists to visit, appointing Tibetans to positions with a modicum of power and permitting refugees to visit families. In February 1978, the Panchen Lama, second only in stature to the Dalai Lama in Tibetan Buddhism, was released from 14 years of house arrest and prison.

The Dalai Lama responded to these changes by calling for the authorities to open Tibet to visitors which Beijing immediately did. The Dalai Lama then tempered his speeches by speaking less of Tibetan independence and more about the economic well-being of Tibetans; "if the six million Tibetans in Tibet are really happy and prosperous as never before," he declared in 1978, "there is no reason for us to argue otherwise."

In December 1978 Beijing contacted Gyalo Thondup and talks resulted in an agreement to send an investigative delegation to Tibet. The Dalai Lama also began to travel around the world more to gain visibility for his cause visiting the Soviet Union, Mongolia and the United States, all for the first time.

In May 1980 the Dalai Lama sent his second and third delegations to Tibet. In the same year Chinese Communist Party (CCP) leader Hu Yaobang travelled to Tibet and found conditions so appalling he immediately ordered dramatic changes. These changes (only partially implemented), and the acknowledgment that there were serious problems in Tibet, continued to set a climate for compromise. In April 1982 The Dalai Lama sent another delegation to Beijing .

Sadly, an accommodation was not at hand as talks broke down.

As long as the Dalai Lama was talking to Beijing third party support was unnecessary. When talks stalled in the latter half of the 1980s the Dalai Lama had to rethink his options. The result was a plan calling for heightening awareness of Tibet by building popular support on moral grounds (independence, religious freedom, environment, etc.) and using the resultant popular protest to compel governments to line up behind the Dalai Lama by pressuring Beijing to be more flexible at the bargaining table. This strategy called for: more openly political travel; establishment of support groups to lobby their governments; recruitment of parliamentary members from the major nations; peaceful civil disobedience inside Tibet; and, continued appeals for dialogue with Beijing.

In March 1988 the International Campaign for Tibet was founded in Washington, D.C. It sponsored visits by Congressional aides to Tibetan settlements in India and Nepal and published Tibet Press Watch, a compilation of news stories on Tibet as well as Tibet Forum, a Chinese language publication written by Chinese educated expatriate Tibetans and aimed at the exile Chinese dissident community.

All of these efforts began to bear fruit, especially in the U. S. Congress where some members were already angry at China over trade imbalance, human rights issues in general, military sales, the export of prison labor, etc.

In 1987 the Dalai Lama addressed the U.S. Congressional Human Rights Caucus and called for: 1. Tibet to be a zone of peace, 2. abandonment of ethnic Chinese migration to Tibet, 3. respect for human rights and democratic freedoms, 4. respect for the environment, and 5. negotiations on the future status of Tibet.

While the Dalai Lama was in the United States the authorities in Lhasa held a public trial, executing two Tibetans accused of being common criminals. Three days later Lhasa saw its first public demonstrations in 28 years. More disturbances followed on 1 October - China's National Day - which led to bloodshed.

Five days after, in response to the turmoil in Lhasa, the U. S. Senate unanimously passed a resolution similar to the earlier bill in the House of Representatives which tied future military sales to China to the resolution of human rights abuses. In December, President Ronald Reagan signed the bill.

But Congressional resolutions do not represent the official view of the United States. Deputy Assistant Secretary of State for East Asian and Pacific Affairs J. Stapleton Roy, testified to Congress that "...the United States Government considers Tibet to be a part of China and does not in any way recognize the Tibetan government in exile that the Dalai Lama claims to head." Moreover the Dalai Lama, "...is the head of a government in exile" which no government recognizes.

In Tibet things remained quiet until 5 March 1988 (10 March is the anniversary of the 1959 uprising) when Lhasa saw its biggest demonstration ever. Several thousand Tibetans were met with tear gas and electric cattle prods. The Dalai Lama had hoped that a little civil disobedience in Lhasa and the internationalization of the Tibet question would help prod Beijing towards compromise. The plan backfired; unrest in a sensitive border area with a history of rebellion coupled with Western interference in what Beijing believes is an internal matter only served to buttress the arguments of those opposing compromise.

Nonetheless, the Dalai Lama took a bold initiative. Speaking to the European Parliament (to highlight his international support) on 15 June he reiterated much of his earlier Five Point Plan and went one step further saying, for the first time publicly, that he would be willing to return to a Tibet that was less than independent. He proposed a Tibetan political entity "in association" with China.

The speech called the Chinese bluff for he had agreed to the one condition China had always placed on the talks. But in the end Beijing rejected the out-stretched hand.

Meanwhile unrest continued in Tibet and Chinese officials who supported less freedoms, more repression and no compromise with the Dalai Lama were becoming more vocal. "We must deal resolute, accurate and rapid blows against the serious crimes of a small number of separatists," read an editorial in Xizang Ribao (Tibet Daily), on 13 March 1988, "... [they] are the cause of this earthquake and a cancer cell in society."

But not everyone agreed. "There are people who think it necessary to strike down the lamas and destroy the monasteries," the Panchen Lama said on 29 March. "We must not fall back to the errors of the past...I must seriously warn against people who have the idea of dealing merciless blows at the lamas and closing all the temples."

Despite, or perhaps because of, the liberalized policies, demonstrations continued and in March 1988 a political rally which culminated months of marches and protests led to a declaration of martial law in Lhasa and its environs which was to last until May 1990.

Hu Yaobang had initiated a decade long liberalization of policies which resulted in increased use of the Tibetan language, the rebuilding of religious structures and a strengthening of Tibetan culture. The goals were to bring stability to Tibet and accommodation with the Dalai Lama.

In January 1989 the Panchen Lama suddenly died and moderate officials invited the Dalai Lama to attend funerary rites in Beijing while letting him know that there would also be political discussions. But the Dalai Lama's advisors were reluctant to accept; he would not be allowed to visit Lhasa, what would he do if he was treated badly, besides the international Tibet campaign was flourishing so going later would give him more international support.

Turning down the invitation was a grave error. In China the moderates were discredited, their policies had resulted in riots in Lhasa and the Dalai Lama refusing to visit Beijing. Hard liners who favored more repressive policies now came to power over Tibet.

For most of the next decade the CCP Party Secretary in Tibet, Chen Kuiyuan, opposed negotiating with the Dalai Lama believing that when the Pontiff died the international campaign would dissolve. Economic development, Chen believed, would make Tibetans forget about the Dalai Lama so to that end he encouraged Chinese (Han) migration and substantial investment in the region coupled with a strict ban on photographs of the Dalai Lama, restrictions on religious institutions, cultural activities and political activities no matter how benign. While economic investment and tourism have brought material benefit to some Tibetans, the migration of perhaps hundreds of thousands of Han into Tibetan urban areas threatens the continued practice of Tibetan culture. By the time Chen was reassigned, his policies had done more to increase ethnic tensions than to ameliorate them.

In Washington the efforts of the Tibet Lobby continued to succeed with Congress passing legislation allowing for cash grants to Tibetan refugees and scholarships to students as well the establishment of a Cold War throwback called Radio Free Asia to beam U.S. propaganda to Tibet and countries of East Asia where governments were seen as hostile to U.S. interests.

But sensitivity to Tibet's status continued so even though the Dalai Lama has met the last three U.S. Presidents in the White House, the visits were "private" and he has never been formally invited to, nor allowed to sit in, rooms where state visitors are received.

Back in Asia the talks broke down completely with China blaming the Dalai Lama's intransigence on the independence issue and arguing that "...we have never changed our eagerness to hold negotiations." and the Dalai Lama insisting that he was searching for a middle way; "I am not demanding complete independence from China," he declared at a press conference on 1 August 1990, for that demand would be "a little unrealistic."

Chinese leaders' worst nightmare is that the Dalai Lama's efforts will contribute to the breakup of China or damage the Chinese economy through the elimination of trade concessions or boycotts. But for all the clamor on human rights foreign investment in China and the economy continue to grow at a healthy pace. In November 2001 China was admitted into the World Trade Organization.

What China wants most in Tibet is stability and economic development. The Dalai Lama has the same objectives along with a reasonable measure of local autonomy so he can work to preserve and advance Tibetan culture. These are not conflicting intentions and the two sides are closer together than it may seem. But more than 20 years of failed talks has engendered considerable distrust on both sides. The internationalization of the issue has made Beijing defensive and weakened the influence of officials most willing to negotiate with the Dalai Lama. A settlement would greatly benefit both sides; the Dalai Lama would return home, end anti-Chinese activities and preserve his culture and the Chinese government's international image would be considerably enhanced. Moreover, the Dalai Lama would attract considerable foreign investment, easing Beijing's current huge subsides to the region.

For the United States Tibet has no political, economic or strategic importance. Washington pays lip-service to moral values but rarely acts on them. Up until 11 September 2001 there was a debate raging within foreign policy circles over U.S. policy towards China. No more. Now China is needed in the battle against terrorism, China's veto in the UN is essential to further U.S. foreign policy interests and there is always the issue of trade and that huge potential market. As Washington and Beijing find that their interests begin to converge, the Tibet issue will subside further and further into obscurity.

As the second phase of the U.S.-Tibet relationship winds down it is apparent that once again the United States has done more to betray the exile Tibetans community than to help them.

Indisputably the Dalai Lama's major success has been his ability to generate world-wide interest and enchantment with himself, his cause and religion. This allure has led to an infatuation with a romanticized and idealized Tibet as well as propelling it to heights unimagined by the originators of the international campaign; Hollywood movies, rock concerts, celebrities practicing Buddhism, have all combined to make the Dalai Lama and Tibet household words. There is a similar phenomena going on in China where the government's attention to Tibet has resulted in a different sort of a fad; an infatuation with Tibetans as 'noble savages' with their curious ways. Things Tibetan, such as traditional medicine, are becoming very popular.

At first glance all the attention in the United States and the West appears to be good for the anti-Chinese cause. But in reality it may be a Pyrrhic victory for American groupies feel far more about Tibet than they know. They would be deeply disillusioned by the real Tibet having created a "virtual" (in Orville Schell's word) Tibet as an icon, like so much else in American popular culture, a temporary fashion whose time will run out when something else becomes stylish. Tibetans – real people, with a real history, with a real struggle, will have been cartoonized by American (and Chinese) popular culture. It could be the third betrayal.

following page
Monks at Sera Monastery.
1998.285.209 (BL.H.182)

The Transformation of Tibetan National Identity

Warren Smith

Contrary to the Dalai Lama's often-expressed opinion that the most essential issue of Tibet is the happiness of the Tibetan people, I would argue that the essence of the Tibet issue is the identity of the Tibetan people. If Tibetans lose their national identity then there is no more issue of Tibet. Tibetans would then be simply minority nationality Chinese and the history of Tibet as a distinct nation would come to an end. Chinese policy is clearly directed toward that goal. Despite China's minority nationality policies' ostensible aim of nationality autonomy, the ultimate goal was and is assimilation. China's claim to full sovereignty over Tibet cannot tolerate a separate Tibetan national identity. A distinct Tibetan national identity is inherently threatening to China's territorial integrity. Even Tibetan autonomy is a threat to China's national security because autonomy favors the preservation of Tibetan national and cultural identity.

In both Chinese cultural ideology and Marxist-Leninist doctrine the merging of nationalities is considered a natural and inevitable process. Chinese cultural ideology justified the expansion of China's borders and the assimilation of non-Chinese frontier peoples as a natural expansion of culture. Traditional Chinese frontier policy aimed to achieve frontier security through the advance of Chinese civilization. Autonomy under the dependent state system was the typical first step, followed by increasing Chinese control, colonization and assimilation. Marxist-Leninist nationality theory and policy aimed at an ultimate goal of proletarian internationalism, to be achieved by means of class struggle. Autonomy was promised to "minority nationalities," but only as a temporary expedient to co-opt their elites and reduce their opposition until firm political, military and logistical control could be secured and long-range policies of assimilation implemented.

The Chinese Communists miscalculated the ease with which Tibet could be politically integrated and culturally assimilated into China. Tibetan national identity and nationalism were underestimated due to Chinese cultural chauvinism, the belief that Tibet had long been a part of China and therefore there was no real issue of Tibetan independence except as invented and exploited by foreign imperialists, and an overconfidence in the efficacy of Marxist-Leninist nationality policies. China attempted to alter Tibetan national identity by its definition of Tibetans as not a nation but only a minority nationality of the Chinese nation. In Marxist parlance a nation deserves independence whereas a nationality does not.

China maintains that there is no political, or national, issue of Tibet and no issue of China's "invasion" of Tibet in 1950 since Tibet was already a part of China. The only issue of Tibet that China recognizes is the social, or class issue of Tibetan feudalism and the exploitation of Tibetan serfs and slaves by the upper class feudal lords. In order to justify China's liberation of Tibetans from class-based exploitation, Chinese propagandists have had to paint a picture of old Tibet as a "dark, barbaric, feudal Hell on Earth" from which Tibetans were liberated by the Chinese Communist Party. This image of traditional Tibet, forcibly inculcated in the minds of both Chinese and Tibetans, justifies the Chinese conquest of Tibet, denigrates Tibetan culture and devalues Tibetan national identity.

Chinese policy in Tibet has varied from an emphasis upon assimilation or upon autonomy as leftist and rightist tendencies have predominated within the CCP. Tibet enjoyed some degree of autonomy until China achieved physical and logistical control in Tibet in the mid-1950s and began altering the Tibetan political and social systems. "Democratic Reforms" in eastern Tibet in 1956 eliminated much of Tibetan traditional autonomy in those areas, but the Tibet Autonomous Region remained relatively immune. China even implemented a retrenchment policy in the TAR in 1957 after revolt had erupted in eastern Tibet. The retrenchment policy included an indefinite delay in reforms and a reduction in the number of Chinese personnel. Eastern Tibet outside the TAR was not included, with the result that the revolt continued there, eventually spreading to central Tibet.

After the 1959 revolt, Democratic Reforms were imposed in the TAR and all aspects of autonomy were virtually eliminated. Democratic Reforms were implemented in the TAR simultaneous with and as an integral aspect of the repression of the revolt. Indoctrination meetings and "struggle" sessions allowed the Chinese to control Tibetans both socially and politically and to identify all those who had sympathized with the revolt or who opposed Chinese rule. Socialist Transformation, beginning with mutual aid teams and progressing through collectivization and communization,
circumscribed and then eliminated Tibetan economic autonomy. During the Cultural Revolution, Tibet suffered massive cultural destruction and intense assimilative pressures. The Cultural Revolution in Tibet was an attempt to replace Tibetan culture and Tibetan national identity with Chinese "socialist culture" and Chinese national identity.

With the exception of the period of the early 1950s, before China consolidated its presence in Tibet, the first three decades of Chinese rule were characterized by intense emphasis upon assimilation and virtually no allowance of autonomy. After the death of Mao in 1976 and the beginning of the liberalization initiated by Deng Xiaoping in 1979, China reverted to a policy on autonomy in Tibet of the type
envisioned by the CCP's system of National Regional Autonomy but heretofore not actually implemented. The new autonomy policy maintained firm Chinese military and political control, but with some tolerance for what were thought to be the non-politically threatening aspects of Tibetan religion and culture.

China's new policy in Tibet assumed that Tibetan nationalist resistance was eradicated and that the Tibetan political issue was forever resolved. So confident were Chinese officials in 1979 that their propaganda themes were the reality of Tibet that they offered to negotiate the Dalai Lama's return and even offered Tibet as a model to Taiwan of the autonomous status that it too might enjoy within the PRC. That this was a mistake is obvious from the reception the Dalai Lama's representatives received in Tibet, Taiwan's scornful rejection of the "Tibet Model," and the revival of Tibetan religion, culture and nationalism that occurred under the liberalized policies of the 1980s. The revival of Tibetan religion and culture, and their contribution to the revival of Tibetan nationalism, came as a profound shock to Chinese officials. The nationalist demonstrations and riots in Tibet from 1987 to 1989 marked the end of China's experiment with autonomy in Tibet.

Since 1989 China has pursued a policy of political repression, economic development and colonization. Economic development was adopted as an essential component of the solution to the Tibetan issue at the Second Tibet Work Forum in 1984, which reversed the decision of the 1980 First Tibet Work Forum to reduce the number of Chinese officials in Tibet. Deng Xiaoping's 1987 statement that a limitation of the numbers of Chinese would no longer be a criteria upon which China's Tibet policy would be judged opened the door to colonization. Chen Kuiyuan's announcement in 1992 that Tibet's "special characteristics" would not be allowed to hinder economic development provided the ideological legitimization for China's abandonment of its promise to allow autonomy in Tibet. Although China continued to proclaim its willingness to negotiate with the Dalai Lama, with certain preconditions, this had become little more than a propaganda exercise.

China's offer to "negotiate" with the Dalai Lama dates from the euphoric period of late 1979 when it was thought that both the Tibet and Taiwan issues could be quickly resolved. Assuming that the only remaining issue of Tibet was the final legitimization of Chinese rule by means of the return of the Dalai Lama, Deng offered to negotiate that issue and that alone. Deng's reported offer to negotiate "anything but Tibetan independence" did not signify a willingness to negotiate the political status of Tibet up to but not including independence. By "Tibetan independence" Deng apparently meant the entirety of the issue of Tibet's political status, based as it is upon Tibet's claim to have been independent before 1950. What Deng, then, indicated was a willingness to negotiate anything but the political status of Tibet. This excluded even the nature and territorial extent of Tibetan autonomy and left only the personal status of the Dalai Lama, which, as the experience of Tibetan negotiators sent to Beijing in 1982 and 1984 was to demonstrate, was all that the Chinese were willing to discuss.

Since the Tibetan political issue had proved to be much less resolved than the Chinese had imagined in 1979, the enthusiasm on the Chinese side for the Dalai Lama's return waned after the last meeting with his representatives in 1984. The last serious overture from the Chinese side came after the death of the Panchen Lama in January 1989. The Dalai Lama was invited to attend memorial ceremonies in Beijing. However, having already recognized China's attempts to isolate the issue of the Dalai Lama's return from the political issue of Tibet and to negotiate only with the Dalai Lama or his personal representatives to the exclusion of representatives of the Tibetan Government in Exile, the Tibetan side declined. Dharamsala may also have overestimated the influence of its recently increased international support in creating pressure upon the Chinese to negotiate. Nevertheless, a general hardening of Chinese policy in Tibet following the demonstrations and riots of 1987-89 and in China following Tiananmen in June 1989 probably precluded any serious Sino-Tibetan negotiations. A subsequent request from some officials of the United Front Work Department to the Dalai Lama to "assist" in the selection of the reincarnation of the Panchen Lama failed to revive Sino-Tibetan dialogue. The Dalai Lama's announcement of Gendhun Choekyi Nyima as the new Panchen Lama was regarded by the Chinese as a challenge to their authority in Tibet.

Since the Third Tibet Work Forum in 1994, the Chinese have engaged in an anti-Dalai Lama campaign within Tibet and internationally that leaves little doubt that China has no intention of negotiating with him about Tibet's future and no longer has any desire to see him return. The Chinese Government continually expresses its willingness to negotiate if the Dalai Lama will give up Tibetan independence and acknowledge that Tibet is an inalienable part of China, as is Taiwan. The Tibetan side also continues to promote negotiations, based upon the Dalai Lama's acceptance of autonomy under China, but this seems an increasingly forlorn hope. Since China apparently has no real intention of negotiating, its expressed willingness to negotiate under certain conditions becomes a convenient screen behind which it can pursue its policies of assimilation in Tibet.

The majority of Chinese officials now apparently regard Tibetan autonomy as incompatible with China's territorial integrity and national security. Having seen what they regarded as a liberal policy of autonomy in the 1950's, especially the retrenchment policy of 1957, lead to the Tibetan revolt, and a similar policy in the 1980s lead to a revival of Tibetan religion, culture and nationalism and the internationalization of the Tibetan issue, Chinese policy makers may quite reasonably argue that China's security interests preclude any form of Tibetan autonomy in the foreseeable future. The belief that "hostile Western forces" are exploiting the Tibet issue in order to contain, weaken and split China only reinforces Chinese resolve to prevent any semblance of actual Tibetan autonomy.

Chinese officials may quite rationally maintain that China's security in Tibet can never be trusted to Tibetans and that the only permanent solution to the Tibet issue is assimilation and colonization. Autonomy would only perpetuate the Tibetan political issue, compromise China's security and delay the final solution. Chinese leaders may say that they have tried autonomy and found that it didn't work, that Tibetans have proved that they are insufficiently loyal to China and that they will exploit autonomy to revive Tibetan nationalism. China condemned the Dalai Lama's 1987 acceptance of autonomy under a status of "association" with China as "semi-independence," "disguised independence" and "failure to give up the idea of independence." Chinese leaders have not forgotten British promotion of Tibetan autonomy under Chinese "suzerainty" in the early 20th century, a proposal that China rejected at the time as an attempt to foster Tibetan independence.

There is a saying in Tibetan: "Tibetans are betrayed by their hopefulness, the Chinese by their suspiciousness." This saying, I believe, defines the current situation. Tibetans cannot give up hope for negotiations because they think that negotiations are their only hope. However, given their suspicions about Tibetan loyalty, the Chinese will not negotiate Tibet's status and will not allow any real autonomy. The Dalai Lama is often quoted as saying he wishes he could convince the Chinese of his sincerity about giving up independence in favor of autonomy. However, the Chinese will not be convinced, given that they believe autonomy inevitably fosters Tibetan nationalism and allows for the survival of the independence issue. There is also the issue of the Dalai Lama's refusal to give up the claim that Tibet was once independent. This is intolerable to the Chinese since if Tibet were independent before 1950 then China's "peaceful liberation" was in fact imperialist conquest.

China's current anti-Dalai Lama campaign, both within Tibet and internationally, should convince anyone not afflicted with unrealistic hopefulness that the Chinese have no intention of negotiating with him. Many Chinese apparently believe that all they have to do to finally resolve the Tibet issue, or at least the Dalai Lama issue, is to await his demise and then chose his reincarnation within China. The Tibetan hope that some future democratic Chinese government will negotiate Tibet's status seems equally futile given that Tibetan autonomy poses the same national security threat to any Chinese government. Another Chinese attempt to allow some cultural autonomy in Tibet in the future is conceivable, under a different Chinese government, but, given the persistence of Tibetan nationalism, the results are likely to be the same as those of the Chinese experiment in the 1980s.

The Dalai Lama may also be excessively optimistic about the potential for the survival of Tibetan culture and identity under Chinese autonomy. China's need for "unity and stability" will always predominate over promises of Tibetan autonomy. Chinese national security considerations will always require the restriction of Tibetan autonomy. The reality of cultural, economic, linguistic and political pressures inherent in Tibet's integration within China will threaten Tibetan national identity. Tibetans' hope for meaningful autonomy within China, by means of negotiations or otherwise, or that autonomy can realistically allow for the survival of Tibetan culture, seem to exemplify the saying about excessive hopefulness being Tibetans' downfall.

The Tibetan Government in Exile's hope for negotiations with China is not only imposed upon Tibetans but also upon international governments that have adopted policies on Tibet. In accordance with Tibetan Government in Exile policy, all such international governments have expressed support for negotiations with China. Perhaps some believe that this is a real possibility. It also serves, however, as a convenient way to show support without doing anything about the issue or anything excessively offensive to China. Pious platitudes about how China should negotiate with the Dalai Lama are certainly easier than a realistic and meaningful policy position. The negotiation strategy also belittles the complexity and significance of the Tibetan political issue, as if the problem between China and Tibet were a simple misunderstanding that might be resolved by friendly talks.

Is there, then, no hope for the survival of Tibetan national identity? One can make the case that hope for the survival of Tibetan identity was abandoned when autonomy under China was accepted, in 1951 and again in 1987. Is hopelessness, at least in regard to negotiations, a better policy than hopefulness? In answer to this question, reality is certainly better than illusion. There is no reason for the policy of the Dalai Lama and the Tibetan Government in exile to be constrained by unrealistic hopes for negotiations with China. Similarly, they should more realistically appraise the difficulties of preserving Tibetan national identity within Tibet under whatever limited autonomy China is likely to allow.

A reading of current Chinese propaganda on Tibet reveals a sense of satisfaction with the policies implemented by the Third Work Forum. China is bothered by foreign criticism, but international criticism about Tibet is considered preferable to the separatist threat that inevitably comes with Tibetan autonomy. China is not concerned about the happiness of the Tibetan people, at least in the way that the Dalai Lama would define their happiness, only in their conformity. China has cultivated a cadre of compliant Tibetan officials whom it considers the best indication of "stability and unity" in Tibet. To the Chinese, economic development along with ever increasing numbers of Chinese in Tibet seems to hold the key to the Tibetan political problem.

China's current policy in Tibet is successful, from the Chinese point of view, on all fronts but one. China has failed to convince the world of the legitimacy and the benefits of its rule over Tibet. Even within Tibet the Chinese Government can never be sure of the loyalty of Tibetans because its repression prevents Tibetans expressing their true opinions. China's only solution to this problem is more propaganda of the same type both internally and internationally. Although it is currently losing the propaganda battle about Tibet, China has not accepted defeat even on this front; its propaganda is still believed by most Chinese and it occasionally finds some international support. China has recently intensified its propaganda campaign about Tibet, with testimonials of the benefits of Chinese rule from Tibetans during the 50th anniversary celebrations of China's "liberation" of Tibet and with the dispatch of numerous delegations of Tibetan officials and scholars on international tours to promote China's Tibet policies.

The international Tibet issue has now become primarily an ideological struggle, one that will presumably continue as long as China rules over Tibet. The subject of the ideological struggle about Tibet, like the political struggle, is Tibetan national identity. The ideological struggle is as important as the political struggle in regard to the survival of Tibetan national identity since national identity is essentially subjective, or ideological. China's annexation of Tibet and all its political campaigns in Tibet have been aimed at the elimination, or at least a transformation, of Tibetan national identity. The ideological struggle has the same aim, to transform Tibetan national identity, past, present and future, into Chinese national identity. China currently has all the power in the political struggle, but the ideological struggle is more evenly matched. China's propaganda machine is hampered by its jargon and its inability to justify Chinese rule over a non-Chinese people. The Tibetan self-determination argument is very persuasive and one that China cannot logically counter.

As to whether Tibetan national identity will survive, only Tibetans themselves can answer that question. Whether this is the end of Tibetan history or not depends upon whether Tibetans can preserve their national identity. The principle of self-determination applies to national identity as much as it does to national destiny. Self-determination has two meanings: the first is a right, recognized by international law, of nations to preserve their culture and identity and to chose their own political organization and representation. However, this theoretical right conflicts with states' rights to territorial integrity. States' interests usually prevail over nations' rights to self-determination since international law is a system of relations between states rather than a system of international justice.

The second meaning of self-determination then becomes more potentially significant. This meaning is that the self in self-determination, the nation, has not only the right but also the responsibility to determine its destiny. Self-determination must be self-determined. Tibetans are responsible for their own self-determination, the survival of their own national identity and their national destiny. Non-Tibetans can play a supportive role, or, in China's case, a non-supportive role, but Tibet's ultimate fate depends upon Tibetans. Tibet's best hope lies in the cultivation of information, knowledge and education that will facilitate the struggle for the survival of Tibetan national identity.

In answer to the usual argument that autonomy is feasible, or that it is all that Tibet is likely to get, whereas self-determination in any form is impossible, I believe that the history of Sino-Tibetan relations has demonstrated that meaningful Tibetan autonomy under China is impossible. The Dalai Lama is himself on record as having said so, in *My Land and My People*. Autonomy of the type that China is likely to allow is no guarantee for the survival of Tibetan national identity; in fact, Chinese policy is clearly aimed at the elimination of Tibetan national identity. Autonomy, unlike self-determination, is a status that is "given" or "allowed" by the dominant power and its parameters are determined by the giver, not the recipient. The British could never give any substance to their definition of Tibetan "suzerainty" under China and had finally to admit that the status of suzerainty, in the words of Hugh Richardson, "had never been defined and, indeed, appears incapable of definition."

The difficulty in defining autonomy is illustrated by the Dalai Lama's recent misadventure in calling for "self-rule" in Kashmir. What the Dalai Lama apparently meant by self-rule was autonomy of the type he envisages for Tibet. However, the Indian media and public interpreted self-rule as equivalent to self-determination, or, in the case of Kashmir, independence or integration with Pakistan. The Dalai Lama had to quickly backtrack and say that he regarded Kashmir as an integral part of India and that he did not regard the political situation of Kashmir and Tibet as similar. The episode illustrates the incompatibility, in the popular conception and, I believe, in reality, of autonomy with self-rule or self-determination. The Dalai Lama's statement to an Indian journalist that, "if the Chinese treat us as equal brothers, there is no reason for us to demand a separate nation," was a reminder of his idealistic political views.

The acceptance of autonomy under China is equivalent to an admission that Tibetans are Chinese. This has an undeniable effect upon Tibetan national identity, one that the Chinese themselves have long been trying to achieve. Self-determination for the Tibetan people may be unlikely at this time, but it is as likely, I would maintain, as is an autonomy that would satisfy the Dalai Lama's definition of self-rule. The self-determination policy has greater potential for the survival of Tibetan national identity because the issue is ideological; a self-determination policy preserves Tibetan national identity in the ideological sense better than does autonomy. Self-determination as a political policy has the advantage that it preserves Tibetan national identity, at least in the ideological sense, whereas autonomy is unable to preserve it in any sense at all.

One may ask the logical question: how long will the negotiations policy be maintained? It is already 20 years old, since Deng Xiaoping's overtures to the Dalai Lama in 1979-80, without achieving any result. Will this policy be maintained for another five years? Ten years? As long as the 14th Dalai Lama is with us? The European Parliament recently announced a deadline of three years for the Chinese to negotiate, after which it will reconsider its policy on Tibet. The Tibetan Government in Exile should consider a similar deadline, after which it would reconsider its policy, including the possible abandonment of the negotiations and autonomy policy in favor of Tibetan self-determination.

Such a change in policy would undoubtedly have an effect upon Tibet's international support. The Dalai Lama's "reasonable" and "conciliatory" policy on negotiations and his acceptance of autonomy, after all, had much to do with his Nobel Peace Prize. Governments that have found it convenient and relatively easy to support a call for negotiations about Tibet will find it more difficult to support Tibetan self-determination. Self-determination is usually interpreted as equivalent to independence, since it is assumed that most peoples, given a free choice, would undoubtedly choose to be independent of foreign control. However, the actual meaning is only that peoples should have the right to choose for themselves their political affiliation and representation. This could mean either independence or autonomy. This caveat gives governments plausible deniability that by favoring Tibetan self-determination they are necessarily supporting Tibetan independence. The US Government at one time (1960) announced its support for Tibetan self-determination while at the same time recognizing only Tibetan autonomy at the United Nations and elsewhere, particularly in US relations with Nationalist China.

In the past, before 1950, even those countries that became aware that China's claims to sovereignty over Tibet were fictitious, such as Britain and the United States, were constrained from support for Tibetan independence out of fear of damaging their relations with and their privileges in China. Those countries now aware that Chinese rule over Tibet is illegitimate are similarly constrained. The Chinese constantly remind us that no country in the world recognizes Tibetan independence, a fact that illustrates China's successful hegemony over the issue of Tibet in the past if not always over Tibet itself. The self-determination policy potentially transcends both international constraints and China's hegemony over the issue.

No doubt, no country will rush to announce its support for Tibetan self-determination. However, except for the era when Tibet was an issue of state policy, for the British during the Great Game and the Americans during the Cold War, Tibet has been a popular issue, driven by popular support, not state interest. Popular interest, activism and lobbying have been responsible for almost all current international governmental support for Tibet. Popular activism will have a more difficult task in achieving governmental support for Tibetan self-determination than for the relatively easier negotiations policy. However, once it is realized on the popular level that the hope for negotiations is futile, then self-determination becomes the only, and, I believe, a better, alternative.

DISCUSSION

QUESTIONS OF NATIONAL IDENTITY

The question was raised as to how we should define Tibetan national identity. Given the complex nature of this issue, one that occupies scholars in many areas, no agreed definition was forthcoming, but a number of possible aspects and considerations were raised. One definition was that national identity did not necessarily equate to territory or culture, but consisted of a group's complex pride and belief that they were a separate nation, a characteristic shared by all national groups. Thus a group might lose territory, land, religion, etc., and still have a national identity.

Confusion over the differences between ethnic and national identity was noted and the view was expressed that 'national identity tends to arise when you are made aware of it by some outside influence or outside stress' – that it is therefore something decided by insiders not outsiders – and that this had happened to Tibetans in the 20th century. Reflecting the wider debate over the origins of nationalism, some observers concluded that Tibetan national identity had early roots, and thus we needed to consider such aspects as their shared ritual language dating back to the 7th century. The understanding that the origins of nation-state identity were a Western phenomenon was not accepted uncritically and refined views of the existence of local, regional and national levels of identity were discussed. There was general agreement over the organic nature of national identity, that ultimately 'identity is something that is growing and changing all the time'. The question for the future perhaps was whether Tibetans would stop feeling Tibetan!

Bell's entry:
"(d) Rug sellers in Gyantse.
Group, mainly women with Gyantse style headdresses."
1998.285.472 (BL.P.143)

On Modern Tibetan History: Moving Beyond Stereotypes[1]

Melvyn C. Goldstein

Introduction

Our understanding of post-1950 Tibetan history has been constrained by an overly simplistic approach that analyzes Sino-Tibetan relations as if "Tibetans" and "Chinese" were really two homogeneous entities. Adherence to this perspective has distorted our understanding of the modern period and obscured essential intra-Tibetan and intra-Chinese differences. This overview essay illustrates the need for a more nuanced approach to modern Tibetan history by briefly examining a major strategic conflict in the Chinese Communist Party in Tibet[2] and its interaction with different elements within Tibet.

The End of Defacto Independence

The victory of the Chinese communist party (CCP) over the Guomindang (GMD) in 1949 began a new chapter in Sino-Tibetan relations that quickly ended four decades of Tibetan de-facto independence.

In 1913, after the collapse of the Qing Dynasty, the 13th Dalai Lama expelled all Manchu/Chinese officials and troops from Tibet and unilaterally declared that Tibet would be ruled without any outside interference. These acts created a de-facto independent Tibet that maintained its own army and government, used its own language and currency and regulated movement across its borders.

This new status, however, was contested by the post-Qing Chinese government which continued to insist vociferously that Tibet was jurally a part of China, although, at the time, it was unable to exercise any authority there. The Tibetan government, therefore, almost immediately found itself faced with a major threat since China might at any time try to reverse the political situation militarily. Key issues facing the Thirteenth Dalai Lama and his government included how to create a military force that could defend its contested status against China, how to secure recognition and/or protection from other countries such as Britain, or, alternatively, how to negotiate a mutually acceptable status with the new Chinese government.

As we know, Tibet successfully maintained its de-facto independence for 4 decades despite continuing Chinese protests and threats. However, it failed to obtain either a negotiated settlement with China or international acceptance of its unilaterally declared status. Moreover, its success in preserving its de-facto independence was deceptive. Beneath the surface, the seeds of Tibet's own destruction were present. Within the Tibetan political and religious elite, anti-modernization views prevailed and created a Tibet that was poorly prepared to defend its contested status. Tibet's success until 1950, in fact, was based more on historical serendipity than effective policies by the Tibetan government. A concatenation of fortuitous historical forces including the fall of the Qing Dynasty, the chaotic early years of the Republican and Nationalist governments in China, the Japanese invasion of China and then WWII, restrained China from imposing its view of the Tibet Question on Lhasa. In a sense, it allowed those in Tibet who feared modernization more than China, an illusion of victory.

The end of WW II began a shift in Tibet's historical "luck." The defeat of the AXIS ended the Tibet government's hope that a victory by Japan over China would solve the threat from Beijing. Similarly, the international community declined to include the Tibetan question in the post-WWII self-determination/ independence discussions despite doing so for Mongolia. And finally, the Civil War in China did not weaken China internally, at least for long.

So as the second half of the 20th century began, although Tibet was still operating as a de-facto independent polity, it now found itself confronted by a powerful and unified China that was committed to immediately incorporating Tibet into the People's Republic of China (PRC). The rest of the twentieth century would be consumed by both sides jockeying to adapt to the new reality.

Incorporation into the PRC

For Mao and the new Chinese Communist government, the key question was how to proceed to incorporate or from their perspective, reunify Tibet. It would have been easy, given the state of Tibet's military ineptness, for China simply to send in the battle-seasoned People's Liberation Army (PLA) and forcefully "liberate" Tibet as it had the rest of China. But it chose not to, except as a last resort. Instead it opted to achieve a "peaceful liberation," which in its jargon meant re-incorporation with the agreement of the Dalai Lama (the Tibetan government). The PRC went through a long carrot-and-stick process in order to compel the Dalai Lama and his government to agree to a formal written agreement accepting Chinese sovereignty over Tibet.

To make this incorporation more palatable, on the "carrot" side, Beijing proposed an ethnically sensitive policy that I have elsewhere called "gradualism."

Mao's gradualist policy for Tibet focused on working through the elites, especially the Dalai Lama, and *gradually* winning them over. Mao felt this strategy would avoid making Tibetans hostile and prone to splittist activities and would gradually convince them to genuinely accept being an integral part of China. It would also minimize the likelihood of attempts at political intervention by India or the West. Consequently, Beijing indicated that Tibetan language, religion and customs would be respected and maintained, and the Dalai Lama's government allowed to continue, at least for some period. Beijing, therefore, repeatedly called on the Dalai Lama to send a delegation to negotiate its "peaceful liberation."

The Tibetan government, however, initially refused to discuss terms of Tibet's incorporation into the PRC. It stalled sending a delegation to Beijing while it sought external military and political support from the West and the U.N. The Chinese responded to this situation by unleashing the "stick." In October 1950 it invaded Tibet's Eastern Province and captured the entire Tibetan army/administration in a two week campaign. This defeat, coupled with the absence of support from the West and India, led the Dalai Lama to finally send a delegation to Beijing in March of 1951. The resultant agreement they signed was called the "17 Point Agreement for the Peaceful Liberation of Tibet." In it, Tibet accepted Chinese sovereignty and China agreed to permit the traditional government to continue to rule Tibet internally until such a time that the leaders and people of Tibet wanted reforms. The Agreement ended Tibet's claim of independence and de-internationalised the Tibet Question, but also gave Tibet a unique, and higher, status within the PRC. It was the only entity incorporated by a written agreement that left the traditional government in power internally.

At the time of the negotiations in Beijing, the Dalai Lama and his top officials were residing in Yadong, a town on the Indian border where they had moved so as to be able to easily flee into exile should the PLA invade central Tibet. The Chinese "gradualist" policy spelled out in the 17 Point Agreement persuaded the Dalai Lama to return to Lhasa, despite strong American pressure for them to flee Tibet and go into exile. This was a great victory for Mao's policy and initiated a new chapter in Tibetan and Chinese history.

The question for the Dalai Lama and the Tibetan government now was what strategy or strategies they should pursue to meet their goals, and more basically, what should their goals be? For example, while the Tibetan government could no longer overtly claim independence, should they covertly continue to contest Chinese sovereignty, and if so how? Should they seek to renegotiate parts of the 17 Point Agreement, or conversely, should they themselves move to rapidly implement reforms to bring Tibet's social system more into line with that of the PRC? Space limitations preclude discussing this aspect of the internal Tibetan situation and it will have to suffice to say that there were different voices and strategies about what should be done.

Instead, let us turn to internal differences within the Chinese Communist Party in Tibet since this aspect of modern Tibetan history is poorly understood. The CCP in Tibet is usually portrayed as a unified entity but from the beginning it was enmeshed in a hotly contested dispute over policy and strategy between officials from the N.W. and S.W. Military-Administrative Bureaus.

Immediately after liberation, China was divided into six large regions, four of which were administrated by Military-Administrative Bureaus. These were considered transitional entities that would quickly be transformed into civilian "people's" governments when conditions stabilized. The N.W. Bureau was headed by Peng Dehuai and was associated with the First Army Corps (c. Diyi yezhang jun). Its catchment area included Qinghai, Gansu, Xinjiang, Ningxia and Shaanxi. The S.W. Bureau was headed by Liu Bocheng and Deng Xiaoping and was associated with the Second Army Corps (c. Diar yezhang jun). Its catchment area included Sichuan, Xikang, Yunnan and Guizhou (and after 1951, Tibet).

The conflict was played out in the Tibet Work Committee (TWC) (c. Xizang gongwei). This was the Chinese government's leading administrative office in Tibet. All important issues on Tibet affairs were discussed and decided by it (in the sphere of the CCP's activities), although final decisions rested with Beijing.

Tensions existed between these two Bureaus going back to the Chamdo Campaign when virtually all of the credit for the victory went to the S.W. Bureau whose 18th Army captured Chamdo. The N.W. Bureau, however, also played a critical role in the victory.

The strategic goal of the Chamdo campaign was not to capture Chamdo per se, but rather to encircle and disable the entire Tibetan army deployed there. The Tibetan troops in Chamdo were the backbone of the Tibet government's army and the Chinese aim was to prevent these troops from returning to Central Tibet as a fighting force. Preventing this, they felt, would make total military conquest of Tibet easier if it came to that, but more importantly, would likely demoralize the Tibetan government and push them to acquiesce to "peaceful incorporation." Cutting off the road from Chamdo to Lhasa, therefore, was an essential goal of the campaign, and doing so required seizing control over the key bridge at Lagong Ngamda (south of Riwoche). That task fell to the 1st Cavalry of the N.W. Bureau under Fan Ming. They marched night and day from Jyekundo (in Qinghai Province) and arrived at the bridge just before Ngabö's forces arrived in flight from Chamdo. Their presence there led Ngabö to stop his retreat and surrender his forces. Ngabö actually surrendered to elements of the S.W. Bureau's 18th Army (who were pursuing Ngabö moving west from Chamdo), but his capture was made possible by the extraordinary effort of the N.W. Bureau's force.

There were also important differences between the N.W. Bureau and the S.W. Bureau concerning the position of the Panchen and Dalai Lamas. In the simplest terms, the N.W. Bureau supported the Panchen Lama (who was resident in their area) and the S.W. Bureau supported the Dalai Lama. In fact, in early November of 1950, the Central Committee had instructed the N.W. Bureau to prepare to accompany the Panchen Lama back to Shigatse and take responsibility for "Back Tibet" (c. Hou zang) and Western Tibet (c. Ali, t. Ngari). The S.W. Bureau would do the same for "Front Tibet" and the Dalai Lama (c. Qian zang). This classification was based on Qing Dynasty history which talks about a Front Tibet (Central Tibet held by the Dalai Lama) Tibet and a Back Tibet (the southwest area held by the Panchen Lama) as separate entities. In early 1951, however, the Central Committee changed their position. Although both the N.W. and S.W. Bureaus would still send troops to Tibet, it now decided that there should be a unified Tibet and that the TWC of the S.W. and N.W. Bureaus should merge into one new TWC after their troops and officials arrived in Lhasa.

Fan Ming's troops entered Tibet in December 1951, a little over a month after the main S.W. Bureau force under Zhang Guohua arrived. From the beginning, there were problems. Fan Ming was unhappy with his reception from both the Tibetan government and the PLA (S.W. Bureau) forces in Lhasa. The Tibetan government sent only a middle level 4th rank official to greet him outside Lhasa as was the custom, and neither Zhang Jingwu or Zhang Guohua went to greet him from the PLA side. While they considered Fan Ming's status lower than theirs, Fan Ming considered himself their equal. He saw himself as head of the N.W. Bureau's TWC just as Zhang Guohua was head of the S.W. Bureau's TWC. The fact that the S.W. Bureau had sent the majority of the troops did not change that for him.

Initially, Beijing appointed Zhang Guohua as the 1st party secretary of the new combined TWC, but almost immediately, due to these tensions, it rescinded this decision and appointed Zhang Jingwu as the 1st party secretary (with Zhang Guohua and Fan Ming as Vice Secretaries). Zhang Jingwu had come from Beijing to Tibet via India as the representative of Mao and the Central Committee to the Dalai Lama. He had been slated to return to Beijing after a few months and had not been attached to either of the two Bureau's TWC, nor was he included in the initial combined TWC. This shift meant that it was Zhang Jingwu who would now remain in Tibet. And it also meant that Fan Ming was not directly under Zhang Guohua's authority.

Fan Ming, moreover, was very successful in placing his people in key positions in the party's administration, in large part because the central government wanted to minimize conflict. Fan Ming, therefore, became Director of the very important United Front Bureau and two other top N.W. Bureau officials, Mu Shenzhong and Ya Hanzhang, became respectively Director of the Organization Bureau (which was in charge of personnel) and Secretary General of the Leadership Committee.

These organizational tensions were paralleled by two very different viewpoints on what should be done in Tibet. Zhang Guohua and the others of the S.W. Bureau followed Mao's position that it is necessary to keep nationality and religion uppermost in mind when working in Tibet and to not push for quick reforms. This view held that the Tibetan Government and the Dalai Lama should be placed in the priority position in Tibet, and that winning over the Dalai Lama was the key to gaining long-term stability and security for China in Tibet. Mao also supported postponing implementation of terms of the 17 Point Agreement that the Tibetan government was uncomfortable with, e.g., the creation of a Military-Administrative Bureau in Tibet.

Mao advocated this because he understood the unique difficulties China faced in Tibet because of its theocratic government, conservative and religious populace and the absence of resident Chinese. Consequently, he felt it was critical to go slow and make a favorable impression on the Lhasa elite in order to secure China's long term interests—i.e., genuinely winning over Tibetans to being part of China. In 1951, for example, when Zhang Guohua was about to leave Beijing for Tibet, Mao told him that when he arrived in Lhasa and met the Dalai Lama he should prostrate before the Dalai Lama in accordance with Tibetan custom. When Zhang Gouhua responded to Mao that he thought a salute would be enough, Mao got angry and told him, " Zhang Guohua, you have sweated and shed blood for the revolution so why can't you prostrate three times for the revolution?" Zhang did not respond (Anonymous interview). [Actually, when Zhang Guohua reached Lhasa and had his initial "ceremonial" meeting with the Dalai Lama, he paid his respects by giving the Dalai Lama a Tibetan scarf and a traditional ritual offering called Mendre tensum. But he did not prostrate. Instead, he asked the ranking Tibetan cadre in the TWC to prostrate in his place.]

Fan Ming (and the other senior officials of the N.W. Bureau in Lhasa), on the other hand, felt strongly that it was futile to try to win over the Lhasa religious and secular elite to reform Tibet. They considered them hopelessly reactionary and splittists, and argued that the best thing for China was to eliminate their power and authority as quickly as possible and implement the 17 Point Agreement fully. The status of the Panchen Lama was a major issue for him.

Based on the Qing Dynasty's notion of a Front and Back Tibet as separate entities, Fan Ming rejected the position that the Panchen Lama was traditionally subordinate to the Dalai Lama politically. Because of this, and because the Panchen Lama and his officials were considered "progressives," he felt that the CCP should be favoring them not the reactionary Lhasa elite.

The Ninth Panchen Lama had fled to exile in China in 1924 together with his top officials after a dispute with the Thirteenth Dalai Lama over taxes and autonomy. After this flight, the Tibetan government took control of the Panchen Lama's many landed estates. In subsequent years, the Panchen Lama tried to negotiate a rapprochement with the Tibetan government from exile in China but was unsuccessful and he died in Qinghai Province in 1937. The search for a new incarnation of the Panchen Lama was started and led to Lhasa identifying several candidates while the retinue of the late Panchen Lama (still in exile in China) also discovered a candidate in Qinghai Province. The Panchen Lama's officials insisted their candidate was the true reincarnation, but Lhasa would not recognize this. Instead it said that the Qinghai candidate must be sent to Lhasa for tests and the Dalai Lama's final decision. The Panchen Lama's retinue refused to acquiesce and unilaterally recognized their candidate as the new Tenth Panchen Lama. Although the Dalai Lama did not recognize this selection, the Panchen Lama's retinue secured China's recognition. In June, 1949, just before the GMD fled the mainland for Taiwan, it officially recognized the Qinghai boy (who was then eleven years old) as the new Panchen Lama. Although this, in large part, was an attempt to persuade the Panchen Lama's retinue to flee to Taiwan with them, they did not. Instead the Panchen Lama's officials opened cordial relations with the PLA in Qinghai (the N.W. Bureau). They supported China's reform policies for Tibet and Tibet's status as an integral part of China. For example, on the inauguration day of the People's Republic of China (October 1, 1949) the Panchen Lama sent Mao a telegram accepting that Tibet was a part of China and pledging, on behalf of the Tibetan people, wholehearted support for the liberation of Tibet. From the beginning then, the Panchen Lama and his retinue had close relations with the N.W. Bureau and the CCP. Thus, Fan Ming's perception of them as "progressives."

Fan Ming felt that China's interests were best met by implementing democratic reforms soon and argued that considering the Panchen Lama's area as an autonomous political entity equal to that of the Dalai Lama would facilitate this. His logic was that if the Panchen Lama headed his own autonomous region (the Back Tibet), he would quickly initiate the process of land reforms in his territory. When knowledge of this spread to the Dalai Lama's region it would raise the consciousness of the peasants there and motivate them to demand land reforms. This, in turn, would force the Dalai Lama's government to yield. This can be thought of as the "hard-line strategy" in the CCP in the 1950s. This faction's strategy held that the best way to create stability and security for the CCP in Tibet was to de-emphasize concerns about religious, cultural and ethnic differences and emphasize class struggle so as to quickly transform Tibet like the rest of China.

Although Mao Zedong had apparently already decided against this, Fan Ming and the Panchen Lama interpreted Mao's call for a "unified" Tibet not to mean unifying the Panchen Lama *under* the Dalai Lama. Rather they argued that there should be two equivalent units (Back and Front Tibet) unified under the higher authority of the unified CCP, as, they claimed, had been the case in Tibetan history.

Zhang Guohua, however, strongly opposed this interpretation, although, to be sure, like Fan Ming, he abhorred the Tibetan feudal-like manorial estate system. Zhang Guohua accepted and supported the Tibetan government's contention that the Panchen Lama's administration historically had been subordinate to Lhasa and consequently felt it was necessary to work through the Dalai Lama. These issues became alive after the Panchen Lama and his entourage arrived from exile first to Lhasa and then, in June 1952, to his seat of power in Shigatse/Tashilhunpo.

Not long after this, a number of disputes and conflicts regarding the status of the Panchen Lama's government arose, and in September, 1952, the Central Committee sent Fan Ming to Shigatse to talk with both the Panchen Lama's officials and the Shigatse Branch of the TWC (that was headed by N.W. Bureau officials) to try to calm the situation. But matters actually got worse since Fan Ming supported their views on the autonomous status of the Panchen Lama.

A quote of one of the actors from the N.W. Bureau will convey a feel for the level of thinking that existed in October, 1952:

> Now they [the TWC in Lhasa] sent ... this telegram, urging Ya Hanzhang [the N.W. Bureau official accompanying the Panchen Lama] ... to persuade the Panchen Lama to surrender to the Kashag unconditionally, and thus to complete the unification of Tibet. ... We believed that Panchen could only unify with a patriotic Kashag, not a pro-independence Kashag. If we sent the two progressive regions [Shigatse and Chamdo] to this pro-separation Kashag, we would actually be helping them. We would hurt our friends and help our enemies. We did not agree with the telegram. We sent a telegram to the central committee with their telegram attached (Anonymous interview).

This is an incorrect depiction of the sequence of events in this incident, but it illustrates the level of discord within the CCP in Tibet, as well as the degree to which different factions in the CCP were allied with different factions within Tibet.

From then on, the conflict between the Fan Ming and Zhang Guohua factions over the Panchen Lama increased in intensity until the Central Committee was forced to convene a meeting to discuss this issue in Beijing in 1953. That Conference went on for about 6 months and was so vitriolic that Deng Xiaoping sarcastically dubbed it "Panmunjom" after the bitter peace negotiations in Korea. In the end, Mao decided this issue by directing that the Dalai Lama was superior and the Panchen Lama was subordinate, and when the Fourteenth Dalai Lama visited Beijing for the first time in 1954-55, he was unambiguously treated as the higher figure. The Dalai Lama's visit to Beijing also played a major role in this CCP dispute. Because the Dalai Lama expressed very progressive views regarding reforms and modernization while in China, Mao, the Central Committee, and the S.W. Bureau people saw this as confirmation that their position of working through him had been correct.

However, soon after the Dalai Lama returned to Lhasa in 1955, the start of democratic reforms in Sichuan Province in January 1956 precipitated a rebellion in Kham (which was part of Sichuan Province). As this rebellion was put down, an influx of Tibetan rebels and refugees straggled into Lhasa from Kham. This set the groundwork for the development of a guerrilla group in Lhasa, and at the same time, led to Tibetan dissidents in India (headed by the Dalai Lama's brother Gyalo Thundrup) linking up with the CIA to train and arm Tibetan rebel forces. Fan Ming argued that the Dalai Lama was secretly behind this. He felt that the Dalai Lama had been duplicitous when he was in Beijing and was really covertly organizing and supporting the rebellion in Kham (and Tibet).

At about the same time, Fan Ming used Mao's 1955 call for rapid collectivization of agriculture in China to justify orchestrating a major effort to begin trial reforms in Tibet. In 1956, he recruited thousands of Chinese cadre from inland China (c. *neidi*), created new Tibetan cadre in Tibet, and developed a plan to start trial democratic reforms in the winter of 1956 (in Chamdo and the Panchen Lama's regions).

Mao and the Central Committee however, were still committed to work through the Dalai Lama, who was then in India attending the Buddha Jayanti Celebration. They terminated the plan for trial reforms in Tibet and ordered major reductions in personnel and activities. Thousands of Tibetan and Han Chinese cadre were sent back to inland China or demobilized. Beijing, therefore, continued to pursue Mao's policy of trying to work through the Dalai Lama.

Soon after this, in April 1958, the Fan Ming dispute was finally set to rest when Fan Ming was arrested in Tibet and sent back to prison in China as Tibet's "ultra-rightist who was trying to split the unity of Tibet".

But while Fan Ming was gone and Beijing's "Dalai Lama policy" retained, Mao's strategy was about to disintegrate. Less than a year later, the March 1959 uprising occurred in Lhasa and the Dalai Lama fled to exile in India. Chinese sovereignty over Tibet was again contested vigorously on the world stage. Mao's gradualist strategy had failed to achieve the goal he had envisioned in 1949-50.

Beijing immediately jettisoned the gradualist policy and implemented a hard-line strategy involving land reforms and the immediate termination of the Tibetan government and virtually all monasteries. For the next 20 years, Tibetan culture and ethnicity would be minimized and prominence given to class struggle and Tibetans adopting the national socialist culture.

Moreover, within the CCP, many now quietly came to accept that it had been a mistake for the communist party to, in their view, "coddle" Tibet's religious elites and institutions, and in particular the Dalai Lama. They blamed the party's gradualist strategy for the 1959 rebellion and the re-internationalization of the Tibet Question, and today some in China consider this gradualist policy one of the party's (Mao's) greatest failures. They argued that the Dalai Lama had duped China's leadership and that if China had eliminated the old system quickly as Fan Ming advocated there would have been *no revolt and no Dalai Lama in exile.*

The Post-Mao era

The rise of Deng Xiaoping raised the question in Beijing of whether it was possible for "reformist" China to settle the Tibet Question by opening a new dialogue with the Dalai Lama. In the course of this reexamination, it became evident to the leaders in Beijing that the hard-line approach of the past two decades in Tibet had been a failure. Tibet was still very poor and a large segment of the masses continued to support the Dalai Lama. This led Hu Yaobang and the Central Committee to launch a new strategy of conciliation in which Tibetan ethnicity, culture and religion would be valorized and allowed to function widely. It was, in reality, a reversal back to something akin to the earlier ethnically conciliatory views of Mao where genuinely winning over Tibetans was the goal. By allowing Tibetans to express their culture and values more fully while helping Tibetans to improve their standard of living, the reform policy in Tibet sought to genuinely win over Tibetans to being "satisfied" citizens of China.

However, like 1951, from the start, there was a hard-line faction within the CCP and Army that warned that this road was a mistake that would end up like the fiasco of the 1950s. They argued that allowing Tibetan religion to reemerge would fan the flames of rebellion and separatism, and should not be done. This faction, which included Han and Tibetan cadres, however, initially was not successful in persuading Beijing to its views (just as Fan Ming had been unsuccessful earlier), and many moves to bolster Tibetan language, culture and religion were implemented.

However, events soon gave the Han and Tibetan hard-liners the leverage they needed. The failure of the negotiations with the Dalai Lama's government in the early-mid 1980s, the start of the Dalai Lama's international campaign in 1987, and the series of riots in Tibet in 1987-89, turned the tables just as the rebellion in 1959 had. The pro-reform Party Secretary (Wu Jinghua) was replaced, martial law was imposed, and from then on we see a return to the dominance of a more hard-line point of view where fostering higher levels of Tibetan religion, language and culture are seen as counter-productive to China's national interests. It also saw the reemergence of the view that the Dalai Lama was acting duplicitously and was untrustworthy to work with. This new hard-line policy promoted what we can think of as a "small ethnicity" model that treated economic development as far more important than ethnic development and aimed at fostering a high degree of integration of Tibetans with the rest of China. That remains the policy today.

Conclusion

This essay has tried to illustrate, cursorily to be sure, that to understand the history of Tibet during the last five decades we have to go beyond simplistic black and white arguments that contrast Chinese views and Tibetans views, and move to a more nuanced approach that examines important alternative views on both sides. We need to go beyond talking about "Chinese" and "Tibetans" as if they were uniform entities and begin to unravel the internal debates, disagreements and conflicts, interpreting how these interacted to drive goals and strategies on both sides – just as we would do for American or European history.

[1] Parts of this paper have been adapted from M. C. Goldstein, *The Snow Lion and the Dragon: China, Tibet and the Dalai Lama*, U. of California Press, 1997, and M. C. Goldstein, *The History of Modern Tibet, 1951-1955*, ms.

[2] Tibet here refers to political Tibet, the polity ruled by the Dalai Lama. It does not include the various ethnic Tibetan areas in Kham and Amdo.

DISCUSSION

THE 1950's

There was considerable discussion concerning the interpretation of events in the 1950s. During the 1912-50 period Tibet had functioned as a de facto independent country, but its independence had not been recognised and China continued to claim Tibet as part of its domains. Following the triumph of communism in China, Chinese forces invaded Tibet in October 1950 and forced the Tibetans to sign the 1951 Agreement by which Tibet was absorbed into the new Chinese state. After a turbulent decade of communist rule in Tibet, the 14th Dalai Lama fled into exile in 1959 with around 80-100,000 of his people, and established a government-in-exile in Dharamsala, north India. This transitional decade, and the decades following it, has until recently been greatly neglected by historians, but was of crucial importance for the future of the Tibetan peoples.

One factor of some historical interest was the question of the respective roles of the Dalai and Panchen Lamas, and their individual interests in and communications with China and India. Both were young men in the 1950s, and relied upon various advisors, whose influences and actions should be assessed.

It was noted that the 1950s were a crucial era in which there were many different factions, ideas of the future, and even a willingness by both parties to reach a successful accommodation. Indeed debate continues within both Chinese and Tibetan systems over the decisions made and actions taken during this period, as it does among historians.

For Chinese communists the events of 1950 represented the reunification of China; but for the Tibetans this was an invasion, and the fact that Tibet was the only entity in China with which the Communist Party felt it was necessary to sign a written agreement demonstrated the unique status of Tibet and the consequent Chinese desire to claim a firm legal justification for their actions. But while there were differences within Chinese policy-making circles over annexation and ruling strategies there were no fundamental differences of intent; all parties within the Chinese elite structure were agreed on the necessity of taking over Tibet.

Bell's entry: "Monks of Gyantse Monastery"
Photographer: David MacDonald
BL.P.323

Chen Kuiyuan and the Marketisation of Policy*

Robert Barnett

Chen Kuiyuan, Party Secretary of the Tibet Autonomous Region from 1992 to 2000, is often seen as the quintessential exponent of the aggressive response to dissent that characterised the policies of the Chinese leadership in Tibet during the 1990s. When he arrived in Tibet, however, many of the policies of those gradualist leaders who (under the leadership of Hu Yaobang) had sought in the early 1980s to encourage local cultural and economic autonomy were still in place. Chen's policies therefore seem to me to deserve notoriety not for so much for their lack of leniency as for the exceptional effort which he had to expend in order to dismantle the gradualist legacy, and for the innovative mechanisms which he deployed in order to do this.

One way to view Chen's achievement is to consider policy in Tibet during the period after 1987 as a three phase operation, with security, economy and culture as the primary focus of policy in each phase. If the years from 1987 to 1990 are taken as the first of these notional periods, it seems to me that policy at that time dealt primarily with security issues, or what Chinese leaders after 1989 referred to as stability – in other words, how to stop demonstrations and dissent. Though it may not have seemed so to outside observers at the time, it is now clear in retrospect that in the first part of that period, from 1987 to 1989, certain leaders were remarkably conciliatory in their responses to protest. They expressed their leniency, in the peculiar rhetoric of inner-Party line struggles, by blaming unrest and even calls for independence on the excesses of unnamed leftists in the administration in Tibet. Even as late as June 1988, Zhao Ziyang, then General Secretary of the CCP, had argued that "the riots in Lhasa were caused by long-standing 'leftist' policies in Tibet."[1] The Panchen Lama used a similar argument to justify the release in January 1988 of the 21 monks who had been detained in the first protest of September 1987. There must, therefore, have been a policy faction or line which was calling for a hardline approach to policy in Tibet, but which at that time could still be publicly denounced. Its proponents remain unidentified, but it is clear that Chen Kuiyuan, here writing an internal report to Beijing, provided the main channel for their response to gradualist policies:

> So far the problem of confusion of thinking has not been thoroughly solved. Some comrades with experience still have a lingering fear. They attributed the riots by the splittist forces to the implementation of policy of the "left". Obviously this is not true. Later on since we did not criticize Dalai and regulate temples, the situation deteriorated and we had to implement martial law.[2]

By mid-1989 the "anti-leftist" or "soft" response to dissent was no longer viable. Zhao had been dismissed for his efforts at conciliation with demonstrators in Tiananmen Square who had gathered to mark the death of Hu Yaobang in April that year. The Panchen Lama had died in January, a week after declaring publicly that Tibet had suffered more than it had gained from the Chinese presence during the previous 30 years. Wu Jinghua, whom Zhao had appointed as Tibet's first non-Chinese Party Secretary in order to symbolise his support for the gradualist approach, had been removed from his position the previous summer.

The demise of gradualist leaders and the crushing of the 1989 protests in China meant that there was no longer any debate over the "hard" approach to security policy, but it did not mean a resort to simple repression. While Zhao had argued for leniency in Beijing, at the local level security management had carried out widespread acts of repression; conversely, although his successors insisted on uncompromising firmness, their methods were deliberately low-profile and non-provocative. We might therefore describe their approach as modern in style and presentation, even if its theoretical basis – the inevitability of Tibetan rebelliousness, solvable only by increased control – was rooted in tradition. Martial law, imposed in Tibet from March 1989 to May 1990, was thus not so much to do with the suppression of dissent in the classic sense of imprisonment, beatings and torture, all of which had been rampant in the previous two years, if not much earlier (these practices in fact subsided dramatically while Tibet was under direct military rule, partly because the military was much better disciplined that the People's Armed Police, the paramilitary force previously in control) as with the implementation of more institutionalised mechanisms of control. Most notable of these was the introduction of the *shengfenzheng* or identity card system, already widespread throughout China, which the martial law authorities were able to introduce into Lhasa and large parts of the TAR. In addition, the informant system was strengthened and the decision was taken to move to a less provocative, low-profile form of military or police presence. This was the shift that the Chinese politicians referred to in internal documents of the time as the move from "passive" to "active" policing.[3] In effect, this meant "actively" using plainclothes police in small teams on the streets, with back-up troops off-street, and focusing on selective pre-emptive arrests of likely activists instead of "passively" using large armed patrols and shooting demonstrators once protests had broken out. By July 1990, when Jiang Zemin, China's new Party Secretary, visited Lhasa, this "active" form of handling unrest was already in place and was beginning to show signs of effectiveness in stopping small demonstrations from escalating into major incidents.

The Second Phase: Economics as Control

The second phase, from 1990 to 1995, began in earnest with Jiang's visit to Tibet: it focused on accelerated economic development as a counter to Tibetan nationalism. This policy was symbolised by Jiang's slogan, "grasping with both hands", a reference to combining the maintenance of stability with the promotion of development. Rapid economic development had been an important part of Tibetan policy since at least the time of the Second Forum on Work in Tibet held in 1984, but it was now linked to security issues, in that raising the standard of living was seen as a way to dilute Tibetan nationalism. This notion corresponded with a social determinist strand in Chinese Marxism which considered local nationalism to be a form of thinking which, like religious belief, arises from a state of consciousness possible only in communities which were economically less sophisticated than the modern Chinese society: it held that people who have evolved to a higher economic plane would no longer be tempted by irredentist notions. Thus plans were announced in 1992 to make Lhasa into a Special Economic Zone, to "open up" the region, and to attract foreign investment.[4] The new zone never came to pass, and it became clear later that the opening up was towards the inner areas of China rather than to the international sector, and that preferred foreign investment was that from east and south-east Asia.

When Chen came to power in Tibet in March 1992, he inherited these policies combining economic propulsion with security control, and to him must be credited the energetic implementation of this hybrid. Significantly, it was in Chen's writings that we can find the most explicit justifications of the use of economy as control. In these he openly articulated the orthodox – and visibly inaccurate – position that this form of development would also diminish the power of religion:

> Only with economic development and improvement of prestige of the country, and with people getting rich and tired of splittist groups can they finally make correct judgments and give up their purpose of splitting the country. [...] If the economy develops well, the spiritual civilization will find a solid ground, and long-term stability within Tibet will be based on very reliable and solid ground. If there is no high-speed development of economy, the basis [for stability] will not be sturdy and far reaching. If the living standard of people is not high, they will not have interest in constructing their homeland, and cannot find much pleasure in their own life, and thus will be sympathetic with the religious illusion that places hope on the next life. With economic development their confidence in the country will be greatly increased, and the trend of unification and loving the central government will be enhanced.[5]

Chen's policies did indeed raise the standard of living in the TAR: the GDP of the area reached double-digit growth shortly after his arrival and stayed at that level for the following decade. The average per capita income soared, so that in the urban areas of Tibet it surpassed the average in inland China. This was achieved through massive investment of public funds from the Central Government or from the inland provinces of China, which were asked from 1994 to assist in financing infrastructural and other large-scale projects in Tibet.

The attempts at foreign development bore little fruit.[6] In April 1992 Chen resorted to simpler methods to rush the Tibetan economy into a new stage: every government office with premises on a main street in Tibet was told to convert the street walls of their compounds into rows of garage-sized shops. At the same time banks were told to give out low-interest loans to local entrepreneurs. The result was an explosion in petty urban private commerce.[7] In December 1992 Chen ordered controls between the TAR and other Chinese provinces to be removed, so that there would be no bar on the flow of migrants, an indication that the boom was aimed at attracting petty Chinese traders. By about 1994 the authorities had begun to give such loans to Tibetans also, instead of mainly to Chinese businessmen. Measures of this kind, however, produced an uneven development focused mainly on the tertiary sector, which expanded rapidly, but which was mainly urban and which brought with it the flourishing of cheap brothels and bars. The class of Chinese immigrant traders, from street-sellers to luxury shop proprietors, expanded rapidly. Again, there was a distinctively modern approach to the use of this mechanism, in that, apart from the case of technicians, administrators, and retired soldiers, it was driven almost entirely by market levers; the term "population transfer" was therefore hardly appropriate to this arrangement.

There was, however, nothing co-incidental about the use of Chinese migrant traders to accelerate the economy: after some years of official denial and evasiveness, it became clear that this was Chen's personal method for stimulating economic development in Tibet. By 1994 he was openly declaring the benefits of this policy:

> All localities should have an open mind, and welcome the opening of various restaurants and stores by people from the hinterland. [...] They should not be afraid that people from the hinterland are taking their money or jobs away. Under a socialist market economy, Tibet develops its economy and the Tibetan people learn the skills to earn money when a hinterlander makes money in Tibet.[8]

There was something more controversial about this blunt approach to economics than merely the fact that it involved intentional if indirect demographic disruption. The economic policy initiated in the early 1980s by Hu Yaobang and nurtured by the Panchen Lama had also stressed development, but with an understanding that it should be led by Tibetans, or at least be centred on advancing the interests of the Tibetan community; it was similar to what Westerners know as "affirmative action", but with more potent political implications relating to questions of autonomy and cultural survival. Necessarily this also involved gradual development rather than chasing fast-growth economic targets. This policy was not stated directly, but indicated through a coded phraseology, again typical of Chinese political discourse, which expressed this idea through the term "special characteristics". The phrase was derived from the writings of Deng Xiaoping, who in his successful effort to displace Maoist universalism had argued that each area in China should develop according to practical, local contingencies. The notion therefore had some canonical sanction and had been used in 1980s Tibet to legitimize the gradualist approach of Hu Yaobang's followers and the attempt to construct a Tibetan-oriented form of development.[9]

Chen's first task when he arrived in 1992, even before his presence had been publicly announced, seems to have been to destroy this notion of indigenous Tibetan priority in the economic sphere. He did this by taking advantage of another Dengist slogan or campaign which had begun only two weeks or so before his arrival in Lhasa: the so-called "spring tide" or "southern tour" of early 1992. This was a call by Deng for rapid acceleration in the marketisation of the Chinese economy. In itself there was nothing in the Spring Tide Campaign that contradicted the earlier notions of "special characteristics" or of local autonomy. But Chen and others were able to adapt the new ideology into a weapon in the attack on those who wanted the Tibetan economy to be primarily in the hands of Tibetans, by depicting this position as disguised resistance to Deng's new policies. Chen's attack rhetorics were inherently more creative and viable than those of his predecessors, who had used primarily anti-leftist and "special characteristics" discourse to criticise their opponents, because he was able to fuse the new policy with notions of modernisation and progress:

> Is Tibet willing to accept the label of " being special" and stand at the rear of reform and opening up? Backwardness is not terrifying. Being geographically closed is not terrifying. What is terrifying is rigid and conservative thinking and the psychology of idleness.[10]

In this way Chen was able to outflank any opposition to his plan to demolish the policy of Tibet-oriented development. After May 1992 the phrase "special characteristics" was rarely seen again in official speeches and statements, and the Tibetan economy became a matter of rapidly integration or "catch-up" with the interior, and thus a largely Chinese affair. The new regime under Chen had dismantled the central economic initiative of the Hu Yaobang era.

In fact, Chen's economic determinism – his contention that raising the level of the economy would automatically render Tibetan nationalism obsolete – was fictive or at best uncertain, and it anyway relied on central subsidies and on the rejuvenation of the tertiary sector. This certainly raised the level of urban wealth in Tibet, but it hugely increased the urban/rural gap, gave little impetus to economic production or to the primary or secondary sectors, and at the same time diverted economic control towards the increasing population of Chinese migrants in the area. Chen's modernism was therefore more rhetorical than actual: speaking the language of the market, he used the methods of the command economy to engineer socio-political results. In this he was not alone among contemporary Chinese frontier administrators. As Nicolas Becquelin has shown in the case of Xinjiang, supposed market policy there also conceals a Leninst centrism, whereby large numbers of Chinese settlers are paid to move to the area to develop cotton, a product for which there is dwindling demand and which is ecologically unsustainable.[11] "We should provide Tibetan people more opportunities to communicate with the inland population of all nationalities and to understand deeply and love the big family of our country," Chen wrote to Beijing in 1993. "We should improve the economic living standard in Tibet, and improve the exploitation of resources. [...] We request the central authorities to arrange a large number of construction projects."[12] The modernist concept of economic integration was fused with the Soviet-style use of centrally-funded projects to boost both the local economy and, somehow, patriotism, to produce a variant of the "socialist market economy" as a form of borderland management.

The Third Phase: Religious and Cultural Control

In his security and economic policies Chen was carrying out the orders of his superiors in Beijing, as far as we can tell, although it seems that he had the vision to adapt central theories of market expansion to his local needs to increase control and loyalty to the state. But if any of his policies were his own creation, it is most likely to have been those that emerged in the third phase of post-1987 policy in Tibet: the phase of cultural control. This phase consisted of two sectors – one dealing with religion after 1994 and the other with culture in the sense of scholarship, the educational syllabus, and the writing of history, after 1996. It was in this second area that Chen developed strategies and rhetoric which had not been seen in post-liberalisation Tibetan before his arrival:

> The continuous expansion of temples and Buddhist monks and nuns should be contained. We shall not allow religion to be used by the Dalai clique as a tool for their splittist activities. This is an outstanding and key issue concerning party construction in Tibet. Under the precondition that we shall mainly rely on education, we shall also take some forceful measures to stop this perverse trend.[13]

Whatever might have been said until then by opponents of Chinese rule in Tibet, the decision to attack Tibetan religion or culture *per se* was unprecedented in the post-reform era. Of course police stations had been erected in the major monasteries, religious teachings had been restricted, and the language policies of the Panchen Lama had not been fully implemented, but these were in essence uncoordinated security moves and restrictions: they were not a policy attack on Tibetan culture or religion as a whole. In this sense, the 1980s reform dispensation was still theoretically in place as far as culture and religion were concerned, albeit hemmed in by numerous and erratic restrictions. The theoretical right of Tibetans to develop their culture and religion as much as circumstances allowed remained intact. Above all, the religious standing of the Dalai Lama was not in question - although constantly criticised for his political views, his religious position remained sacrosanct. It was Chen's achievement to change all this, and to sweep away the notion that Tibetan culture and religion were too sensitive to be openly targeted for political and ideological control, just as he had proved for the first time in the reform era that Chinese immigration into Tibet could be openly encouraged as an aim of policy.

The Anti-Dalai Lama Campaign

The outside world had no inkling of this radical move until it became public policy in 1995, but it appears from the 1993 "Request", only published six years later, that the attack on Tibetan religious culture had been carefully planned almost from the time of Chen's appointment. The first public signs of this policy shift appeared in May 1994 when Party members in Tibet were reminded of the Party's commitment to atheism and told to remove any altars, rosaries, Dalai Lama pictures or signs of religious devotion from their homes. In the last week of May 1994 government officials – including those who were not party members - were told that no photographs of the Dalai Lama would be allowed in their offices or vehicles. In the second week of June further meetings were held in government departments forbidding display of the photograph. In July the ban was extended to cover semi-official agencies, including tourist agencies, business co-operatives and taxi companies. At the end of August notices were circulated in Lhasa which made it clear that the ban had been extended to apply not just to the offices but also to the homes of government employees. On the 28th of September that year police for the first time confiscated Dalai Lama photographs that were on sale in Lhasa markets: this marked the extension of the campaign from officials to ordinary Tibetans. These moves were not publicly declared, and it was only from January 1995 that the newspapers began to carry lengthy articles attacking the Dalai Lama's religious standing. These attacks were elaborations of the internal rulings made by the Third Forum on Work in Tibet, the policy conference chaired by Jiang Zemin in July 1994 which gave Chen a national-level mandate in these words:

> We must be able to reveal the true colours of the Dalai clique. Due to the traditional religion, Dalai has a certain prestige amongst monks, nuns and devotees. But Dalai and the Dalai clique have defected and escaped to a foreign country, and have turned into a splittist political clique hoping to gain Tibet's independence and have become a tool of international hostile forces. [...] The struggle between ourselves and the Dalai clique is not a matter of religious belief nor a matter of the question of autonomy, it is a matter of securing the unity of our country and opposing splittism.[14]

In other words, the Centre had formulated an explanation for ignoring the distinction between the religious and political aspects of the Dalai Lama. Their decision led to an article in the *Tibet Daily* a month later describing "the Dalai" as "no longer a religious leader [but] a naked anti-China tool".[15] The concession to the Dalai Lama's religious status that had in effect been granted by Deng Xiaoping in 1979 had been withdrawn, and religion was no longer considered too sensitive for direct attack. Chen was later to hint in an internal speech that the leadership before him had failed by not taking this step earlier:

> The Dalai clique's capability in creating damage is to some degree also a reflection of our failures in recognition, in striking power, and in political discrimination. Some party members believe that denouncing the Dalai would offend God and the masses; they not only [do not] engage in the struggle, but also uphold differences between the struggle of the masses and that of party; this is completely incorrect. Communists are atheists. If we see the Dalai as a religious ideal and avoid denouncing him in the process of the anti-splittist campaign, then politically we will not be able to lead the masses to fight effectively against the splittist group headed by him. We must denounce him fundamentally and not recognise his religious authority.[16]

The TAR leaders waited, however, another year before moving to full implementation of their new policy, which was imposing it on the monks. This came on 5th April 1996, when the *Tibet Daily* formally announced the ban on public display of Dalai Lama photographs:

The hanging of the Dalai's portrait in temples should gradually be banned. We should convince and educate the large numbers of monks and ordinary religious believers that the Dalai is no longer a religious leader who can bring happiness to the masses, but a guilty person of the motherland and people.[17]

It was a high-risk move, and led to conflict in several monasteries, including Ganden, where a monk was shot dead by troops suppressing protests against the ban. It was followed by a massive exercise in political education called the *dgon sde'i nang rgyal bces ring lugs kyi slob gso spel ba* or "Carrying Out Patriotic Education in all Monasteries" across the entire region, with teams of officials sent to every monastery and nunnery in Tibet to extract written denunciations of the Dalai Lama from all monks and nuns. More importantly, new administration committees were set up in each monastery, sometimes with lay or even party membership. Hundreds of monks and nuns were expelled from their institutions or fled to India, and a few were imprisoned following small incidents of protest. By the time Chen left office four years later he was able to claim that his drive to curb monastic unrest had been successfully enforced without significant repercussions.

The Attack on Intellectual Culture

It was understandable that Chen would target the Dalai Lama as an enemy, but it was his larger attitude to religion and to Tibetan culture in its more intellectual aspects that was more exceptional. He went on to rule that all government officials should renounce not just worship of the exile leader, but any form of religious practice. By 1997 this ruling had been extended to the family members of officials, and to all state employees including drivers, janitors, caretakers and the like. At about the same period – no clear date is known for the promulgation of this order, since it too was never made public – the rule was extended to all students and schoolchildren. In doing this, he went beyond any obvious security argument and set aside the promise of religious freedom given in the Chinese Constitution. It was the ban on religion among the extended family members of government officials that is rumoured to have finally led to him being criticised (extremely mildly) by the Chinese leader Lan Lanqing during the latter's visit to Lhasa in August 2000, some six weeks before Chen was removed from his position in Tibet (the ban on religion among schoolchildren and students does not seem to have been questioned). But it was a speech that Chen gave in July 1997 on legitimate art, acceptable tradition and the role of Buddhism in Tibetan culture that made him most notorious among Tibetans:

> Some people say that the Tibetan national culture is connected to religion in form and essence. Some others say that college teaching material will be void of substance if religion is not included and that in that case, colleges would not be real colleges. […]
> Is only Buddhism Tibetan culture? It is utterly absurd. Buddhism is a foreign culture. […] The view of equating Buddhist culture with Tibetan culture not only does not conform to reality but also belittles the ancestors of the Tibetan nationality and the Tibetan nationality itself. I just cannot understand

236

that. Some people, claiming to be authorities, have made such shameless statements confusing truth and falsehood. Comrades who are engaged in research on Tibetan culture should be indignant at such statements. Making use of religion in the political field, separatists now go all out to put religion above the Tibetan culture and attempt to use the spoken language and culture to cause disputes and antagonism between nationalities, and this is the crux of the matter.[18]

In this argument we can again see the harnessing of a modernist, progressive notion – the critique of the "Buddhification" of Tibetan history leveled in recent years by modern historians such as Namkhai Norbu and Samten Karmay – to support an ultra-conservative attack on the role of religion in Tibetan culture. That agenda was more readily discernible from another startling innovation in the same speech – Chen's announcement that the 17th century Tibetan writer and politician Sangye Gyatso was "a separatist chieftain" whom it was no longer permitted to praise. There was no particular reason or precedent for the Party Secretary to issue bans on the study or description of incidental historical figures: it seemed rather to have been intended as a sign that Chen, after much study and reading, had familiarised himself with Tibetan history and was now prepared to take on Tibetan scholars and intellectuals publicly, something that his predecessors had also never attempted, as far as we know. There was a deeper theoretical shift behind this: Chen was rumoured to have made a statement at an internal meeting 18 months earlier saying that Tibetan nationalism was rooted in Tibetan religion, and that Tibetan religion was rooted in Tibetan culture and language. This implied that Tibetan culture and language had to be restricted, or at least closely monitored, as well as Tibetan religion, a radical departure from existing policies. Shortly afterwards, the experimental Tibetan-medium school classes that had been started by the Panchen Lama some six years earlier in four secondary schools were closed down, the offices in charge of Tibetan translation were downgraded, the Tibetan Department of Tibet University was told to suspend all intake for some two years while it revised its textbooks, and a number of distinguished Tibetan scholars were encouraged to take early retirement.

This was not a policy of eliminating Tibetan intellectual culture – in fact the Centre decided in 1999 that in order to offset exile and foreign allegations that Tibetan culture was being destroyed, large amounts of money should be spent on developing the departments of Tibetan language and history in Lhasa, Chengdu and elsewhere. But Chen had brought into the policy arena a theoretical position whereby Tibetan intellectual endeavour was considered a threat to security, and thus in need of control. He had taken on Tibetan scholars directly, even though there was little evidence that they directly threatened China's interests, and even though there had been no call for a purge of this sort in the internal rulings of the Third Forum, which were supposedly Chen's policy guidelines.[19] The third phase of China's post-1980s policy regime in Tibet, the attack on the cultural front, was thus an attempt to contain or corral Tibetan intellectual life, and it led to much closer management, and even the truncation, of some academic activities in the Tibet Autonomous Region.[20] It also marked an important shift in Chinese ideology regarding the rights of minority cultures.

But, above all, it represented the final stage in the programmatic dismantling of the reforms that had been put together by the Panchen Lama and others during the time of Hu Yaobang in the early and mid-1980s. By October 2000, when Chen Kuiyuan moved to Henan Province in Central China to take up the position of Party Secretary there, the gradualist approach of the 1980s had been finally supplanted in the arenas of security, economy and culture in the TAR. It had taken much longer to achieve than might have been expected.[21] Chen's rule was thus notable not for so much for repression as for the extensive and thorough way in which he dismantled the earlier policies, and for the modernist and market-oriented mechanisms which he developed for implementing and justifying what were, at base, deeply traditional premises of official distrust towards unruly natives and their beliefs.

NOTES

[*]A version of this paper was presented at the History of Tibet Seminar held at St Andrew's University, Scotland, August 2001. I would like to thank the organisers of that Seminar, plus the East Asian Institute of Columbia University, the Oesterreichischen Fonds zur Foerderung der wissenchaftlichen Forschung, and the Society for the Protection of East Asian Human Rights for their assistance and support during the research and preparation for this paper. In particular, I am indebted to Heather Upadhyay for her help with translation, and to TIN (London) and the BBC Monitoring Service (Caversham) for their extensive help with source materials, as well as to many others who contributed materials over the years.

[1]"CCP Encounters Tremendous Resistance in Attempting to Eliminate Pernicious Influence of Leftism in Tibet", *Ming Pao*, Hong Kong, 2nd June 1988, p.6, in FBIS, 2nd June 1988, p.32.

[2]"Several Requests and Hopes for the Third Third Forum on Work in Tibet (June 28th, 1994)" in *Xizang de Jiaobu* ("Tibet's Steps"), Gaoji Ganbu Wenku ("High Level Cadre Documents Series"), Zhonggong Zhongyang Dangxiao Chubanshe, Beijing, 1999, pp. 190-200. Chen also specifically blamed Tibet's problems on Hu Yaobang's 1980 policy of withdrawing Chinese cadres from Tibet: "From 1980, between 10,000 and 100,000 cadres and working staff hastily left Tibet in a short time. This made Tibet, which already lacked human talents, suddenly lost more of them. [...] This is the key factor that prevents all kinds of undertakings from fast development." Chen Kuiyuan, "Request to Convene the Third Worker's Forum on Tibet to Ensure a Prosperous Tibetan Economy and Long Term Peace and Stability", *Xizang de Jiaobu*, Beijing, 1999, pp. 118-124ff. This passage includes one of many examples of Chen's recurrent distrust of Tibetan cadres, a view I discuss in "Beyond the Collaborator-Martyr Model" in Barry Sautman and June Dreyer (eds.), *The Tibet Question*, forthcoming.

[3]For the internal instructions on the passive-active shift, see my *Security Policy in the TAR, 1992-4: Analysis of a Speech*, TIN Background Briefing Document No.24, TIN, London, March 1995.

[4]"The action is part of Tibet's efforts to open its door wider to the outside world and step up economic development in the wake of Deng Xiaoping's urge for bolder reform," said Gyamtso, vice governor of the TAR (see "Economic Zone Status for Lhasa", Reuters, Beijing, 12th May 1992, citing *China Daily* of the same day). The article noted the TAR was considering setting up a second economic zone in Gyantse.

[5]Chen Kuiyuan, Requirements and Hopes for the Third Working Meeting on Tibet (June 28th, 1994)", *Xizang de Jiaobu*, 1999, pp. 194, 196-197.

[6]"The economic sources of Tibet mainly comes from the central government. How much we can do depends on how much appropriation we can get [from the central government]. [...] The foreign investment in Tibet is very small. In the last year, there have been only 24 foreign joint ventures from countries and areas such as Hong Kong, Taiwan, Thailand, Nepal whose registration and projects have been approved, and the agreement amount is only 0.12 billion yuan," Chen wrote in 1993 ("Request to Convene", *op. cit.*, pp. 118ff.).

[7]See "Construction Boom for Chinese Migrants in Tibet" in "Tibet Policies Designed to Attract Chinese Traders", *TIN News Update*, TIN, London, 3rd December 1992 and Tibet People's Broadcasting Station, Lhasa, 3rd February 1994, published as "Private Businesses Develop Rapidly in Tibet", BBC SWB,16th February 1994.

[8]Tibet People's Broadcasting Station, Lhasa, 28th November 1994, published in translation as "Tibet;

Chen Kuiyuan in Qamdo Says Prosperity Will Drive Out Religion", BBC SWB, 5th December 1994.

[9] The term again had its own tradition in Party history as a school of policy often linked with Deng Xiaoping: "The validity of the "special characteristics" theory was again disputed, as it had been in the Great Leap Period", wrote June Dreyer of the leftist policy shift under Mao in 1968 ("Traditional Minority Elites and the CPR Elite Engaged in Minority Nationalities Work" in Robert Scalapino (ed.), *Elites in the People's Republic of China*, University of Washington Press, Seattle, 1972, p. 447.

[10] *Renmin Ribao* (People's Daily), 16th May 1994.

[11] Nicolas Becquelin, "New Mediums of Xinjiang's Integration by the Centre since the Emergence of Post-Soviet Central Asia," Paper presented at the Association of Asian Studies Meeting, Boston, 1999.

[12] Chen Kuiyuan, "Request to Convene", *op. cit.*, 118ff.

[13] Chen Kuiyuan, "The Situation of Tibet and the Problems We Request the Central Authorities to Solve (February, 1994)", *Xizang de Jiaobu*, pp. 131-136.

[14] "Document No.5: Seize this Good Opportunity of Having 'The Third Forum' [and] Achieve in an All-Round Way a New Aspect on Work in Tibet," a speech given by Deputy Party Secretary Raidi (Ragdi) on 5th September 1994 at the Seventh Plenum of the Sixth Standing Committee Session of the TAR Communist Party.

[15] Li Bing, "Dalai is a tool of hostile forces in the West", *Xizang Ribao*, Lhasa, 11th December 1995, p.2, published in translation by the BBC SWB as "Tibet Daily' Calls Dalai Lama "Tool" of West", 8th January 1996.

[16] Chen Kuiyuan, "Speech made at the Party Section Meeting within the [combined] Fourth Plenary Session of the Sixth TAR Regional Congress and the Fourth Plenary Session of the Sixth TAR Political Consultative Conference", 14th May 1996.

[17] *Xizang Ribao*, 5th April 1996, p.1.

[18] Chen Kuiyuan, *Xizang Ribao*, 16th July 1997 pp. 1,4; published in translation by the BBC SWB as "Tibet party secretary Chen Kuiyuan speaks on literature, art", 1st August 1997.

[19] The Central authorities also took a more activist position on the priorities of Tibetan scholarship after 1999. "Academics have a responsibility to provide powerful, scholarly argument in support of our external propaganda for public opinion on Tibet. [...] The[ir] argument should prove that Tibet is an inalienable part of China, that the democratic reform was absolutely necessary, that the present autonomous arrangement for Tibet is the best and most effective way to protect the equality of nationalities and to guarantee the right of autonomy to the Tibetan people, and that the atheist Communist Party of China gives religious freedom." The prescribed method was again modernist, in the sense in which I have used that word, in this case with a conscious indication of anomaly: "However, such works should be factual with ability to strike the important views of foreign adversaries; the arguments should be clear and credible; sources quoted should be reliable; there should be footnotes and bibliographies." See "Tibet-related external propaganda and Tibetology work in the new era – Zhao Qizheng's statement at the meeting on national research in Tibetology and external propaganda on Tibet, [Beijing,] 12 June 2000", internal document issued in translation by International Campaign for Tibet, Washington D.C., May 2001.

[20] The undeclared policy of banning religious practice among schoolchildren remained in place after Chen's departure, as did the close management of academic study. In July 2001 Chen's successor Guo Jinlong, quoting Chen's July 1997 speech on cultural policy, outlined a similar set of priorities for Tibetan scholars: see, *Bod rjongs nyin re'i tshag par* (the Tibetan language edition of *Tibet Daily*), 11th July 2001.

[21] Tenzin, widely regarded as the last of the 1980s gradualists to retain a leadership position in the TAR, at least on cultural issues, was not removed from his position as a Deputy Party Secretary in Tibet until 2001, when he was sent to Beijing to take up a position in the National Federation of Writers.

following page
Bell's entry:
"(f) Golok man and his wife, back view.
On the woman's back large engraved discs of silver;
turquoises and corals down her hair."
1998.285.313 (BL.H.284)